A Novel Marketplace

A Novel Marketplace

Mass Culture, the Book Trade, and Postwar American Fiction

Evan Brier

PENN

UNIVERSITY OF PENNSYLVANIA PRESS

PHILADELPHIA

Published by
University of Pennsylvania Press
Philadelphia, Pennsylvania 19104-4112

Printed in the United States of America on acid-free paper

10 9 8 7 6 5 4 3 2 1

Library of Congress Cataloging-in-Publication Data
Brier, Evan.
  A novel marketplace : mass culture, the book trade, and postwar American fiction / Evan Brier.
    p. cm.
  Includes bibliographical references and index.
  ISBN 978-0-8122-4207-2 (alk. paper)
    1. American fiction—20th century—History and criticism. 2. Fiction—Publishing—United States—History—20th century. 3. Literature publishing—Economic aspects—United States—History—20th century. 4. Authors and publishers—United States—History—20th century. I. Title.
PS379.B675 2009
813′.5409—dc22

                                                                        2009023569

For my parents

Contents

Introduction
Selling the Novel in the Age of Mass Culture

The age of American mass culture and its attendant anxieties has come and gone. Today, books, music, and news outlets are available to suit any individual's narrow tastes and outlook. Chris Anderson, editor of *Wired* magazine and an unabashed celebrant of the emergent niche culture, puts it this way: "The era of one-size-fits-all is ending, and in its place is something new, a market of multitudes" (5). For Anderson, these multitudes signal the technology-aided triumph of the forces of cultural democratization; others express anxiety about our lack of unity and stability, the loss of an American "common culture" that connects people of disparate backgrounds and perspectives. There are now, it is said, too many channels on the television, purveyors of news, and means of communication, and this surfeit of choices threatens America's literature, its culture, its democracy, and even, in an age of anxiety about sleeper cells, its national security. "Diversity," Cass Sunstein wrote in 2002, "is a wonderful thing, but fragmentation carries serious social risks" (206).[1]

The current conversation between fragmentation's partisans and opponents would likely surprise mid-century culture critics, for many of whom the one-size-fits-all mass culture of the 1950s appeared to be a quasi-apocalyptic end, the inevitable result of the marriage of technology and capitalism. Thus for fifteen years after the end of World War II, the urgent cultural and political problem was said to be the opposite of fragmentation: too much manufactured unity, too little diversity, too few choices, a too-passive populace. As Louis Menand notes, television sets in the mid-1950s "had twelve VHF channels, all except three of which probably broadcast static" (115). The result was a uniformity that might now seem inconceivable: whereas the top-rated television show of 2005, *CSI*, drew 15 percent of the television-watching audience (Chris Anderson 37), Milton Berle in 1948 drew 87 percent (Baughman, *Same*

Time 51), and the top-rated show of 1954, *I Love Lucy*, 74 percent (Chris Anderson 29). Definitions of mass culture are frequently contested, but there seems little question that television in the mid-1950s is an example of it: a moment that in retrospect seems singular, when an unthinkably large audience of culture consumers, made possible by the combination of the postwar economic boom's expanded middle class, the prewar technology of the cathode ray tube, and the paucity of viewing choices in the precable television age, could and routinely did tune in to the same show.[2] It was this unusual and by no means inevitable confluence of factors—caused by, among other things, a series of missteps by the Federal Communications Commission (FCC), which was ill-equipped to regulate such a massive cultural and economic shift—that inaugurated what James L. Baughman calls the "republic of mass culture" and what Menand deems network television's "empire" (116).[3] For a brief moment that has now passed, network television ruled, and the result was mass culture.

The emergence and temporary dominance of mass culture exerted itself powerfully on American novels, shifting the cultural and economic space they occupied as surely as television did to movies, magazines, and newspapers. But unlike these latter shifts, the story of postwar mass culture's effects on novels has largely gone untold.[4] These effects, which this book sets out to describe, are most easily—but still incompletely—seen in the stories told in the novels themselves. In the 1950s, numerous scholars have noted, novelists and contemporary critics turned their attention from the class issues that galvanized novelists of the 1930s to cultural and psychological concerns: disillusioned with radicalism in 1949, Lionel Trilling wrote, "Nowadays, it is no longer possible to think of politics except as a politics of culture" (xi), and Norman Mailer noted with disdain three years later in *Partisan Review* that "it has become as fashionable to sneer at economics and emphasize 'the human dilemma' as it was fashionable to do the reverse in the 1930s" (*Advertisements* 189).[5] The novelistic effort to represent mass culture in the 1950s is one little-discussed example of this shift in focus. Throughout the decade, the emergence of mass culture provided novelists with a new topic not just to depict but also to critique, bemoan, and satirize. As the works I discuss in this book exemplify, such depictions are found not only in those novels that have dominated the critical conversation about postwar American fiction but in a range of novels that span what is conventionally but regrettably understood as the cultural spectrum: from Paul Bowles's avant-garde depiction of the flight from banal American "mass society" in *The*

Sheltering Sky to Ray Bradbury's nightmare science fiction portrayal of a future dominated by television in *Fahrenheit 451* to Sloan Wilson's reputedly conventional novel, *The Man in the Gray Flannel Suit*, about a man who begins work in a debased profession (public relations) for a debased institution (a television network). Even Grace Metalious's *Peyton Place*, itself typically though again regrettably viewed not as a novel but as a mass-culture scandal, mocks the conventional, mass-produced romance novel.

These representations are essential to the story this book tells, but the impact of mass culture on American novels was more far-reaching and less obvious than any or all of them might indicate. Between 1948, when television began its commercial ascendancy, and 1959, when Random House, an American publishing house founded in the commercial heyday of literary modernism, became a publicly owned corporation, the way American novels were written, published, distributed, and marketed changed considerably, in ways rarely visible to the reading public at the time and rarely discussed since by cultural historians or literary scholars. This absence of discussion might reflect a continuing scholarly-critical discomfort with viewing novels as participants in a cultural and an economic arena that also includes movies and television shows. Although it is conventional to treat Hollywood movies or American magazines from an economic perspective, as competitors vying for an audience with limited amounts of money and leisure time—both topics have been the subject of numerous scholarly studies—postwar novels, at least in discussions by literary scholars in relation to other forms of commercial culture, are still often studied as though they exist outside the realm of commerce; they are still often treated *solely* as commentators on the commodification of culture.[6] Novels are indeed commentators, and they should be treated as such, but they are also themselves commodities that inhabited the cultural and economic field that the emergence of television unsettled in the 1950s.

The idea that literature exists outside the economic realm is in a sense inherited from the prewar modernists, whose project of separating so-called high art from commerce—as a matter of ideology, not fact—was carried into the postwar era in the form of famous attacks on mass culture by such figures as Theodor Adorno, T. S. Eliot, and Clement Greenberg.[7] These attacks have rightly been read as corollary to the postwar novelist's concern with culture over class, and they have become a touchstone of scholarship about the 1950s.[8] In the early postwar era, mass culture (or the culture industry, or masscult, as it was also known), along with its detested offshoot middlebrow culture, was inevitably depicted in essays and symposia, by critics with vast political differences, as a threat to American democracy or to the brand of high culture that the modernists had created or to both. In one of several iterations of his evolving theory, Dwight Macdonald wrote in 1953 that what he called masscult "threatens high culture" ("Theory" 61) and that its creators "exploit the cultural needs of the masses in order to . . . maintain their class rule" (60). The standard-bearers of anti–mass-culture theories were followed by many critics who, in sometimes painstaking detail, delineated the ills of mass culture through close examination of its artifacts. *Mass Culture: The Popular Arts in America* (1957), edited by Bernard Rosenberg and David Manning White, is one collection of these critiques; it features four essays on detective fiction (two on Mickey Spillane alone), four on comic books, six on movies, and five on television and radio. The degree of attention that so many critics devoted to forms of culture they ostensibly deplored prompted art critic Harold Rosenberg, in a review of the anthology, to accuse: "They play in this stuff because they like it, including those who dislike what they like. I never heard of one who to meet his duty to study best-sellers or Tin Pan Alley tore himself away from Walden Pond" (260).

This same spirit of suspicion is found in Richard Yates's novel *Revolutionary Road* (1961), an example of the cultural concerns shared by critics and novelists in this era. In Yates's corrosive account of suburbia, the television set has already seduced not just the children but also their purportedly highbrow parents. In the Wheelers' living room, "the wall of books . . . might as well have been a lending library" and "only one corner of the room showed signs of pleasant human congress . . . the province of the television set" (31), this despite the fact that Frank Wheeler is himself a mass-culture critic, or a parody of such a critic, given to lengthy assaults for his wife and neighbors on the ills of suburbia, where "the television droned in every living room" (65). As Yates describes the Wheelers' social rituals: "With the pouring of second or third drinks they could begin to see themselves as members of an embattled, dwindling intellectual underground. . . . Even after politics had palled there had still been the elusive but endlessly absorbing subject of Conformity, or The Suburbs, or Madison Avenue" (59). But they are frauds. Late in the novel, Frank and his wife April watch a television show together, "which he found wholly absorbing and she declared was trash" (206). In satirizing these reactions—his presumably undeclared absorption and her felt need to declare the television show trash—Yates, like Rosenberg, has it both ways, savaging mass culture while mocking its most vociferous critics for doing the same. By the end of the 1950s, Yates's novel and Rosenberg's essay suggest, the mass-culture critique, as a topic for novels and essays, was itself a cliché. For Yates, though, as for Rosenberg, casting it as a cliché seems an effort to present himself as a more authentic critic, purer than his characters in his contempt for television and for the suburbanites who watch it. The consequences of the characters' hypocrisy, moreover, are severe: "The children," Yates writes of Frank and April's son and daughter, "lay silenced by television" (135).

Over the course of decades, the attitudes of Greenberg and Macdonald and Rosenberg and Yates have come to seem old-fashioned at best, but to a considerable and lamentable degree they continue to dictate the terms of our conversation about American culture. The rhetoric of cultural crisis in which, Rosenberg suggested, critics wallowed has since been called the discourse of the "great divide" (Andreas Huyssen's term), which purportedly separates high culture from mass culture: the idea that high art and low art exist not on a continuum but on separate planes, that there is a "categorical distinction" between them that it is the critic's role to guard and maintain (viii). The discourse's unabashed snobbery has made it an irresistible target. Contemporary cultural-studies scholars and theorists of popular culture have drawn attention to mass culture's subversive potential, what Andrew Ross calls its "contradictory power and significance . . . for its users and consumers" (52). In this revisionist account, the artifacts of mass culture are seen to have uses beyond the control or intentions of their makers, who are as nefarious as Macdonald suggested they were in the late 1940s but far less powerful. Mass-culture products may be intended, as Macdonald suggested, to function as instruments of class rule, but their makers cannot control the way they are ultimately used by their audience, and that audience—the people, not an unthinking mass—create, in a process John Fiske calls "excorporation," their own authentic culture out of game shows or romantic comedies (15); it is for this reason that "mass" culture is advisedly renamed "popular" culture.[9]

Where do novels fit into this intergenerational debate about the relationship between and the relative values of mass and high culture? It depends, and that fact in itself reveals something of the debate's inadequacy to the story of the postwar novel. As Thomas Hill Schaub and others show, the postwar era brought renewed attention to the novel, from both New Critics and the New York intellectuals, as a form of high culture.[10] But as Rosenberg and White's *Mass Culture* anthology makes plain, the

1950s also brought attacks on certain novels as examples of mass culture; in addition to the essays on detective fiction, a separate group of chapters focused on the problems posed by "mass literature." According to both the original and the revisionist mass-culture critics, some novels qualify as high culture whereas others are defined as popular, and the criteria for classifying a novel as one or the other are elusive; as C. W. E. Bigsby observes, "Popular culture . . . can apparently be transformed into 'high' art by a simple act of critical appropriation . . . a fact which applies not only to individual artists but to genres (theatre, novel, film), subgenres (farce, science fiction, detective fiction) and styles" (qtd. in Kammen 6). The idea of a cultural division between high and low (or mass) forms of literature is sometimes helpful: for one thing, it enables making the case for the specific value of literature once deemed low on terms different from the ones used to celebrate high culture. But this division, to the large extent that it is merely evaluative, obscures rather than clarifies the relationship between American novels and mass culture in the 1950s. Novels of the 1950s—regardless of whether they were deemed high or low culture at the time or since—were always also a form of commercial if not mass culture; to examine the effects of the emergence of mass culture on American novels, it is necessary to consider these novels not as high or low culture, categories so fluid as to be useless except as historical markers of critical opinion, but as commodities produced in the pursuit of admittedly varying amounts of both prestige and profit.

Doing this work, I argue throughout this book, entails shining a brighter light on the postwar book trade, that set of institutions that produced, marketed, and sold novels, occupying crucial but neglected intermediate space between the much discussed twin extremes of mass-culture corporations and highbrow critics and, in a literal sense, sometimes, negotiating with both of them. The specifics of these types of institutional negotiations have gained the attention of literary scholars in recent years. Influenced by Jürgen Habermas's study of the transformation of the public sphere, Pierre Bourdieu's sociology of culture, and the idea of the institution as that which mediates between the individual and society, institutional accounts of twentieth-century literature and of the novel as the product not just of an author but of assorted institutions, including publishers, literary agents, critics, booksellers, and readers, have gained in prominence.[11] To date, these accounts have focused primarily on either genre fiction once deemed lowbrow or the production of literary texts in the first half of the twentieth century: Lawrence Rainey on high modernists Eliot, James Joyce, Ezra Pound, and H.D.; Janice

A. Radway on romance novels and on the Book-of-the-Month Club as a quintessentially modern, middlebrow institution; and Catherine Turner on the successful marketing of modernist texts in America during the 1920s and 1930s.

This book extends the institutional focus into the postwar era, from which it has, with a few important exceptions, been absent, and uses it in two related ways: first, to sketch a necessarily episodic narrative of postwar novel production, of modernization in fits and starts, during the postwar mass-culture explosion; and, second, to explore a paradox that ran deep in literary culture throughout the decade but has yet to be examined.[12] The 1950s is likely the time during which alarm over the fate of both reading in general and high literature in particular was at its apex. These were, in fact, two distinct forms of alarm: as I discuss throughout this book, those intellectuals concerned with the fate of culture for the few—Macdonald, Harold Rosenberg, and Greenberg—had little interest in, if not outright hostility toward, more humanistic assertions of the importance of mass literacy, concerns that were more properly the purview of secondary school English teachers, mainstream commercial publishers, and Rudolf Flesch, author of the best-selling literacy jeremiad *Why Johnny Can't Read* (1955). There was a tension between the missions of self-appointed protectors of high culture and those who wished to spread literacy, promoters of the value of reading for everyone.

But the tension was easily elided in the light of shared assumptions about declining literacy in the age of television, and the two forms of alarm were easily conflated in the face of the common enemy that mass culture represented. "Who is to blame," *Saturday Review* asked in 1956, "for the plight of contemporary reading?" ("The Battle" 5). The premise of the question, the idea that there was a plight, was taken as self-evident, the point of departure for much of the discussion of the future of reading and literature in the 1950s. At the same time, as contemporary issues of *Publishers Weekly* and the recent study *Literacy in the United States* suggest, in the 1950s more books than ever before were produced and sold to a growing population of educated consumers. "The increase in trade book sales during 1956," *Publishers Weekly* reported in January 1957, "will top the 7 per cent increase which 1955 registered over 1954" ("Highlights of 1956" 47). *Literacy in the United States* confirms *Publishers Weekly*'s conclusions, citing the "widespread popularity of book reading by the 1950s" (Kaestle, Damon-Moore, Stedman, Tinsley, and Trollinger 150) and noting that reading expenditures, controlled for both inflation and population growth, rose throughout the decade (153–54), despite the fact that, for much of the 1950s, spending on magazines and newspapers was in steep decline. This rise is not merely an effect of the economic boom, either; at the same time that book sales were increasing, borrowing from libraries was also increasing, "contrary," the study notes, "to all the dire predictions" (165).[13] In 1959, *Publishers Weekly* reported the happy news that the book-publishing business was "approaching a billion-dollar level" ("A Year of Reading" 79). In short, throughout this decade of alarm over the plight of reading, the book trade was benefiting from the public's growing consumption of books, mostly nonfiction but also fiction.[14] This raises two important and, as it turns out, related questions: Why did the public buy more books than ever in the 1950s? And what produced the disconnect between the rhetoric of crisis and the reality of increasing book production and sales?

To the latter question, the Cold War is one inescapable and essential answer, but in broaching its role, caution is advised. As Deborah Nelson has noted, we are likely past the point where the "containment" metaphor for an anxious postwar culture needs to be asserted and defended as a counternarrative to what was once the standard, idealized version of the content 1950s.[15] Now that the cultural power of Cold War ideology has been established by Ross, Donald Pease, Elaine Tyler May, and Alan Nadel, among others, the opportunity exists to shine a light on how that ideology intersected with other, also formidable, cultural, commercial, and institutional imperatives. It is important to recognize the Cold War's role, but it would be a mistake to view the concern about literacy after World War II as another instance of perhaps manufactured Cold War paranoia, whereby fears of the consequences of illiteracy, fed by anxiety about Communist infiltration, the masses, and totalitarianism, overwhelm empirical evidence that suggests those fears are baseless if not, at least, premature.

For one thing, such a view misses how interlocked were the articulations of alarm and the book trade's commercial success. As I discuss throughout this book, and in depth in Chapter 2, about Ray Bradbury's fantastically successful science fiction paperback *Fahrenheit 451*, institutions of the book trade, the ones that were benefiting most from the increase in reading expenditures, did much to disseminate the idea that the literary sky was falling, suggesting that what seems to be a disconnect between perception and reality might be better understood as a successful and shrewd, but not cynical, marketing strategy, one that paid off in the form of the sizable increase in book production and sales throughout the era. All of this is meant not to deny but to complicate the

Cold War's considerable role in the marketing of culture during a tense historical moment. Anxieties about Communism did in many instances script the marketing of novels, sometimes directly but often indirectly, as a consequence of government and educational efforts to promote national literacy as a bulwark in the battle against Communism. Although the Cold War plays an essential role, it does so only alongside and in conjunction with other factors that demand but have received little or no attention from literary scholars, such as the previously mentioned modernization of the book trade after World War II and the exponential growth of America's college-educated population in the middle decades of the twentieth century, a process that began before the Cold War.[16] Rebecca Lowen's assessment of the "Cold War university" applies as well to this study of early Cold War culture: "While America's research universities . . . were undoubtedly shaped by the more than forty years of cold war . . . other forces, which are not neatly bound by the beginning and end of the cold war, were shaping them as well" (1).

Shining a light on these "other forces" that shaped novel production at this crucial moment and on their intersections with Cold War ideology is one of this book's primary aims.[17] Throughout the 1950s, institutions of the book trade engaged in a paradoxical project: using the genuinely felt alarm over the emergence of mass culture as a means to carve and define a space for the novel within a newly crowded commercial field, not just articulating a Cold War–inflected rationale for novels in the age of mass culture but also disseminating that rationale more widely and effectively than had ever been done before. That project—how it came about; how and why novelists, critics, and the book trade participated in it and how they were affected by it; and how it has affected the critical conversation about postwar novels—is the subject of this book.

Institutional Change

The cultural and commercial project of redefining the novel for the television age occurred at a moment that in retrospect, like the era of mass culture itself, was transitional rather than final: when literary institutions, flush in the late 1940s with the end of wartime paper rations and the start of the postwar boom, first contended with television but before America's publishing houses were consolidated into mass-media empires, as they would be in earnest in the 1960s. An institutional account of the book trade during this transitional moment might include the following developments. In 1939, Robert de Graff and Simon & Schuster together formed Pocket Books, resulting, after World War II's paper rations ended, in the unprecedented ubiquity of books in America, both lowbrow genre fiction and literary classics, which were now sold not just in bookstores but also in train stations, pharmacies, and anywhere magazines were sold. The mass-market paperback would be followed by the more upscale trade paperback, which was more expensive, printed on higher quality paper, and sold in bookstores only, in the early 1950s: first Doubleday's Anchor Books, and later Knopf's Vintage and others. In 1943, the William Morris Agency, then the second-most powerful show business agency in the United States, established a separate department for representing authors of books, signifying both the growth of the literary agent's profession and, just as important, a mass-culture institution's belief in the profit-making potential of the book trade. As this book shows, the literary agent, whose role shifted markedly in this era, is a persistent symbol and presence in accounts of novel writing of the 1950s yet has received little attention. That William Morris represented not just commercial writers like James Michener but also literary stars like Paul Bowles, Ralph Ellison, and Robert Penn Warren hints at an untold story of 1950s literary culture: the continued growth of the audience for fiction marketed and received as literary. Another important moment occurred in 1944: Pocket Books and Simon & Schuster were merged into a small multimedia conglomerate called Field Enterprises, which included four radio stations, a newspaper, and a textbook publishing company. The merger was not an immediate trendsetter, but it was a harbinger of the widespread consolidation of the book trade that was to come and to which this era served as crucial prologue.

Running roughly parallel to this set of developments, the impact of which was felt throughout the 1950s, was a set of institutional initiatives begun in 1946, when American publishers joined forces to form the American Book Publishers Council (ABPC). The ABPC was a successor to numerous earlier attempts to modernize and organize the book trade, and it was the first one that effected genuine change.[18] Its explicit aim was twofold: first, to unite competing publishers in pursuit of their common commercial interests and, second, just as important, to unite publishers with other institutions that had an interest in getting people to read. These included, of course, other commercial institutions of the book trade like bookstores and book manufacturers. But more meaningful alliances were formed with institutions outside the commercial field, including English teachers and professors (who perceived a strong interest in promoting the value of literature); religious institutions; and private-sector, concerned-citizen cold warriors, who believed that an educated, literate populace was a key element in the struggle to contain Communism. These new alliances reflected the dual status of the book as commodity and form of artistic expression with both civic and aesthetic value beyond its value as commerce. As Frederic G. Melcher, longtime editor of *Publishers Weekly*, put it in 1953, "Books have some advantages over steel in gaining public attention, for a million and more teachers and librarians serve daily, explaining to the new generation what books are and how to use them" ("An 'Industrial Family'").[19]

Aiming to harness these advantages for the first time during a moment of extraordinary economic growth, the ABPC was instrumental in forming organizations with such names as the Committee on Reading Development (established in 1950) and the National Book Committee (established in 1954) ("Summary 1950" 224; "Review" 322). The latter committee exemplifies the collaboration that took hold during the decade. Its original officers included a university president, representatives from publishing houses, and the former Secretary of the Air Force, and its mission statement sets into relief the Cold War context of its effort to market books: "In a time of tension like the present, it is especially needful for citizens to see to it that books are made available for all . . . and above all, that they are read, so that we may understand the complex issues of our time and see our current crises in perspective" (qtd. in Grambs).[20] To promote the buying of books, these committees established symposia and conferences on the value of reading and the need to promote it in both urban and rural areas, and they published volumes on the social and political importance of reading with titles like *Wonderful World of Books* (edited by Stefferud) and *The Development of Lifelong Reading Habits* (edited by Grambs). The ABPC was also instrumental in creating, in conjunction with other institutions of the book trade, the National Book Awards, which were first awarded in 1950, and which were designed in part to be a literary alternative to the Pulitzer prize (English 58). The ABPC and the materials it produced have yet to figure in accounts of postwar American literary culture, but they provide crucial clues not just to the literary institutions' emerging ideology of the book but also to its increased ability to disseminate that ideology.

In these two lists of generally neglected institutional developments (only the story of the paperback has received a lot of attention; the rest have received either little or none), two overlapping stories are being told.[21] The first is the story of the book trade's emerging relationship with mass-media institutions. In the decade or so between the emergence of postwar mass culture in 1948 and the publishing industry's own consolidation triggered by Random House's purchase of Knopf in 1960, both sets of institutions recognized common commercial interests, or ways in which they could achieve their separate commercial interests through collaboration. The creation of the William Morris Agency's literary department, which was headed by Helen Strauss, a former executive at Paramount Studios, and the merger of Simon & Schuster into Field Enterprises, a product of Field's belief, after seeing the sales of paperbacks, that the book trade would be increasingly profitable in the second half of the twentieth century, exemplify this nascent, mutually beneficial collaboration (Tebbel 4: 70–71). So too does the sharp increase, largely driven by the paperback, of movie tie-ins during the 1950s, whereby new books, or new versions of older books, and their movie versions are promoted together. As Emory Austin, the ominously titled "director of exploitation" for MGM told *Publishers Weekly* in 1956, "When the publisher is willing to spend the money and make the effort required, then we, for our part, are happy to do the same" ("Paperback Movie" 151).

But the story of collaboration between literary and mass-media institutions in the 1950s—the story of the institutional absence of a great divide—has been obscured in large part by the second story, that of the book trade's increasingly unified and centralized public response to mass culture's emergence, a response that, in the light of the first story, needs to be understood as largely rhetorical rather than substantive and thus as deeply ironic. At the historical moment in which the book trade's ties to the institutions that produced mass culture were strengthening, it had both a commercial and an ideological interest in positioning itself as separate from and opposed to mass culture, in language not dissimilar from that of the harshest and most uncompromising highbrow critics. This was a delicate rhetorical strategy, for to advertise novels as works of art or as works of transcendent social or political importance or as both, the book trade had to speak loudly about them without being noticed, without drawing attention to the fact that the production of books, whatever their artistic value and whatever their civic value, was always also a commercial enterprise.

This was one of the charges of the ABPC. As Pierre Bourdieu describes it, in the cultural world, "The less visible the investment, the more productive it is symbolically." Thus promotions within that world, "which in the business world take the overt form of publicity, must here be euphemized" ("Production" 77). In 1955, George Brockway, a vice president of Norton, addressed the convention of the Modern Language Association, a crucial partner in the project of promoting the book as a cultural good: "The road to salvation is, however, a simple one: all one needs to do is to increase the reading of books. . . . Publishers would not be much better off than they are today, because oddly enough a publisher doesn't make much more on a sale of 10,000 copies than he does on a sale of 5,000. But authors and booksellers would be vastly better off, and so would the country" (123). The book trade's challenge, made explicit in Brockway's address, was to minimize the visibility of its investment in books as a form of commerce—publishers, Brockway says, do not even benefit from increased sales, but the country does—because the perception of its distance from the commercial world was one crucial source of its value as a commodity. One way of doing this, as this book shows in some detail, was to embrace works that themselves presented novels as a bulwark against a threatening mass culture. Mass culture may have been, as Huyssen famously put it, "the hidden subtext of the modernist project" (47), but by the 1950s it was out in the open, an "enemy" uncovered, which is to say a rhetorical foil; the book trade, by its own design, was what was hidden.

Thus an inevitable irony of the book trade's promotional responses to mass culture is that they also, wisely, exploit the enormous commercial opportunities that mass culture offered; in the 1950s, books were advertised as never before on the radio and of course on television, in the form of both actual advertisements and book-related programming. "Publishers," Priscilla Coit Murphy notes, "embraced new media for the new advertising opportunities—even if they were competitors for their readers' time and money" (41). The first National Book Awards ceremony was broadcast on the radio (television coverage also was sought), and it featured musical numbers to enhance the ceremony's entertainment value, but what it aimed to advertise most of all was its literary credibility (Melcher, "1000" 1508).[22] In promoting novels, the line between mere advertising and what Bourdieu calls the "production of belief" in the value of the novel beyond its market value was beginning to blur because the idea that the novel transcends commerce became a chief selling point to an increasingly educated audience in the age of mass culture.[23] To the extent that the audience for fiction marketed as literary had grown, announcing the novel's distance from commerce and especially mass culture could quickly pay commercial dividends.

Spheres of Cultural Production

My aim in describing how novel-producing institutions marketed their products, here and throughout this book, is decidedly not to criticize them for engaging in commercial activities; rather, it is to show the specific commercial uses to which the idea of the literary was put into the age of television, an issue that scholarship of the era has yet to address. Nor is it my aim to suggest that because novels are always commodities and because in the 1950s the institutions that produced novels developed relationships with mass-media corporations, those novels are somehow artistically compromised. On the contrary, although it is important to recognize novels as commodities in order to appreciate how mass culture's emergence affected them, it is just as important to recognize that not all commodities are alike: the concrete differences between the institutions of the book trade and those of mass culture affected what they produced, and those effects matter.[24] By Michael Kammen's useful definition, mass culture is that which is "nonregional, highly standardized, and completely commercial" (18). The book trade, for a variety of reasons, could never be thus. For one, barriers to entry into the trade have always been relatively low: it is far less expensive to publish a book than it is to produce a movie or television show, so the possibility of "mass control" over output by a small number of well-capitalized institutions (like the major Hollywood studios or three television networks) is diminished. According to sociologist Paul M. Hirsch, "Conglomerate middlemen do not have the capacity to transform diverse readers of books into a controllable market with an oligopolistic or monopolistic structure" (114); in short, novel production could never be like television production was in the 1950s or movie production in the first half of the twentieth century.[25] Books are therefore inevitably a more "producer-oriented" than "consumer-oriented" trade, a distinction Hirsch borrows from Herbert Gans's study of the relationship between high culture and popular culture, and this is a sociological insight with consequences for both literary output and institutional studies of it.[26]

In particular, Gans's insight has significant implications for this study of the postwar American novel and its institutions. Institutional studies of the arts have sometimes disdained close readings of texts themselves, on the grounds that the answers the studies seek are better found elsewhere (in the structures that distribute and legitimize those texts, for example).[27] Throughout the 1950s, as the logic of modernization dictates and as this book shows, the machinery of literary production—the number and size of those structures, the institutions that stood between the novelist and the reader—was indeed growing, as publishing became less of a cottage industry and individual houses became more like conventional businesses. But one of the primary aims of this book is to show the degree to which novelists of the 1950s, as producers in a producer-oriented trade, participated *within their novels* in the promotion of the novel in general as a cultural and political good, often in terms that echoed the industry's promotional campaigns and the rhetoric of culture critics.

To view postwar novels in this light is, hopefully, to take a step toward overcoming what Pascale Casanova calls "the supposedly insuperable antinomy between internal criticism, which looks no further than texts themselves for their meaning, and external criticism, which describes the historical conditions under which texts are produced, without, however, accounting for their literary quality and singularity" (4–5). As there is no categorical separation between mass culture and other forms of culture, there is no such divide between the marketing of postwar American novels and the novels themselves; marketing went, as it were, all the way down, and novelists were, in effect rather than by design, essential collaborators in the project of producing belief in the novel's cultural value, cocreators of a promotional pitch that was inscribed into the novels themselves in ways that have yet to be appreciated. For this reason, this book is neither exclusively a marketing or business history nor exclusively a study of novelistic representations of mass culture. Either project, on its own, misses something essential about the complex relationship that developed between American novels of the 1950s and the emergent mass culture, which was alternately, if not at once, a marketing partner and a foil, a collaborator and a Cold War bogeyman. This relationship is better grasped by reexamining what and how novels communicated in the context of the book trade's slow, unsteady, largely neglected modernization, a story of a relatively small set of businesses capitalizing on an opportunity for growth, in part by collaborating with mass-media corporations and in part by advertising their distance from them.

Advertisements for Themselves

The novelist's role as promoter—his or her participation in the project of articulating the specific cultural value of the novel in the age of mass culture, typically by announcing his or her aloneness—was always paradoxical in ways that rarely found expression. These paradoxes are explored in the first two chapters of this book, which outline the emergence and novelistic articulation in the late 1940s and early 1950s of a strategy for advertising the literary novel and the emergence of an institutional apparatus for implementing that strategy, a network of relationships among publishers and between publishers and a range of other institutions. In the story of how Paul Bowles's avant-garde literary excursion became a best seller—with help from the William Morris Agency and Doubleday— and how Ray Bradbury's version of a little-esteemed form of genre fiction, published by paperback upstart Ballantine, became a staple of high school English classes, we find far more institutional continuity than institutional divide among supposedly disparate literary spheres. Literary institutions of the postwar era—publishers, teachers, and critics— embraced works that celebrated the idea of the writer's solitariness and juxtaposed that solitariness against a corrupt, decadent, or totalitarian mass culture, precisely because those novels did the work of producing belief in the cultural and political value of the novel.

Conversely, the novels discussed in Chapters 3 and 4—Sloan Wilson's *The Man in the Gray Flannel Suit* and Grace Metalious's *Peyton Place*, respectively—seemed to fail or refuse to do this work, and they were critically derided in the mid-1950s, the former as a "quintessentially middlebrow" compromise and the latter as a lowbrow scandal that precipitated a supposed cultural decline from which we have yet to recover. Both novels benefited from the increasingly sophisticated machinery of literary promotion that developed over the course of the 1950s, early examples of the synergy that would be one of the rationales for media mergers in the 1960s and after, and their marketplace success does indeed constitute the realization of a modernized book business's commercial potential, which had only begun to come to light in the late 1940s. But the to-date unexamined stories of the making and marketing of both novels confound the still-too-prevalent modernist narratives that connect the book trade's growth and the rise of mass culture to literary decline; it is one of this book's aims to unsettle the hold that these narratives of decline have had on accounts of cultural change after World War II. Between *The Sheltering Sky* and *Peyton Place*, two novels on opposite sides of an old version of the cultural spectrum, there exists, again, not a divide but a continuity that was obscured in the service of the myriad goals of collaborating cultural and economic institutions.

That continuity, and the growth of the book business that fostered it, was exposed late in 1959, when Random House sold 30 percent of its shares to the public and months later bought Knopf; the merger was front-page news in the *New York Times* (Talese 1). At almost the exact moment of the stock sale, Norman Mailer's unorthodox, early career retro-spective *Advertisements for Myself* was published and, as Chapter 5 shows, its relentless exposé of the business of publishing is itself both a some-times blinkered comment on what had become of the book trade over the period this book covers and a prescient example of how its transfor-mation into a high-profile business might affect the ideology of the novel going forward. With Mailer's unorthodox example in mind, this book ends where it begins, in the twenty-first century. With hindsight, truly *mass* culture is a brief moment, the result of an unlikely set of circum-stances that shifted the cultural ground beneath the novel and allowed it to be defined a certain way. Even as publishing houses have continued to consolidate, to be bought and sold by multimedia corporations over the past two decades, the number of choices for culture consumers has grown exponentially, and the mass audience, if it ever existed, has be-come ever more a fiction. Our current era, featuring a conceivably un-limited number of cultural niches, has shifted the ground beneath the novel yet again and in ways that we have only begun to consider.

Chapter 1
Constructing the Postwar Art Novel:
The Making and Marketing of
The Sheltering Sky

I'm sorry about my agent—both for your sake and mine.
—Paul Bowles, in a letter to his publisher, James Laughlin,
April 7, 1949 (In Touch 201)

Keep up your standards. It is better to be read by 800 readers and be a good
writer than be read by all the world and be Somerset Maugham.
—James Laughlin, in a letter to Delmore Schwartz
(qtd. in Gussow D19)

He was one of the least troublesome, most gentlemanly clients I had, really a
nice man. Despite our friendship, he always addressed me as "Miss Strauss."
—Helen Strauss, Bowles's agent, on Paul Bowles (152)

Apologies for his agent, Helen Strauss, are a recurring feature of Paul
Bowles's letters to James Laughlin in the months leading to the publication of *The Sheltering Sky*, Bowles's first novel, by New Directions, Laughlin's company, in December 1949. The apology above, like most of the
others, is given for no apparent reason. There is no sign that Strauss did
anything that warranted an apology; if Bowles complained to her about
her conduct with Laughlin, there is no record of it. As it turned out,
Bowles's association with Strauss far outlasted both his friendship and
his business relationship with Laughlin, suggesting that the apologies
are better understood not as genuine expressions of regret (or not solely
as such expressions) but as Bowles's attempts to affirm his detachment
from business matters—the agent's purview—and thereby ingratiate himself with his publisher, who, as his advice to Delmore Schwartz indicates,
counted himself not as a businessman but as a patron of avant-garde

artists.[1] At the time of these letters, Bowles had not established himself as a novelist, and before Laughlin agreed to publish *The Sheltering Sky*, the manuscript had been rejected by numerous publishing houses, so Bowles's desire to stay on Laughlin's good side is understandable. Long before the publisher markets a novel to the public, the novelist, particularly the yet-to-be-published novelist, must market himself or herself to the publisher.

In his letter, Bowles goes on to say, "I should have known better than to sign up with Eddie Cantor's and Jack Benny's agent. Except that I was ignorant at the time of the entire species" (*In Touch* 201). In fact, Strauss did not represent either star, but her employer, the William Morris Agency, did. Bowles defends his decision to hire Strauss on the grounds that his lack of interest in such things left him incapable of making the "right" decision; paradoxically, according to this logic, only someone interested in such mundane matters (only someone of a commercial bent) would know enough to not hire an agent so invested in the commercial. Bowles's next letter, dated April 30, 1949, continues in this vein: "I'm sorry the agent business has been so harassing for you. . . . I do need some sort of link with New York, naturally" (203). The agent is here cast as the necessary consequence of Bowles's expatriation to Tangier. Again, the novelist justifies his attachment to the world of commerce by presenting it as the necessary consequence of his self-imposed detachment from that world.

If Bowles's apologies for his ties to commerce are paradoxical, they are not idiosyncratic. As Pierre Bourdieu writes, "The literary and artistic world is so ordered that those who enter it have an interest in disinterestedness" ("Field" 40). Perceptions of the writer's artistry depend in part on the perceived distance he or she maintains from what Bourdieu calls the "economic world"; it is thus in the writer's interest to *disavow* this world, to announce his or her lack of interest in the commercial.[2] More specifically, Bowles's apologies reflect the changing cultural and economic status of the novel at the start of the 1950s. Between 1948 and 1955, two-thirds of American homes acquired television sets (Spigel 1), spurring predictions of the demise of the literary novel and high culture.[3] At the same time, notwithstanding these predictions, the combination of the postwar economic boom with a sharp increase in college attendance—and even the growth of the mass-media industries themselves—presented the book trade with an unprecedented opportunity to expand, to sell more books to more people than ever before.[4] The book trade, in a transitional moment between its prewar past as a decentralized cottage industry and its post-1960 future as a small piece of multimedia corporations, exploited this opportunity in part by marketing individual novels, and at times the novel in general, as something other than—something more special than—a mere commodity.[5] In this regard, the book trade's response to the emergence of mass culture throughout the 1950s mirrors the gesture of Bowles's apologies to Laughlin in 1949—strategically, if somewhat disingenuously, advertising to a growing, increasingly literate audience of consumers the book's separateness from the world of commerce.

In this chapter, I treat not just Bowles's apologies but also the story of the writing, publication, and reception of *The Sheltering Sky* as a means to illuminate the complicated set of negotiations among the book trade, culture critics, and mass-culture institutions in the early postwar era. After falling out of print in the 1970s, Bowles's first novel has been of interest to scholars over the past decade as a recovered masterpiece of postwar alienation, conducive to revisionist studies of the 1950s as an anxious rather than a placid decade; Bowles's entire oeuvre, now back in print, has garnered renewed attention as texts well suited to queer and especially postcolonial readings.[6] In its own time, however, the novel was something different: a best-selling "art novel"—to borrow Mark McGurl's term for the post–Henry James, self-consciously artistic novel—sprung from what was then an unusual and in some regards accidental collaboration between mass- and high-culture institutions. *The Sheltering Sky* was hardly the first art novel in American literary history to achieve immediate commercial success. But when viewed in its institutional context, the context of what Theodore Ziolkowski calls "the totality of agents performing specific tasks in the production, distribution, or promotion of literary works" (10), the story of Bowles's success is emblematic of a generally overlooked aspect of its moment in literary history, a moment when both high- and mass-culture institutions began to realize the salability of the *idea* of the avant-garde or "art" novel—the growth, that is, of a market large enough to support a novel marketed as such. It is not surprising that the emergence of this type coincides with the emergence of the art-house cinema; in the era immediately after World War II, the book and movie businesses found relatively small but reliable audiences for products marketed as art rather than as entertainment.[7]

Bowles is an ideal figure with which to trace this development because the trope of detachment (what Bourdieu calls "disinterestedness") was a hallmark of his life and literature. But only because he was a well-known figure in avant-garde artistic circles long before he had published a novel was he able to make that detachment work for him. When Bowles first left the United States in 1929, after a single semester at the University of Virginia, he was already a published poet, having had his work included in the March 1928 issue of *transition*, a little magazine, alongside James Joyce, André Breton, and Gertrude Stein. He was seventeen years old at the time. Bowles idolized Stein; when he visited her in France in 1931, it was as a fledgling poet in search of a mentor. Stein, happy to oblige, exerted her influence in two important ways. First, she effectively shattered his poetic ambitions by telling him his poetry showed no promise.[8] Second, more constructively, it was on Stein's advice that Bowles visited Tangier for the first time, in 1931. He made that trip with his other mentor, Aaron Copland. Copland showed interest in Bowles's music, and Stein showed none in his poetry, so Bowles abandoned poetry and became a full-time composer on his return to New York in the 1930s. He now divided his time between work for the Broadway stage and "serious" composing—working in the same artistic and sometimes the same social circles as Copland, Virgil Thomson, and Benjamin Britten (with whom he briefly shared an artist's residence in New York, along with, among others, W. H. Auden). Bowles was inspired to write again by his wife, Jane Bowles, whose novel *Two Serious Ladies* was published in 1941. He wrote short stories in which, as in his novels to come, his own detachment was inscribed. This is true not just in the sense that they portray alienated Americans searching for a more authentic existence in northern Africa and Central America but also in the sense that the narrative voice always stands far apart from the sometimes grotesque violence it describes. Before he became a novelist, Bowles's distance from conventional American culture was already a pronounced aspect of both his biography and his writing.

The Agent

One way of considering the postwar relationship between mass culture and the novel in the early postwar era is to ask how and why an avatar of detachment like Bowles became associated with Helen Strauss and the William Morris Agency, and, equally important, why Strauss and the agency showed interest in Bowles. The answers to these questions can be found in the simultaneous growth of the book business and the mass-media industries over the first half of the twentieth century. Before writing his novel, Bowles wanted to publish a volume of short stories, but editors at Dial Press told him that to publish such a volume an author needed two things. First, the author needed a published novel. The reason seems clear enough: short-story collections by unknown authors rarely sell well. Collections by established novelists, however, at least have a chance to justify the publisher's investment.[9]

Second, the author needed an agent. "According to them," Bowles writes in *Without Stopping*, "an agent was essential; they offered to telephone then and there to make an appointment with one for me" (274).[10] In itself, this requirement suggests a significant but infrequently noted shift in the literary field. The original purpose of agents was protection, to make sure that the publisher treated the author fairly. The advent of the literary agent is in this sense a consequence of the modernization of the book business: as the business grew more profitable and more complicated, the relationship between publishers and authors became more impersonal. Authors, according to the agents' pitch, as artists and not businesspeople, needed representatives to ensure that publishers did not exploit them. Not surprisingly, therefore, when literary agents first appeared on the scene in the late nineteenth and early twentieth centuries, publishers denounced them as the scourge of the book business, in terms that mirrored antiunion rhetoric from factory owners of the same era. The agent's interest, so the publishers' rhetoric went, was neither in the well being of the book business (without which there could be no books) nor in the quality of the individual finished product, the book. From the beginning, publishers and sometimes authors negatively identified agents with the commodification of culture, casting the agent as the serpent in the book business's familiar fall narrative, who corrupts the previously pure process of book production by interfering in what was a gentlemanly and nurturing publisher-author relationship.

By mid-century, however, as Dial Press implicitly told Bowles, the publisher-agent relationship had changed: agents, although still charged with protecting the business interests of the authors they represented, had come to serve a necessary function for publishers as well; agents did much of the work of finding commercial writers and weeding out unsuitable ones. As the publishing industry expanded after World War II and as the number of prospective authors and manuscripts increased exponentially, agents came to be useful as "screens" for publishers, "winnowing good books from bad" (Coser, Kadushin, and Powell 287). By mid-century, as Bowles's experience suggests, the agent served a double role. Now that the agent no longer served just as a protector of the writer, the hiring of the agent became an important part of the process of novel production and an added hurdle in the construction of a literary career, necessary to legitimize the writer in the eyes of the publisher.[11]

This consideration of literary agents from the publisher's and author's perspectives should not obscure the basic truth about them: their trade is opportunistic, and their existence signals the belief that there is money to be made. That agents became increasingly prominent in the literary field shows the commercial potential of that field, and that potential was tied not just to the growing reading public but also to the growing connection between the book and mass-media forms. A telling and little-noted sign of the growth of the book trade is the fact that, in 1944, the William Morris Agency formed a literary department.[12] William Morris, then the second-largest theatrical agency in the United States, was noted not just for its sizable stable of talent but also for its ability to adapt to shifts in the cultural market; not only did it leave its competitors behind in making the transition from vaudeville to movies, but it was also the first agency to recognize television's potential.[13] The agency's decision to establish a literary department signifies both the growth of the reading audience and the book trade's developing relationship with mass-media industries. The decision to hire Helen Strauss to head the department reflects these two developments: in her previous job as a story editor for Paramount, she was charged with finding and buying from authors stories that were suitable for filming and with convincing writers to write such stories.[14]

Strauss's decision to leave Paramount for William Morris testifies to both the growing commercial opportunities afforded by the literary field and the opportunism of the agent. In her memoir, Strauss characterizes the relation between Hollywood and the book business at the time of this decision: "Each of the big film companies was buying approximately fifty pieces of material annually—novels, plays, magazine serials and short stories. . . . They bought more than they needed, more than they could produce, not knowing what they would or could do with it. They bought everything. They gobbled up the best-seller lists and the bulk of magazine fiction" (39). Strauss left Paramount for William Morris because she felt it would be more lucrative to represent authors than to work for the studio, given the studios' seemingly unending willingness to spend on movie material. Her choice to become a literary agent was a winning bet on the economic future of the book business.

That Strauss's motives were explicitly financial puts her decision to represent Bowles in its proper context: she evidently saw in his literary endeavors a chance to make money. In the light of Bowles's unconventionality and relative anonymity—he had at the time no commercial credentials, but he did have what might be called highbrow credentials—that judgment is fairly striking. When an agent takes on a client, that agent is gambling that the client will succeed commercially. Business capital comes with the ability to make salable recommendations to publishers, who then make the financial investment in publishing the book. If the book fails commercially, the agent's ability to secure advances for other authors, and thus the agent's bottom line, will be damaged. Bowles, moreover, was not the exception among Strauss's clientele; her list of authors would come to include such literary stars as Archibald MacLeish, Ralph Ellison, James Baldwin, Robert Penn Warren, Edith Sitwell, Dylan Thomas, and Leon Edel. Fears of mass culture in the 1950s were often based on the notion that the masses would coarsen or debase literary culture (if they had not already done so). But just as the emergence of the art cinema signified the emergence of an audience for serious film that Hollywood studios would soon try to exploit, Strauss's decision to take Bowles and other literary stars on as clients suggests that institutions of mass culture perceived (rightly, it turned out) a growing audience for the literary, a niche market waiting to be tapped.[15]

Not only the agent saw commercial potential in Bowles: within ten days of her hiring, Strauss secured for him an advance for a novel from Doubleday, "one of the authentic colossi of the industry," in the words of publishing historian John Tebbel (112). Bowles's new position in the field of literary production was enviable: he was represented by the biggest Hollywood agency and was to be published by one of the biggest houses—all without having written a word of his novel or even come up with the idea for it. The idea did not come until *after* he received word of the advance, which he used to fund the trip to Tangier and the Sahara that inspired the writing of the novel. This chain of events (the hiring of the agent, who secures the advance, which pays for the trip that leads to the inspiration, idea, and writing of the novel) suggests again how integral these disavowed aspects of novel production—agents, advances, commercial publishers—had become to the construction of the novel, even for, if not especially for, the novelists most vigorously engaged in efforts to suppress their ties to them. The kind of detachment embodied by Bowles's sojourn to the Sahara is not cheap; it can only occur in the context of some attachment to the business world. At the moment in literary history when the novel was receiving from both New Critics and the New York intellectuals its closest critical attention as a distinctive form of artistic production, its institutions were becoming increasingly intertwined with other, more consumer-oriented forms of culture.[16]

Bowles's literary career was set back when Doubleday rejected his manuscript for *The Sheltering Sky*. The publisher told Bowles that what he had submitted was, simply, not a novel.[17] It is best not to make too much of this assessment; as Bowles himself concluded with evident satisfaction in his autobiography, Doubleday's rejection was likely a (regrettable) assessment of *The Sheltering Sky*'s commercial prospects, a curious one at that, given that the novel is much like the short stories on the basis of which, presumably, along with Strauss's recommendation, Doubleday gave him the advance. Doubleday's assessment of the book, that is, is likely not an intentional application of genre theory to a specific text. But the language of the rejection does suggest the role of publishing houses in the construction of genre conventions, in determining what constitutes a novel and what does not. In strictly material terms, if no publisher is willing to deem *The Sheltering Sky* a novel, then it is not one.

New Directions

Doubleday's rejection, a footnote in most accounts of Bowles's career, nonetheless triggered a chain of events that altered the reception of his first novel and probably altered perceptions of his entire career.[18] In the short term, it put Bowles in a precarious position because, as a first novelist with no commercial track record, he was asked to return Doubleday's advance.[19] The manuscript then "went through a bad year of being turned down by every publisher who saw it." Finally, Bowles reports, he "sent it to James Laughlin, at the other end of the publishing spectrum" (*Without Stopping* 292). In his preface to the novel, Bowles emphasizes that "it was I, and not my agent, who finally sent the typescript to New Directions, and fortunately he liked it and agreed to publish it" (6).

Bowles's version of this story is noteworthy. By signaling that his manuscript was accepted only when the agent was bypassed, Bowles links the story of the novel's publication with the mythic bygone era alluded to earlier, before agents arrived on the literary scene, when publishing was gentlemanly and the author's relationship with the publisher was direct, personal, and concerned solely with art. The makers of art novels and the owner of the avant-garde publishing house in the early postwar era would repeatedly connect their productions to an earlier age of purportedly unmediated aesthetic judgment, to a time when there was no institutional apparatus and no intermediaries (agents, for example) whose concern might be something other than the aesthetic quality of the text. In this respect, the key phrase of Bowles's account is "he liked it," where the assessment of commercial prospects (if not application of genre theory) that governed Doubleday's decision to reject is replaced by something more ineffable: the taste of a single, discerning reader.

That reader is James Laughlin and, to understand the making of *The Sheltering Sky*, one needs to take stock of Laughlin's unusual place in the postwar literary field. Although it is important to understand that New Directions occupied a different place in that field than did Doubleday (it was, as Bowles rightly puts it, "at the other end of the publishing spectrum"), it is equally important to see that the marketing strategies used by New Directions proved to be not all that different from those of the larger companies. A useful point of departure is the grammar of Bowles's above account—"I . . . sent the typescript to New Directions, and . . . *he* liked it" (emphasis mine). Bowles's use of the pronoun "he" to refer to New Directions is understandable; the publishing house was perceived to be a one-man operation. "I don't have any business acumen," Laughlin once said. "I am not good at deals and can't cope with agents" ("History" 222). Just as Bowles, in his letters to Laughlin, disavowed the agent in order to maintain his avant-garde status in the eyes of the publisher, New Directions achieved its cultural status in part by disavowing the trappings of the modernized publishing house. Laughlin, heir to a Pittsburgh steel fortune, had founded the company in 1936 after his mentor Ezra Pound told him he had no future as a poet (his experience with Pound is much like Bowles's with Stein) and would be more "useful" (Pound's term) as a publisher of Pound and his friends (Laughlin, "New Directions" 21). Starting as Pound's patron, Laughlin cultivated a reputation as the publisher who would publish what no one else would, a patron to the avant-garde whose interest was neither in best sellers nor politics but in art itself.[20]

This reputation suggests in broad strokes what Bowles's account of Laughlin's decision to publish his novel suggests in miniature: that without the aid of financially motivated intermediaries Laughlin discovered great, unpublished writers, and that through his discernment and concomitant indifference to financial matters put them into print.[21] Laughlin and New Directions writers have an interest in telling this version of events, as it allows both to accrue maximum symbolic capital from their association with one other, and they have done so frequently over the years.[22] Laughlin in particular railed against the literary world's collaborations with mass-media corporations, railed that is against the very apparatus that Helen Strauss represented: "Every day," he wrote in 1946, "some new and more disgusting ulcer forces its way into the skin of the putrefied body—just yesterday I read in a trade journal that Warner Brothers have established a special department to 'inspire ideas' for writers to make into books and later into pictures" (qtd. in Barnhisel, *James Laughlin* 96–97). The poet Donald Hall summed up this version of Laughlin-as-aesthete best in saying that Laughlin chose which works to publish based on two assumptions: "the assumption of quality and the assumption that these books would not sell in the marketplace" (275).[23]

But two, related ideas are left out of this assessment of Laughlin's importance, and both need to be considered if we are to understand the story of *The Sheltering Sky*. First, the network of writers who recommended other writers to Laughlin muddies the picture of him as the solitary man of taste. Second, the surprising profitability of New Directions by the end of the 1950s—after almost two decades of losses, Laughlin's company began to turn a profit—must alter our view of Laughlin as a nonbusinessperson whose books would not sell. Some New Directions books did sell, and the method of advertising the book by not advertising it (Hall's description of Laughlin, first printed in the *New York Times*, as someone who cared only about aesthetic quality and who presumed failure in the marketplace, exemplifies this method) would prove an effective marketing strategy for novel producers in general. It was a way to distinguish the book from the mass culture that intellectuals attacked, even as, as Bowles's example suggests, the emergence of mass culture enabled the composition and publication of literary novels. The situation of New Directions in 1949 was analogous to Bowles's fledgling career as a novelist: on the verge of finding commercial success by producing works that were, as Leslie Fiedler derisively described Bowles's fiction, "intendedly highbrow" (502). *The Sheltering Sky*, published at the end of 1949 as New Directions entered its first profitable decade, was to become a prototype of a kind of literary-commercial success in the 1950s.

Toward the end of his life, Laughlin spoke proudly of his willingness to publish writers other than the ones Pound recommended, but almost every writer he published was recommended by a more established writer: "Most of our writers have come to us through recommendations of another writer friend" ("New Directions 34).[24] Most famously, Pound recommended his friend William Carlos Williams.[25] Djuna Barnes's *Nightwood*, already out of print and little acclaimed when New Directions reprinted it in 1946, was recommended by T. S. Eliot (31). Delmore Schwartz brought in John Berryman. Kenneth Rexroth brought in Denise Levertov (Rexroth 61). Edith Sitwell recommended Dylan Thomas, and Williams recommended Nathanael West (Hall 274). A telling example is the one that did the most to make New Directions a profitable company after twenty-three years of losses: Henry Miller, himself recommended by Pound years before, advised Laughlin to publish Hermann Hesse's *Siddhartha*, which Laughlin professed to dislike.[26] On Miller's advice, Laughlin published the novel in 1951, and it went on to become New Directions' best-selling book.

The William Morris Agency's decision to establish a literary department and Helen Strauss's decision to leave Paramount to become a literary agent together constitute one version of the story of the postwar growth of the book trade, one clearly linked to the growth of the mass-media industries. The surprising profitability of New Directions in the 1950s—propelled by sales of *Siddhartha*, the popularity of Lawrence Ferlinghetti's *A Coney Island of the Mind*, and the academic acceptance of Pound (itself triggered, according to Laughlin, not by the inherent greatness of Pound's poetry but by New Directions' publication of Hugh Kenner's *The Poetry of Ezra Pound* in 1951 ["History" 224])—is another version of the same story, linked to the growth of the educated reading public and surely the growth of the modern English Department.[27] And although New Directions might seem far removed from the economic world of William Morris, the role of intermediaries in the company's success somewhat belies the notion of Laughlin as the solitary man of taste. Laughlin asserted that he couldn't "cope with agents," yet he relied on Pound, Miller, Rexroth, and Schwartz, all of whom fulfilled the double roles of the agent that arose as the book business expanded over the course of the century. As Strauss was for Bowles and Doubleday, they were at once advocates for writers and screens for publishers, helping to get the writer into print and assuring the publisher that the writer was worthy.

Thus New Directions' rise to profitability is not just a story of talent, good taste, and indifference to commerce winning an underdog's battle against the forces of homogenization, commercialization, and bad taste, though there were elements of all that, and though Laughlin's belief in the aesthetic superiority of the works he published, his dislike of *Siddhartha* notwithstanding, is unquestionable. New Directions' rise is also a story of independent wealth; the publishing industry's low barriers to entry; and, most important, a network of poets, playwrights, and novelists functioning as agents and scouts, legitimizing one another's work, and then capitalizing on one another's success and on a growing market for serious literature. New Directions did not "find" avant-garde writers; writers who wrote for New Directions *became* avant-garde by virtue of their association with fellow New Directions writers and the New Directions imprint (which stood for nonideological, noncommercial aestheticism), and they did so at a time when conditions for writers deemed such were most favorable.[28]

All of which brings us back to Bowles, who as a first novelist in 1949 linked the commercial field of William Morris with the aesthetic field of New Directions. As noted earlier, Bowles's account of how New Directions came to publish his novel excludes any mention of intermediaries between him and Laughlin and in fact emphasizes that Strauss was not involved, attributing the company's decision to publish to an old-fashioned notion of aesthetic appreciation. But this account leaves out the role of Tennessee Williams, probably the most important player in the story of the publication and reception of *The Sheltering Sky*.

Williams was a close friend of both Laughlin and Bowles. Laughlin became Williams's publisher after they struck up a conversation at a cocktail party ("his only literary discovery with a social origin," according to Hall [275]) and discovered a common interest in Hart Crane's poetry.[29] Bowles, who first met Williams in Acapulco in 1940, years before the latter achieved literary success, had done what amounted to an enormous favor for him, composing music for *The Glass Menagerie* for its Broadway production in 1944 on short notice (one weekend) and perhaps without a contract.[30] Just after Bowles had submitted the manuscript of *The Sheltering Sky* to Doubleday, he returned to New York to compose music for Williams's *Summer and Smoke*.[31] According to a lengthy *Publishers Weekly* feature on Laughlin drawn from an interview with him, it was Williams who asked Laughlin to read Bowles's manuscript after Doubleday and many others had rejected it: "*The Sheltering Sky* had been turned down everywhere when . . . Williams brought it to [Laughlin]. Laughlin read the novel, was delighted by it" (Berkley 28).[32] Williams was, in short, Bowles's agent in deed if not name and, if not for his intervention, it is likely that New Directions never would have published Bowles's novel, not because Laughlin did not like it but because he probably never would have read the manuscript.[33]

It is impossible to know how *The Sheltering Sky* would have been received had it been published by Doubleday, but it seems fair to say, at least, that with the New Directions imprint *The Sheltering Sky* became a *different* novel than it would have been had Doubleday published it, legitimized by a different set of institutions within the literary field and thus received differently. In the week of its publication, in December 1949, none other than Tennessee Williams wrote an exceptionally favorable review of it in the *New York Times*, never mentioning his friendship with the author and the publisher or any role he may have played in getting the novel published. In that same issue of the *Times*, the New Directions poet William Carlos Williams, with whom Bowles had corresponded as far back as 1931, included *The Sheltering Sky* at the top of his list of the year's best books.

In the context of this story, it is not hard to understand why Bowles apologizes to Laughlin for his agent. After all, Strauss was hired specifically to get Bowles published, but in the end Bowles secured a publisher only when he bypassed Strauss—a publisher, moreover, who disdained the commercial anyway, rendering the Hollywood agent superfluous if not detrimental to Bowles's literary career. So it might have seemed, at least, to Bowles, who had already been rejected by numerous publishers and likely saw Laughlin as his last chance to become a novelist (to say nothing of whatever animus he might have had toward more mainstream parts of the book business, of which Strauss was his last remaining tie, after those rejections). Just as an art film gains status as such by being shown in an art-house theater, the failure of *The Sheltering Sky* to be accepted by the modern world of book publishing and the subsequent embrace it received from New Directions, so-called patron of the avant-garde, mark *The Sheltering Sky* as an art novel even before its publication and regardless of its form and content. The story of its tortuous path to publication, moreover, seems like a prewar, modernist parable about the marketplace's inability to recognize high art and the subsequent need for some form of patronage if high art were to survive.

Promoting the Novel

As it turned out, the market did recognize *The Sheltering Sky*, quickly rendering the modernist parable inapt. Commercial success was immediate, and the novel spent ten weeks on the *New York Times* best-seller list. Less than two months after *The Sheltering Sky* arrived in bookstores, *Life* magazine, much maligned as a bastion of middlebrow culture, featured Bowles, complete with photograph and a factual error (the caption says that he is unmarried) in a two-page spread as one of "four new writers." Bowles, according to *Life*, "hit a financial jackpot" with *The Sheltering Sky* ("Four New Writers" 35). By the time the novel left the best-seller list, it had sold nearly 40,000 copies, at a time when the average debut novel sold 2,000. In 1951, Signet published a paperback version that sold 200,000 copies in a year (Sawyer-Lauçanno 287).

This success needs to be contextualized in a few ways. First, accounting for the sales of a novel, particularly a first novel by an unknown author, is tricky. Publishers cannot reliably predict which of their products will sell. For this reason, they overproduce, publishing more books than they know the market can support, assuming that of ten titles, one or two will sell well. This is publishing's version of the Pareto-Zipf distribution, or the 80/20 rule, according to which "20 percent of products account for 80 percent of revenues" (Anderson 130–31). Once the publishing house gets an indication that a book is selling, it can throw its promotional muscle behind it in an attempt to ratchet sales upward and, if the system works right, the sales of that book subsidize the others that failed to sell.[34] It is a mistake to draw firm conclusions about the literary world from the sales of a single novel.

In addition, in the context of the postwar explosion of mass culture, it is worthwhile to remember just how small 40,000 purchases really is. That *The Sheltering Sky* was a best seller means simply that it sold a lot of books relative to the sales of others and it attained enough success to be profitable because the production of books is relatively inexpensive. Bowles's association with the William Morris Agency exemplifies the links between the literary and mass-culture fields, but even as these links grew the readership for a typical best seller would be dwarfed by the audience for a television show; only in the rarest of cases would a book achieve what might be called "mass" success. The novel's success, however, is of interest as an example of the way disavowals of the market could be commercially exploited. The relative success of *The Sheltering Sky* suggests that, contrary to the hand-wringing over the emergence of mass culture in the 1950s, the conditions that produced the emergence of mass culture were not antithetical to an increase in the number of readers or the survival of serious fiction; that hand-wringing—a significant aspect of both the promotion of the novel and the novel itself—would prove a good way to reach the book-buying audience.

Laughlin once remarked, "Advertising is useless for highbrow literary books, a waste of money. Word of mouth is what sells books, and it is reviews that get word of mouth started" ("History" 224).[35] But when the reviewer is a friend of both the publisher and the author and functions as the de facto agent for both, the line between advertising and reviewing becomes blurred. (In fact, the text of New Directions' paid advertisements for Bowles's novel draws on Williams's review.) Williams, moreover, trades on his literary fame to promote his friend's novel; Gore Vidal writes that Williams "wanted to be helpful to *The Sheltering Sky* so he asked the *New York Times* to let him review it" (*Point* 238).[36] At the time of the review, *A Streetcar Named Desire* had only recently completed a two-year run on Broadway. An assessment of the success of *The Sheltering Sky* and of the role that the review played must begin with Williams's own literary celebrity.

The review serves as an unusually clear window onto the way the art novel could be promoted in a commercial context: advertising the author's "disinterestedness," his disavowal of audience. At the heart of the review is an idea about art in the age of mass culture and corporate capitalism; the idea is that artists and art are becoming rare because career demands and career possibilities interfere with the aspiring artist's development. Williams begins his review by generalizing about the career of the American writer: "In America the career almost invariably becomes an obsession. The 'get-ahead' principle, carried to such extremes, inspires our writers to enormous efforts. A new book must come out every year. . . . I think that this stems from a misconception of what it means to be a writer or any kind of creative artist. They feel it is something to adopt *in the place* of actual living, without understanding that art is a byproduct of existence" ("Allegory" 7).

The implication is that whatever writers produce in an age of intense career pressures and career opportunities, it is not art. Williams's notion that the career precludes the production of genuine art combines the discourse of Huyssen's "great divide" (the idea of a "categorical distinction between high art and mass culture" [Huyssen viii]), most famously promulgated by Macdonald, Greenberg, and Horkheimer and Adorno, with ideas later famously articulated in popular sociology texts like David Riesman's *The Lonely Crowd* (1950) and William H. Whyte Jr.'s *The Organization Man* (1956), critiques to which the American reading public proved enormously responsive. According to Riesman and Whyte, Americans had lost what had been their defining trait—"rugged individualism"—as economic changes (particularly the ascendancy of the corporate business structure) conditioned them to be far more responsive to the needs and desires of others than were nonconforming Americans of the nineteenth century. American writers, in Williams's review, have analogously lost the ability to produce "art" (categorically distinct from the nonart they do produce) for similar reasons. Artistic expression is rare because the career has erased and replaced the self.

What makes Bowles special, according to Williams, is his willful avoidance of this self- and thus art-destroying careerism: "Bowles has deliberately rejected that kind of rabid professionalism," enabling "his growth into completeness of personality" ("Allegory" 7). Williams draws attention to Bowles's advanced age of thirty-eight and asserts that his artistry results from the fact that Bowles has waited until the time was right *for him* to produce a work of art—though we know that he set out to write a novel at the time that he did as a means to getting his short stories published and only after Helen Strauss secured an advance for him. The point here is not to deny Bowles's artistry on the grounds that he fails to meet Williams's criteria; rather, it is to point out that the idea of detachment from career concerns is perhaps less a precondition for artistry, as Williams would have it, than a constitutive aspect of artistry in Williams's time, one that springs from the actual growing connection between the literary field and other cultural and economic fields, and as such a selling point. The review reflects and depends on Bowles's place in what would prove to be a commercially viable network of literary production, and in it Williams celebrates an ideal of artistic detachment and congratulates Bowles for meeting that ideal. This irony is compounded as the thrust of Williams's praise is repeated in the full-page advertisement for *The Sheltering Sky* that New Directions placed in the *Saturday Review* on December 31, 1949. "Bowles is that rare thing," the advertisement declares, "a writer who waited to live life before he began to write it."

If the New Directions advertisements take their cue from Williams's book review, Williams might be said to take his cue from the novel he was reviewing. In the review, Williams's attack on the contemporary writer and his notion of the conditions that make art possible—"They feel it is something to adopt *in the place of* actual living, without understanding that art is a by-product of existence" (7)—are nearly identical to Bowles's narrator's account in the novel of why Port, the novel's protagonist, who has pondered a career as a novelist, does not write: "As long as he was living his life, he could not write about it. Where one left off, the other began, and the existence of circumstances which demanded even the vaguest participation on his part was sufficient to place writing outside the realm of possibility" (200). The two passages appear to express opposite ideas. Williams asserts that "actual living" is a prerequisite of writing, while Bowles's narrator suggests that living and writing are mutually exclusive, that as long as one is living one cannot be a writer. The confusion stems from the fact that Williams and Bowles use the word "living" in opposite ways. In Williams's review, "living" signifies detachment, whatever one does when not pursuing one's career. The novel suggests that Port could not be a writer because he was not detached enough; here "living" means engagement, the "vaguest participation." The point for Williams and Bowles (or at least for Port) is that engagement of a certain kind is fatal to artistry.[37]

Thus the novel itself articulates a version of the "great divide" discourse that Williams used to promote it. Indeed, the novel is more uncompromising than the review: whereas Williams finds art to be possible provided one ignores the demands of the career (thus allowing for the possibility of Bowles's achievement), the novel seems to assert that even deep in the Sahara, good writing will be impossible. Port's decision to forgo a necessarily compromised kind of writing signifies at once his capacity for artistry and the impossibility of artistry, a contradiction made possible by the equation of artistry with the refusal to engage. If Port, the self-proclaimed "traveler" (as opposed to mere tourist, a distinction crucial to the novel as a whole) who chooses death in the Sahara over life in New York, is not detached enough to write, no one could be. But where does this leave Bowles, and what does this say about the status of *The Sheltering Sky* as a work of art? That somehow the novel's declaration of the impossibility of art becomes a source of the novel's artistic stature, rather than an implicit statement of the novel's inevitable artistic failure, is itself a kind of marketing triumph.

That triumph rests on the problematic notion that Port and Bowles are alter egos. Williams was the first of many to make this claim: "Were it not for the fact that . . . [Port] succumbs to an epidemic fever, it would not be hard to identify him with Mr. Bowles himself" (7). But Port's death is not an accidental difference between author and character. The novel hints that it results from his refusal to be immunized by Western medicine before the trip; to the extent that this refusal constitutes another, supreme rejection of the West, it is an important part of Port's character. The novel's view of art is more extreme than the review's, ultimately because Port, by virtue of his quasi-suicide and his refusal to write, is a more detached version of Bowles. The paradox is that, as the romanticizer of Port's detachment, Bowles gains symbolic capital from it, even as he exemplifies, in writing and publishing a novel, what Port rejects. Symbolic capital accrues not from detachment but from the representation of and advertisement for detachment.

The Commercial Interruption

The relationship between this symbolic capital, or artistic prestige, and the representation of detachment becomes clearer in the chapter in which Bowles delineates Port's attitude toward writing, not just because of the view of art it espouses but also because of the way it interrupts the narrative and thereby undermines what is distinctive about its form. At this point, Kit and Port are in a truck on their way to Sba, alone, and Port is sick with the typhoid that will eventually kill him. The chapter opens this way: "As he lay in the back of the truck, protected somewhat from the cold by Kit, now and then he was aware of the straight road beneath him. The twisting roads of the past weeks became alien, faded from his memory; it had been one strict, undeviating course inland to the desert, and now he was very nearly at the center" (198). The description of the "undeviating course inland" captures not just Port's feelings about the trip but also something of the logic of the novel and the process by which it was composed: "It would write itself, I felt certain, once I had established the characters and spilled them out onto the North African scene" (*Without Stopping* 275). As Bowles described his own method, he never knew what would happen next in his novel because it always depended on what happened to him that day.[38] A distinctive feature of this method, and an important part of Bowles's aesthetic, is that he does not attempt to develop his characters' pasts. In the plot of the novel as in Port's own conception of his journey, memory is faded and the story moves forward only.

In one of the first looks at the novel, John W. Aldridge suggested that Port and Kit's lack of a past was a sign of the author's immaturity; to Aldridge, the novel's nihilism was unmotivated and therefore uninteresting (186–87). But there was a rationale for it. On principle, Bowles disdained the idea of character development. He conceived of the Sahara as the main "character" of the novel; his purpose was to show the ways in which the desert could make any of us, regardless of our history, culture, or class, submit, and he appeared to regard the awareness of this fact of human existence as supremely important: "The destruction of the ego has always seemed an important thing. I took it for granted that that was what really one was looking for in order to attain knowledge and the ability to live" (qtd. in Stewart 152–53). The kind of Jamesian character development that Aldridge sought would undermine the point Bowles was trying to make about the ego because it would draw attention to those aspects of human existence—job, personal relationships, class—that Bowles deemed superfluous and deceptive.[39] The ties between his disinclination to develop his characters' pasts and the form of the novel are summed up by the Kafka quote that serves as the epigram for the final section of the novel: "From a certain point onward there is no longer any turning back. That is the point that must be reached"; that Bowles identified with this kind of forward movement is apparent in the title of his autobiography: *Without Stopping*. Port's unwillingness to stop traveling signifies his (the character's) detachment from conventional American life; the novel's unwillingness to stop—that is, Bowles's refusal to develop his characters—signifies the same for Bowles.

At just this point in the novel, however, two-thirds of the way through and immediately after announcing Port's journey as "strict" and "unde-viating," Bowles does what both his aesthetic and his characterization of Port would seem to dictate against: he stops and turns back, offering the novel's only glimpse of Port and Kit's pretrip past. Much of what one might expect in the first chapter of a more conventional novel, about Port's family and career, for example, is given to us here, and these are just the kinds of details that Bowles would be expected to disdain as irrel-evant to his thesis about what we are beneath the dress of Western civiliza-tion. Something about this flashback is decidedly unnovelistic, as it comes without any impetus from the plot. So what is this scene—this unchar-acteristic look back—doing here? Coming so late in the novel, Bowles's decision to "stop" cannot be said to serve the conventional character-developing function that he disdained; rather, it serves the strategic func-tion of advertising Port's (and, by extension, Bowles's) detachment by transforming it into a theory of the (im)possibility of art in the postwar age. The point would hardly be worth making but for the fact that the flashback constitutes a concession to the conventional storytelling meth-ods the novel otherwise eschews and the absence of which, throughout the rest of the novel, is meant to signify the novel's artistic integrity. Art requires a kind of detachment made impossible by the demands of con-temporary Western culture, the novel suggests, but Bowles can only make that point, and implicitly make his case for his own artistry, by using those conventional, nonartistic methods. The flashback is like a commercial interruption, a built-in advertisement for the novel and its author.

In that advertisement, the narrator recounts actions that took place be-fore the start of the novel: first, Port's rejection of a career in New York, then the insistence of immigration officials that he identify his profession on his arrival in Africa. Port's refusal to answer brings to mind Williams's assertion that Bowles "has deliberately rejected . . . rabid professional-ism"; the episode as a whole recalls Williams's assertion that Bowles has achieved artistry by forgoing career concerns. Kit tells the immigration officials that he is a writer, and Port is intrigued: "The idea of his actually writing a book had amused him. A journal, filled in each evening with the day's thoughts, carefully seasoned with local color, in which the absolute truth of the theorem he would set forth from the beginning—namely, that the difference between something and nothing is nothing—should be clearly and calmly demonstrated" (199). Port's vision of a writer is a solitary teller of unpleasant truths, a notion of a piece with Bowles's own reputation but far removed from the growing network of literary production that enabled Bowles's sojourn. Just how solitary is soon made clear: "He had not even mentioned the idea to Kit; she surely would have killed it with her enthusiasm." Writing is serious work; the remark suggests that Port is rejecting the trappings of literary success, the admiration of a fan thrilled not necessarily by the quality or "truth" of the writing but by love of the romantic figure of "the writer." Port elaborates moments later: "Kit would be too delighted at the prospect; it would have to be done in secret—it was the only way he would be able to carry it off" (199). Port conceives that the fan's admiration precludes good writing.

Tunner presented a greater obstacle than Kit to Port's literary ambitions. Port attempted to write at the beginning of the trip but found himself unable to produce anything because "he could not establish a connection in his mind between the absurd trivialities which filled the day and the serious business of putting words on paper." He attributes his inability to write to Tunner's presence, which "created a situation, however slight, which kept him from entering into the reflective state he considered essential" (199). Tunner constitutes "the circumstances which demanded even the vaguest participation on his part," the engagement fatal to artistry. In this respect as in many others in the novel, Tunner is crucial. The novel's explicit theory of art in "the mechanized age" is a theory of the cultural problem that Tunner purportedly represents. But to the extent that Tunner is a problem in the novel, the representation of Tunner as such constitutes a profitable solution to the problem of how to preserve an idea of high art in the age of mass culture; it is through the depiction of the flight from Tunner that Bowles shows Port and Kit's—and his own—escape from the West.

From the start of the novel, Port and Kit cast themselves as sophisticated travelers (again, as opposed to tourists) whose desire it is to find a place as yet untouched by the war and, more generally, by the West. The tourist "accepts his own civilization without question; not so the traveler, who compares it with others, and rejects those elements he finds not to his liking" (14). The distinction matters not so much because it accurately captures Port's essence but because it is so clearly essential to Port's own sense of his identity. Port and Kit are highbrows, members, as Williams notes in his review, of the New York intelligentsia. After Kit laments that "the people of each country get more like the people of every other country. They have no character, no beauty, no ideals, no culture," Port replies, " 'You're right. . . . Everything's getting gray, and it'll be grayer. But some places'll withstand the malady longer than you think. You'll see, in the Sahara here' " (16). Port is the expert, the artist, the intellect, and Kit—the fan—submits to his intellectual vision of the world, responds emotionally and intuitively to it, and attempts to live up to Port's ideals.

Tunner occupies the bottom rung of the hierarchy, and it is often through their attitudes toward him that Port and Kit define themselves. Moreover, although Tunner has not received close attention from Bowles scholars, the entire plot of the novel turns on Port and Kit's attraction to and repulsion by him.[40] What attracts and repulses Port and Kit is best captured in Kit and Tunner's exchange as the trio arrive in a town even less civilized than the one from which they'd come. Says Tunner, "One thing I can't stand is filth," to which Kit replies, "Yes, you're a real American, I know" (112). This is the role Tunner plays in Port and Kit's lives—the American, the reminder of what they have tried to escape, the reminder of what they are better than. Tunner is, finally, the tourist (which is just another way of saying he is an American). He has not, as Port and Kit perceive that they have, abandoned the identity his home country has given him. Thus the novel's first description of him: "He was a few years younger [than Port and Kit] . . . astonishingly handsome, as the girl [Kit] often told him, in his late Paramount way. Usually there was very little expression of any sort to be found on his smooth face, but the features were formed in such a manner that in repose they suggested a general bland contentment" (15). Bowles's intention seems to be to paint Tunner as the unworldly American, but if Tunner is so American, what is he doing in the Sahara? Why does he want to listen to Port and lust after Kit? The narrator's answer to this question is typically abstract: "With them as with no one else he felt a definite resistance to his unceasing attempts at moral domination, at which he was forced, when with them, to work much harder; thus unconsciously he was giving his personality the exercise it required" (67). Far from being an intellectual, Tunner enjoyed the company of those he perceived as such: "Tunner was essentially a simple individual irresistibly attracted by whatever remained just beyond his intellectual grasp." Port and Kit are in Africa to see the Sahara. Tunner is in Africa to see Port and Kit. He is a step removed from their highbrow primitivism; he is their audience, and it is as such that Port both wants him near and ultimately runs from him.

Tunner's character is at least nominally modeled on George Turner, an American whom Bowles had met during an earlier foray into the Sahara. A more meaningful source for Tunner's character might be the idea of the "middlebrow," a staple of postwar American culture. The great fear of postwar intellectuals was not mass culture itself; for Macdonald and Greenberg, lowbrow fare for those who had no interest in (or ability to appreciate, as they would probably put it) "real" culture was just fine. As Macdonald put it, "If there were a clearly defined cultural *elite*, then the masses could have their *kitsch* and the *elite* could have its High Culture, with everybody happy. But the boundary line is blurred" ("Theory" 61). Middlebrow was what blurred that line. As such, it was a threat to the categorical distinction between art and nonart so crucial to the novel, the review, and the idea of highbrow art in the age of mass culture. "A tepid, flaccid Middlebrow Culture," Macdonald wrote, using rhetoric that seems borrowed from anti-Communists, "threatens to engulf everything in its spreading ooze" (63–64); the image clearly suggests, as does Port's refusal to write, that soon "high" art will vanish, in this case consumed by what Macdonald called midcult and masscult. The metaphor also suggests that middlebrow needs to be understood as both a demographic fact and an artistic problem, a form of cultural production and an audience that would happily consume it. Macdonald cited Ernest Hemingway's *The Old Man and the Sea*, the work of Thornton Wilder, and Mortimer Adler's Great Books volumes as examples of middlebrow culture, all commercially successful products for educated people. It was the growth of the market for products such as these—the same growth that led Doubleday to give Bowles an advance and that made New Directions a profitable company—that, to Macdonald, threatened high culture.

Port's refusal or inability to write while engaged with Tunner is telling in this context. For if Tunner is attracted to the intellectual challenge of Port and Kit, it is equally clear that for Port, at times, Tunner serves as a surrogate American audience. At the start of their journey, against Kit's wishes, Port offers a detailed account of a dream he has just had. Afterward, when they are alone, Kit upbraids him for telling "'that dream in front of Tunner.'" Port responds incredulously: "'In *front* of him! I told it *to* him, as much as to you'" (19). And Tunner wants to hear about it. Not long after Port shares his dream with Tunner, Kit is seduced by Tunner on the train. Bowles's narrator notes that "Kit and Port . . . both resented even the reduced degree to which they responded to his somewhat obvious charm, which was why neither would admit to having encouraged him to come along with them" (67).[41] Both Kit and Port wanted Tunner to join them in Africa; neither wants to admit it. In Port and Kit's relationship with Tunner we see both the middlebrow audience's desire to consume high culture and the debased desire of the supposed highbrow for an audience. Until Port and Kit flee from Tunner, the novel suggests, they have not truly left bland, contented America.

Port and Kit's solutions to the problem Tunner presents are extreme: not just not writing but also madness (in Kit's case) and death (for Port). Bowles's narrator seems to endorse this result: "It was all right to speed ahead into the desert leaving no trace" (200). Without stopping, as it were: leaving no trace is preferable to necessarily compromised communication or engagement. But Bowles is attuned to the paradoxes of this view and the economics on which they depend. Ultimately, there is one reason that Port has the opportunity to not write. That reason is mentioned just once, in the middle of the novel's out-of-place look back, so quickly it might be missed: "Since the death of his father he no longer worked at anything, because it was not necessary; but Kit constantly held the hope that he would begin *again* to write" (199, emphasis mine). This is the only allusion in the novel to Port's having aspired to being a *professional* writer at one time. Bowles thus marks the all-too-prosaic point at which it becomes possible to detach oneself from careerism: when one can afford it. Port's inheritance functions as a kind of antipatronage. Usually, patronage is understood to free the artist from the demands of the commercial marketplace and thus to pursue his or her own artistic vision. Here, Port's inheritance prevents him from the need to write at all in a world where even writing for no one in the Sahara is corrupt. As noted, the promotion of *The Sheltering Sky* depends on the association of Port with Bowles; in that Port's financial situation allows him to detach himself from matters of commerce, he is also, coincidentally, a bit like James Laughlin.

Career Moves

Port's flight from the Tunners of the world resonates in the context of the publication and success of *The Sheltering Sky*. The growth of middlebrow America, understood as a demographic fact rather than a cultural judgment—that is, as the growth of the population of educated culture consumers—was the condition of possibility for Bowles's career as a novelist and for the writing of his first novel, the reason that Helen Strauss and Doubleday (however briefly) showed interest in and invested in him, the

driving force behind New Directions' commercial success. Bowles capital-
ized on the opportunity afforded him by the growth of this audience by
writing a novel depicting the uncompromising flight from it and, in so
doing, created a blueprint for intendedly highbrow novelistic success in
the 1950s—a novel that achieves success in the consumer-culture market
by depicting the bankruptcy of that market. Ironically, the cultural problem that Port and Kit try to escape was more than just subject matter; it
was what enabled the novel's writing and publication in the first place.

The links between the novel's meditation on art and audience, on the
one hand, and the shifting institutional relation between novel production and the larger economic and cultural fields, on the other, become
clear in the story of *The Sheltering Sky*'s rocky path to the best-seller list.
The novel was an immediate success when it arrived in bookstores in late
1949, but it did not reach the best-seller list until January 1950. The reason for the delay is that Laughlin had only 3,500 copies printed when the
book was first released; they sold out quickly, but he did not print more
until the year's end. It is at this point that Bowles grew disenchanted with
Laughlin's disavowals of the market. As Bowles recounts in the preface,
written fifty years later yet with his ire for Laughlin still evident: "Because
his accountants had already filed income tax returns for 1949, he could
not risk showing a profit on an item that he had already written off as a
loss (since his interest in publishing was literary and not commercial),
and so he restricted the edition to 3,500 copies instead of the 10,000
which *Publishers Weekly* had recommended. It came out the second week
of December, but holiday sales were limited to what was available" (6).[42]
The story Bowles tells is confusing because it offers two separate reasons
for Laughlin's initial refusal to print more copies. First, he suggests a
curious tax-related reason, that because Laughlin had already written
the novel off as a loss, increased profits would mean he would have to
redo his tax returns. Parenthetically, however, and perhaps sarcastically,
Bowles hints at a second reason: Laughlin did not want to print more
copies because his interest was "literary," not "commercial." The rest of
Laughlin's career, and of course his subsequent printing of more copies
of *The Sheltering Sky*, suggests that Laughlin was not averse to selling a lot
of books. He was, however, noted for being a lax businessperson, prefer-
ring skiing to taking care of business matters. It is possible that he simply
missed the opportunity to sell more books in December due to inatten-
tion or because he underestimated the demand for the novel. Whatever
the cause, the dispute over the printing of the novel likely accelerated
Bowles's departure from New Directions.

As noted earlier, Bowles hired an agent and decided to write a novel only after Dial Press told him he could not publish a volume of his short stories without having first published a novel. The success of *The Sheltering Sky* put Bowles in an ideal position in which to have this volume of short stories published. The details here are sketchy but suggestive: we know that Bowles orally agreed to let Laughlin publish the volume and then reneged and moved on to Random House, a much larger publishing house, prompting Laughlin to threaten a lawsuit (which he apparently never filed). Bowles's stated reasons for leaving New Directions vary. He tells the early version of the story in an April 1950 letter to Vidal: "It was orally understood that the volume was to be done by [New Directions], until I got a cable from [Helen Strauss] saying that she had a far better offer from Random House and strongly advised me to take it" (*In Touch* 218). Characteristically, Bowles shifts the burden of a financially motivated decision onto his agent. But in another letter, written thirty-four years later, Bowles offers another explanation for his move: Laughlin's "principal reader, David McDowell, left at the end of December [1949] and went to Random House" (521).[43] Bowles here claims he left avant-garde New Directions for powerhouse Random House for specifically literary reasons, to maintain a tie with a literary collaborator. Bowles's two explanations for his move to Random House are not irreconcilable; both may be true. The luring of both Bowles and McDowell away from New Directions by Random House—Bowles as an established, now legitimate novelist and McDowell as a legitimizer of texts, himself now legitimized in and by the mainstream book world—epitomizes how ripe the postwar book market was believed to be for avowed avant-garde detachment from the market.

The moves of Bowles and McDowell barely affected New Directions; its formula—literary writers and an avowed indifference to commerce—had met its historical moment and its success continued throughout the 1960s and 1970s. Moreover, although larger publishers poached talent and marketing strategy from New Directions, New Directions cemented its own profitability by following the leads of some of those larger publishers. As Greg Barnhisel notes, Laughlin's decision to produce New Directions books in the new "trade paperback" format in 1954 ensured the company's commercial success (161–62). As conceived by Jason Epstein at Doubleday, who developed the idea for Anchor Books in 1953, soon to be followed by Knopf's Vintage Books, trade paperbacks were less expensive than hardcover books, so they could reach a wider audience of readers; unlike mass-market paperbacks, however, which were produced on a cheaper grade of paper and which had attached to them a lowbrow reputation, trade paperbacks were printed on higher-quality paper and were sold in finer bookstores.[44] The trade-paperback format allowed New Directions to market its highbrow fare to a wider audience. In the early 1950s, the distance between mainstream and avant-garde publishers was shrinking as the audience for books produced by both was growing. As the next chapter shows, even publishers of mass-market paperbacks would reach for that audience.

Chapter 2
The "Incalculable Value of Reading":
Fahrenheit 451 and the
Paperback Assault on Mass Culture

You're probably tempted, as we were at first, to work up a sputtering head of indignation about this . . . this . . . indignity. But hang on a second. Ray Bradbury got the medal in 2000, and while he can now be painted as a man who gave a popular genre a literary flair, were they saying that when "The Martian Chronicles" made its debut in 1950?

—*From "The Shining Moment," a* New York Times *editorial,*
October 16, 2003[1]

In suggesting that a recent decision to honor Ray Bradbury's writing constitutes a revisionist attempt to deem literary what was once considered mere genre fiction, the *New York Times* had it backward. The answer to its question is yes: as early as 1950, Ray Bradbury was credited with the feat of making literature of science fiction, using strategies similar to those used by James Laughlin and Tennessee Williams to promote *The Sheltering Sky*. But when, in 2000, the National Book Foundation (NBF), the organization that gives out the annual National Book Awards, awarded Bradbury the Medal for Distinguished Contribution to American Letters, its version of a lifetime achievement award, it was not for accomplishing this feat. In fact, as the NBF's announcement of the award attested, the honor had little to do with the perceived artistry of Bradbury's literary output. Bradbury's "life work has proclaimed the incalculable value of reading," the announcement said, adding that "these values are the bedrock of the National Book Foundation. Our mission is to promote the reading and appreciation of great American literature among audiences across the country."[2]

The decision to honor Bradbury and the reason given for that honor resonate in the context of two distinct, parallel, and seemingly unrelated institutional shifts in the American book trade in the era immediately after World War II: the emergence of a network of institutions, both commercial and nonprofit, designed to promote the value of reading, represented well by the formation of the National Book Foundation, and the emergence of science fiction as a commercially viable literary genre in book (as opposed to pulp) form. The NBF, officially established in 1954 (though the National Book Award, with which it would soon be attached, was first given in 1950), is the kind of literary institution that was new to postwar America, an example of the modernization of the book trade and, more specifically, of the trade's efforts to capitalize on the postwar economic boom and the growing population of educated consumers that made *The Sheltering Sky* a best seller and New Directions a profitable company. This modernization coincided with Bradbury's crossover from the world of American science fiction pulps to the more mainstream literary world: *Fahrenheit 451*, Bradbury's first novel, was published in 1953, a consequence of both his own high standing and of the book trade's new interest in science fiction and the emergence of the paperback.

One indication of the separateness of these two institutional developments (and thus, perhaps, an explanation of the *Times*'s incredulity in 2003) is that in the more than fifty years since the NBF was founded, it has not awarded a single one of its annual National Book Awards for Fiction to a science fiction novel.[3] Critical acceptance for science fiction as literature has been elusive and, in this context, it is notable that in its announcement the NBF does not explicitly honor Bradbury as a writer of the "great American literature" that it is the NBF's stated mission to promote; rather, it locates Bradbury's achievement in his promotional activities. In and of itself, this is unexceptional. As the NBF's general explanation of the Distinguished Medal makes clear, specifically literary accomplishment is not a necessary criterion: "The recipient is a person who has enriched our literary heritage over a life of service, or a corpus of work."[4] Past winners include esteemed novelists Toni Morrison (1996), John Updike (1998), and Philip Roth (2002), as well as more peripheral literary figures, such as Clifton Fadiman (1993), Oprah Winfrey (1999), and James Laughlin (1992). The presence of these latter figures suggests that the service criterion encompasses any work that in some way contributes to the dissemination of literature, the promotion of its importance to the reading audience, or both, and it further suggests im-

licit, rarely articulated connections between the mid-century projects
lisparate figures Bradbury and Laughlin.

dbury's promotional activities are ample. In interviews and essays,
ever shied away from proclaiming the cultural importance of the
ok.[5] His remark, quoted in the NBF's announcement of the honor, that
his job is "to help you fall in love" (with the book) is but one example of
many such pronouncements over the past half century. It is in the service
of this cause that, as Bradbury himself notes, he has "spun more stories,
novels, essays and poems about other writers than any other writer in history that I can think of" (Afterword 168).[6] But undoubtedly Bradbury's
most important work in this regard is *Fahrenheit 451* itself, the novel that
followed *The Martian Chronicles*, the "seminal book-lover's book," as Steve
Martin put it at the NBF ceremonies honoring Bradbury, a star-making,
moneymaking novel about what the NBF calls the "incalculable value"
of books.[7] The unusual place in the literary field that Bradbury has occupied since *Fahrenheit 451* was published, as the genre writer who has
made the importance of literature a primary topic, helps to explain the
ambiguity surrounding the reasons for which the NBF honored him in
2000. What distinguishes Bradbury's "service" from that of Laughlin and
Fadiman is the fact that it is located within and is inseparable from his
literary output, his corpus of work. His work is at once literature and
promotion, and it is this that marks Bradbury as an emblematic figure of
the rapidly changing book trade of the early 1950s.

Fahrenheit 451, which imagines or predicts a future American society
dominated by television and largely devoid of books, is thus an emblematic text of this era in two crucially related senses. First and more obviously, it takes as its subject the much discussed threat to the book posed
by the emergence of postwar mass culture, a fact that links it to classic
texts of its decade's mass-culture debates, though this fact has received
little attention in Bradbury scholarship and in scholarship of the mass-
culture debate itself.[8] Second, it is enabled by the generally neglected,
if not deliberately and necessarily obscured, opportunity that accompanied the threat, an irony that also has received little attention but which
is crucial to an understanding of the novel, its reception, and the larger
issue of the shifting cultural and economic status of American novels in
the early 1950s. As a dystopia that links the destruction of Western civilization to the predicted decline of the book, *Fahrenheit 451* might be the
best advertisement for the book ever devised. Although the novel has
received a great deal of scholarly attention since its publication, mostly
in the form of close readings of its quasi-allegorical plot and mostly in

sources devoted to science fiction specifically, its effectiveness as a promotional piece—and the way that effectiveness situates it in the context of similarly themed book promotion efforts of the time, complicates its relationship to mainstream intellectual culture and the genre from which it emerged, and sheds light on a developing network of 1950s literary institutions—has yet to be examined.[9] Bradbury's honor in 2000, and the decades of unlikely recognition it embodies (in 1952, *Time* magazine called Bradbury the "poet of the pulps"), might be explained as a result of his defense of timeless literary values—certainly the NBF would like to explain it this way—but it demands to be understood as well as a time-bound product of the twin institutional shifts in the literary field noted earlier: the emergence of science fiction and the emergence of a sophisticated network of promotional institutions. These shifts, moreover, though seemingly unrelated, are connected at the root, both products of the growing market for books in the United States in the postwar era and in particular of the triumphant emergence of the paperback after the war.

To draw these connections and to tell this largely untold story, this chapter reconstructs the rapid emergence of the institutional structures that could enable both the writing and the recognition of *Fahrenheit 451* in the late 1940s and early 1950s. As the NBF's decision to honor both Bradbury and Laughlin attests, it is a story inseparable from the rise of New Directions to profitability; in both we see the emergence of a distinctive strategy for selling literary fiction in the age of mass culture, the emergence of a promotional apparatus that could implement that strategy, and the growth of an audience receptive to it.

National Book Awards

In 1949, the Book Manufacturers' Institute (BMI), a trade association of American book manufacturers, awarded what was billed as the first annual Gutenberg Award—it turned out to be the only award so named—to Robert Sherwood for *Roosevelt and Hopkins* because, according to the BMI, the book "most progressively influenced American thought in 1948" (qtd. in "Roosevelt" 8). Covering the event, *Publishers Weekly* discussed the ways in which the BMI sought to publicize the event and the award, which now seem modest to the point of quaintness: "The BMI has run full page ads about the award and the ten books named as candidates for it, in the *Herald Tribune Weekly Book Review* and the *Saturday Review of Literature*, and has secured extensive publicity, samples of which

column space in the *New York Times Book Review* ("Re

That the Gutenberg Awards are long gone and that two of the pu̲
cations they used to publicize their awards, the *Herald Tribune* and the
Saturday Review, are also long gone, might look like yet another version
of a familiar postwar narrative: that of the decline of "book" or literary
culture and along with it the decline of culture itself. But that appearance is misleading because the modest Gutenberg Award of the BMI did
not disappear so much as it metamorphosed and expanded. One year
later, it was replaced by the bigger, better, and more patriotically named
National Book Awards, now with single, separate awards for nonfiction,
fiction, and poetry, suggesting that, in a sense, the often-told story of
the mid-century death of print culture is not distinct from the fact of its
growth; and this is a fact that the enduring success of *Fahrenheit 451*, itself
a story of the death of print culture made possible by its growth, attests
to well. The transformation of the Gutenberg Award was precipitated by
an increase in the number of its sponsors and planners. *Publishers Weekly*
reported in 1949 that, in addition to the BMI, planners would now include the American Booksellers Association (ABA) and, crucially, the
American Book Publishers' Council ("Gutenberg" 1980). This kind of
collaboration among the different strands of the book trade was rare before World War II. Indeed, it was one of the goals of the ABPC, founded
shortly after the war, not just to unite competing publishers in pursuit of
their common interests but also to unite publishers with other institutions that had an interest, whether profit or the public good, in getting
people to read.

The National Book Award is properly understood as a fruit of these efforts. When the January 21, 1950, *Publishers Weekly* deemed the National
Book Awards "the first official awards to be made to American authors
by the entire book industry" ("First" 245), the unstated emphasis was on
the word "entire." The collaboration matters in a broad sense as a sign
of a developing strategy on the part of the book trade, and it matters
specifically because it triggered a dramatic increase in the scale and ambition of the awards. The Gutenberg Awards were attended by authors
and industry insiders; the "toastmaster" was the general counsel of the
BMI, and other speakers included representatives of other institutions
of the book trade. The highest profile speaker was New York City mayor
William O'Dwyer, who presented the award to Sherwood.

The first National Book Awards banquet was, in a word, bigger, and not merely because more books were honored, though in itself that suggests a belief that the market can accommodate a greater number of heavily promoted books, a belief, that is, that the investment made in those books will be returned. (In addition to the three winners, five citations were awarded to other nonfiction books.) The banquet was described in *Publishers Weekly* as "probably the largest assemblage of book trade personnel and authors in the industry's history" ("National Book Awards Given"); more than 1,000 people attended to see Nelson Algren, William Carlos Williams, and Ralph L. Rusk (for *The Life of Ralph Waldo Emerson*) honored. At the 1950 event, Fadiman was the master of ceremonies, and speakers included Eleanor Roosevelt, Senator Paul Douglas of Illinois, and Frederick Lewis Allen, editor of *Harper's*. "An atmosphere of glamour attended" the awards presentation, reported the *New York Times* ("Three" 12), and the event was broadcast on the radio (though not on television, apparently to the chagrin of the organizers) (Melcher, "1000" 1508). It even featured a musical performance to enhance its entertainment value. It was, in multiple senses, a multimedia event.

The emergence and rapid evolution of the awards is telling, less for its ultimate effect on the book trade, which is not momentous, but for what it signifies about the business at what was evidently a transitional moment. The increasing pomp suggests again that the book business was growing (the awards, as an obvious promotional event, should be understood as both a reflection of that growth and an attempt to further it) and that growth meant not just increased production and sales but also that the trade was attempting to adopt marketing techniques used to great success by institutions of mass consumer culture. The fact that the event was broadcast on radio, and that television coverage was sought, anticipates the book business's later alliances with mass-media corporations, and it was this aspect of the event that triggered Frederic Melcher's lone criticism of it: "There was one flaw in the planning. The book trade did not quite have the faith that a program built of such elements would bring together and hold such a large audience, and it turned to lesser arts than literature for aid . . . in reaching for a television audience . . . night-club features were given a half hour of precious time. The book trade will want to carry on this series of annual dinners, but next time needs to have more faith in books" ("1000" 1508).

These remarks, particularly the snobbish references to "lesser arts" and "night-club features," delineate an elusive but deeply felt tension within the book trade, between maintaining its dignity as purveyors of literature on the one hand and achieving greater commercial success by trying to

tension: if the event was a spectacular one, the choices, happily, were not. The three winners are serious writers, shy of personal publicity, who have reflected on the meaning of America" ("Three" 12). In making this reference to the literary dignity of the event, both Melcher and the *Times* might have been treating the National Book Awards relative to the Pulitzers, which had lost credibility as a literary prize-giver.[10] But the notion of a choice between literary dignity and mass success was always a false one and thus something of a rhetorical gesture: first, because the attempted reach for a larger audience was a market-driven inevitability and, second, because as noted earlier books never could compete with television anyway. In short, both the worst fears and most optimistic hopes of a genuine, sustained mass success within and without the book trade were always unfounded. But while the idea of such a choice was always false, the articulation of the possibility of this choice served useful purposes.

This last point has been made frequently with respect to literary critics in the 1950s, as a way to understanding the fierce reaction to mass culture at the time, but the limited degree to which it holds as well for the book trade has received less attention. Janice A. Radway has noted that the alarm expressed by 1950s intellectuals over the purported erosion of cultural standards, the assertion, that is, of what Huyssen calls the "great divide" between art and mass culture, helped those intellectuals make a case for their own relevance as mass culture emerged.[11] Concern within the book trade about the appearance of commercialization, about the glitziness of the inaugural National Book Awards ceremony, suggests the degree to which the book business similarly sought to maintain a distinction between the world of books and the world of mass culture: the argument above that mass culture degrades the book, far from signifying the book trade's retreat from consumer culture, in fact constitutes what would become one of its primary marketing pitches, a fact made clear in Laughlin's marketing of *The Sheltering Sky*. Rather than choose between snobbery on the one hand and advertising on the other, the book trade inevitably and wisely chose snobbery (that is, the moral, political, and aesthetic superiority of books to other forms of culture) *as* advertising. This was not, in itself, a new development: what was new was the centralized institutional structure, embodied by the ABPC and the development of the National Book Awards, for disseminating this message.

At the 1950 ABA convention, for example, "Speakers adopted the point of view . . . that while television was another claimant for readers' leisure time, it also offered opportunities for book promotion" ("Summary 1950" 223); one year later, the ABA announced that "the book trade's fear of television is unjustified" ("TV Effect" 38). And the ABPC later reported that "TV programs, especially those systematically focused on books, do help sell books" ("Reading Promotion" 215). But the point is not that television was not a threat or that television was both a threat and an opportunity. The point is that the idea of the threat, properly exploited, constituted the opportunity, as can be seen in this anecdote reported in *Publishers Weekly*: "A television company's advertisement stating that children who were deprived of television were being abused by their parents was widely condemned; Harper countered with a full-page *Times* ad promoting Harper Juveniles for the 'poor little waifs' without television" ("Summary 1950" 223). Here an egregious television advertisement was made a symbol for an increasingly crass culture, the very idea that people *need* television an insult to the book and to book culture and to the sensibilities of the reading audience; through an advertisement of its own, the book business was happy to foment and exploit whatever ill will was generated by the television advertisement.

Wonderful World

Some of the paradoxes of this approach to mass culture, paradoxes that are embedded in *Fahrenheit 451*, can be found in a volume called *The Wonderful World of Books*, also published in 1953 (Stefferud). *Wonderful World*, a collection of essays that grew out of a 1951 conference on the fate of the book in rural areas, caused considerable excitement within the book trade. As a measure of the similarities and differences between the book trade and high-culture intellectuals, it is appropriate that the book was published so close to the publication in *Partisan Review* of the famous "Our Country and Our Culture" symposium, in which the editors cited mass culture as a primary threat facing American life, in part because "its tendency is to exclude everything which does not conform to popular norms; it creates and satisfies artificial appetites in the entire populace; it has grown into a major industry which converts culture into a commodity." The editors went on to note that the "increasing power [of mass culture] is one of the chief causes of the spiritual and economic insecurity of the intellectual minority," suggesting the specific threat that mass culture posed to the financial well-being of professional intellectuals (285).

Wonderful World expressed a similar view of mass culture, but from an institutional perspective it was something different, essentially a com-

considered high literature) and for a generalized notion of the importance of reading (not solely the importance of a small list of great texts), written and produced not by high-culture critics (the "intellectual minority") but by representatives of the book trade and other institutions that perceived an interest in expanding national literacy. This is another way of saying that whereas *Partisan Review*, famously the champion of modernist culture, was exclusionary, *Wonderful World*, aiming to spread the book far and wide, was inclusive; the best thing for America, the book suggested, was for *everyone* to read and read more of whatever it was that booksellers were selling. In this respect *Wonderful World* embodied an advertising strategy that became particularly crucial in the postwar era; rather than try to create advertisements for individual books (an expensive proposition), the book trade would seek to promote the value of reading in general.[12]

Backed by what the ABPC called "one of the most intensive promotion campaigns in book history" ("Widespread" 112), *Wonderful World* was billed as a nonprofit effort on the part of no less than eleven organizations, including, of course, the ABPC, ABA, and BMI, along with other peripheral literary institutions like the American Library Association (ALA) and the National Council of Teachers of English (NCTE); even more than the National Book Awards, it stands as the quintessential example of the ABPC's efforts to unite institutions in and out of the book trade for the common goal of promoting the value of reading.[13] All proceeds were to be "put back into a national campaign for books and reading" (112). For the book business, *Wonderful World* surely functioned as an advertisement, though to call it such is not to deny the civic virtues of reading or of books. Whereas a television advertisement that asserted that children needed television was crass and unseemly, no one would suggest that the book trade should feel shame for positing the necessity of the book for children or adults. This is the payoff of previously produced belief in the value of reading.

"Now, more than ever," is the portentous beginning to the introduction of the volume, "we felt a reminder is needed that books can instruct and help us in a competitive world, in which more and more knowledge is needed to keep up with scientific developments . . . in a world of television, radio, automobiles, of getting and spending and laying waste our powers, books can give us perspective and depth and fulfillment" (Stefferud 13). This passage could easily function as an introduction to and advertisement for not just the book in general but the new science fic-

tion novel and *Fahrenheit 451* in particular: the terms of the promotion of
the science fiction genre are encapsulated in the notion that "more and
more knowledge is needed to keep up with scientific developments." But
the terms of a far more general (that is, non-genre-specific) book promotion are here clearly laid out as well—in a world of emergent mass culture, consumer culture (William Wordsworth's "getting and spending"),
and the threats of the Cold War ("In view of the current world situation,"
begins another equally portentous explanation of why reading is so important now), the book is both more endangered than ever and more
important than ever, a message that Bradbury's *Fahrenheit 451*, published
just a few months later, would echo. The fact that the book is itself a
commodity, one of those products we can get and spend on, is not mentioned in a volume designed to elevate the book to something more than
a commodity—not a product with mere exchange value but an object
with what the National Book Foundation would later call, in the course
of honoring Bradbury, "incalculable value" for the person who buys it.
But the relationship between the book and the financial self-interest of
the contributors and publishers of the volume is not exactly unacknowl-
edged: as the introduction notes, "For some of us—publishers, editors,
booksellers, writers, teachers, librarians, and Extension workers—books
are connected with the way we make our living" (13).

This was probably true for all of the contributors. The point, however,
is not that a crass motive underlay the involvement of all contributors
to the project. As the introduction continues: "But job and pocketbook
were not mentioned during those three days [of the conference] . . .
rather, the word 'missionary' was used often" (13). As with the assertions
of the "great divide" between high art and mass culture by academics and
high-culture critics, this commerce-averse appeal to an Arnoldian notion
of literature as secular religion no doubt reflected deeply held beliefs on
the part of the participants in the conference and contributors to the
volume, and this again suggests something of the power of a culturally
constructed, internalized belief in the importance of the book. In terms
of content, *Wonderful World* is at once a testament to the effectiveness of
earlier efforts to produce belief in the value of the book and a piece of a
new, larger-scale postwar effort to further this goal.

If the profit motive was obscured within the text or suppressed in the
minds of the contributors, something of *Wonderful World*'s financial subtext was in evidence in the way the book was published: simultaneously
as a hardcover by Houghton Mifflin and a paperback by New American
Library (NAL) in February 1953. The logic of this decision is simple:

chet, a space in their bookstores, and perhaps media attention from middlebrow or highbrow sources; paperbacks, however, which are much cheaper, are far more likely to actually be bought, and they spread the word about books not just to bookstores but to department stores, train stations, newsstands, and even vending machines everywhere. ("Good Reading for the Millions" was NAL's slogan.[14]) In terms of content, *Wonderful World* was one of the book business's answers to the threat of mass culture, the embodiment of a marketing strategy; materially, the paperback was the book business's version of mass culture, its attempt to exploit the opportunity that mass culture presented. As a version of mass culture used to respond to the threat of mass culture, the paperback stands as the ultimate symbol of the paradoxes of the 1950s book trade, the sign of its actual growth at the moment it was said to be most threatened. Neither the postwar emergence of science fiction in book form in general nor the particular story of *Fahrenheit 451* itself can be fully understood without taking its impact into account.

Paperbacks and Science Fiction

The paperback, as Kenneth C. Davis describes in depth in *Two-Bit Culture: The Paperbacking of America*, made its famous entry into the book world in 1939, when Robert de Graff, in partnership with Simon & Schuster, created Pocket Books, selling mass-produced paperbacks for twenty-five cents. But like the impact of television, its cultural and commercial effect was not fully felt until after World War II, when paper rations ended and an unprecedented economic boom and increase in college attendance ensued. Although much has been written on the paperback as a cause of major change in the book trade, its emergence needs to be understood as an effect as well. Davis notes, "Like Hollywood and television, this undertaking was another amalgam of that peculiar American genius for combining culture, commerce, and a little technology" (13). But what the paperback required most of all to succeed was an audience. The true American ingenuity regarding the paperback was as much demographic insight as it was technological advance: the recognition that there are enough people who will buy them. (It should not have been greatly surprising that high-culture texts appealed to a wide audience; before the paperback revolution, both the Modern Library and the Everyman's Library had demonstrated the popular appeal of relatively low-cost reprints of classic texts).[15] The economic logic of the paperback was that of mass production: producing large quantities of books created economies of scale that lowered the cost of production per book. Not only did this enable books to be sold cheaply, it also aroused the ire of high-culture critics; the arrival of the paperback marks a moment where the book trade and high-culture critics, united in their distaste for mass culture, parted ways. Intellectuals who wrote for the *Partisan Review* might have agreed with the sentiments expressed in the book trade's *Wonderful World*, but they found cause for alarm in the manner of its dissemination.

According to Cecil Hemley's "The Problem of the Paper-backs," published in *Commonweal* magazine in 1954, there were in fact two problems with paperbacks. First, they degraded what used to be high culture by placing quality books right next to low-quality fare, thus diluting their standing as high culture. In this sense, paperback sellers are the book trade's version of *Life* magazine, famously mocked by Dwight Macdonald in his essays on middlebrow and mass culture. "The same issue," Macdonald complained about *Life*, "will contain a serious exposition of atomic theory alongside a disquisition on Rita Hayworth's love life . . . an editorial hailing Bertrand Russell on his eightieth birthday . . . across from a full-page photo of a housewife arguing with an umpire at a baseball game" ("Theory" 62). The implication, of course, is that Hayworth diminishes atomic theory and the housewife diminishes Russell. Similarly, in Hemley's view, paperback vendors degrade Shakespeare by selling him alongside Mickey Spillane. By failing to pay proper tribute to the greatness of high-culture texts, paperbacks contribute to the erosion of cultural standards in America, even as they demonstrate the appeal to the masses of what were once considered high-culture texts—if not precisely *because* they demonstrate that appeal. That Hemley's article was later published in *Mass Culture: The Popular Arts in America* (1957), a collection of some of the decade's most famous attacks on mass culture ever published (including Macdonald's attack on *Life*, first published in *Diogenes* in 1953, a year replete with attacks on mass culture), a volume that stands as perhaps the primary document of the debate over mass culture, suggests something of the way the paperback was looked at by intellectuals (Rosenberg and White).

For Hemley, the second, more pertinent problem with paperbacks is that they encourage the production of lowbrow genre fare. As he notes, the paperback publisher "must fall back on genres, such as the mystery or the western, which have wide, ready-made audiences waiting for them" (141). Throughout the first half of the twentieth century, publishers lamented that books could not be advertised the way other products were,

sell, and required its own advertising campaign, which made advertising not cost-effective.[16] A different advertising campaign was not needed for each McDonald's hamburger, but each book did require one; indeed, the individual book's uniqueness was a selling point, but it was a point that publishers asserted they could not profitably afford to make. This is one reason it was so valuable for publishers to promote "reading" instead of individual books, and this same set of circumstances helps make the book critic so important to the book trade; each book needs individual attention to determine its worthiness, and the cost-ineffectiveness of advertising individual books creates a cultural and an economic space for the critic to fulfill this role. In this sense, the uniqueness of the individual literary work is the source of the literary critic's cultural authority.

Genre fiction was one way to combat the seller's problem that uniqueness posed. To the extent that individual genres relied on a set of received conventions, they could be sold and advertised as a group rather than as individual texts. But to the extent that genres were a boon to publishers, they were a bane to critics. Because genres rely on a set of conventions, they contribute to the diminution of the importance of the critic in determining what is read and what is not. As Kammen usefully puts it, in the 1950s the cultural authority of critics and intellectuals began to be usurped by the "cultural power" of institutions of mass culture, paperback publishers included. The tragic dimensions of this lost battle—more precisely, the idea that this lost battle has tragic dimensions and dire consequences—is crucial to the plot of *Fahrenheit 451*, even as the novel itself is a direct consequence of the rise of the much lamented usurper, the paperback publisher. *Fahrenheit 451*, like *Wonderful World*, is a quintessential product of the convoluted web of paradoxes in which the postwar book trade was enmeshed.

Science fiction, in any event, is a notable omission from Hemley's list of problematic genres, but it is likely omitted not because it was more respected by critics than were westerns or mysteries but rather because, until the mid-1950s, it was scarcely represented in book form. The genre existed almost exclusively in pulps, and the few science fiction books that were published in the late 1940s and early 1950s were anthologies of material first published in pulps; the term "science fiction novel," much less the idea of science fiction as literature, was largely unheard of, not just in literary circles but within the community of science fiction writers as well. The origins of science fiction as a self-conscious genre, with its own conventions and its own publications, at least in the United States, are usually traced to the founding of *Amazing Stories* by Hugo Gernsback in 1926 (it was Gernsback who popularized the term "science fiction" after his first choice, "scientification," failed to ignite).[17] Thus science fiction is younger than the western and the detective story, and as Reginald Bretnor wrote proudly of his genre in 1953, "Since Gernsback . . . it has developed independently, owing almost nothing to our main literary streams" (ix). At the time of Hemley's essay, in other words, science fiction was only beginning to find its way onto the critics' radar; prior to the 1950s, no analog exists in the science fiction genre for either Edmund Wilson's famously curmudgeonly attack on the detective fiction genre ("Who Cares Who Killed Roger Ackroyd?," also included in the 1957 *Mass Culture* volume) or for the attempts to deem detective fiction literary that prompted Wilson's rebuke.

That that was about to change—that a dialogue of sorts was about to open between science fiction writers and editors and more mainstream intellectual culture—signifies science fiction's postwar emergence and perhaps exemplifies what high-culture intellectuals most feared as they worked to maintain the great divide between an exclusionary high culture and mass culture. Bretnor's remark appeared in *Modern Science Fiction: Its Meaning and Its Future* (also published in 1953, around the same time as *Wonderful World* and months before *Fahrenheit 451*), a collection of essays edited by Bretnor that grew out of a symposium on the genre that featured numerous science fiction superstars, including John W. Campbell, editor of the seminal pulp *Astounding* and author of the early science fiction classic *Who Goes There?* (1938); Robert A. Heinlein; and Isaac Asimov. Described by Seymour Krim in a generally derisive review in *Commonweal* as "the first book of its kind . . . a serious symposium on this new medium," *Modern Science Fiction* is, like *Wonderful World*, another little-noted but significant complement to the famed *Partisan Review* symposium of 1952, in part because it signifies the emergence of one version of the mass culture that the "Our Country" participants feared, in part because, like those texts, it celebrates the distance of its subject from mass consumer culture.

Indeed, one fact that *Modern Science Fiction* makes clear is that science fiction writers, rightly, did not consider themselves mere mass entertainers. Part of the stated aim of the book, in fact, is to make the case for the intellectual heft of the genre. Bretnor deems the volume "the first attempt to examine modern science fiction in its relation to contemporary science, contemporary literatures, contemporary human problems" (x-xi), and at the same time suggests, in a manner not different from high-

consumer culture. It has attracted a wide, intelligent readership without the benefit of high-pressure publicity or pathological sensationalism" (ix). Thus, Bretnor concludes, "its presently increasing popularity is a result of its own special merit—its validity for the age in which we live" (ix). Science fiction is defined by its aim to give a plausible account of the future based on what is happening in the present; what makes it especially relevant is the increasing degree to which technology is determining our present and will continue to do so. As they are in *Wonderful World*'s celebrations of generalized reading and *Partisan Review*'s celebrations of modernist difficulty, both the Cold War and the problem of mass consumer culture are prominent subtexts to *Modern Science Fiction*'s explanation of the importance of science fiction. Campbell, often cited as the most important figure of the golden age of science fiction pulps of the 1930s and 1940s, elaborates on some of these ideas and specifically connects the importance of science fiction to the Cold War in his essay: "The atomic bomb has had a great deal to do with the increased interest in science fiction—but only indirectly. Atomic bombs are explicitly a scientific device; they involve the most advanced and esoteric understanding of the basic nature of the universe—the sort of ideas that people have, for years, shrugged off with, 'What's that got to do with me, huh?'" (17).[18]

As a bid for mainstream critical respectability, *Modern Science Fiction* was at best a qualified success. Krim's review of it in the June 12, 1953 issue of *Commonweal*, which describes science fiction as "a phenomenon which has been growing like Pinocchio's nose and has far-reaching literary and cultural consequences" and which treats the book as an occasion to assess the genre as a whole, is distinctly double-edged. Krim accepts the notion that science fiction "brings that future to us by making both logical and imaginative deductions from the [specifically scientific and technological] temper of our times" (252). As a result, he writes, it is "often more provocative entertainment than will be found in the ordinary detective story," in large part because it "has brought to light and dramatized aspects of the contemporary imagination which our better-equipped writers, qua *writers*, have left untouched." Although science fiction fills a conceptual void, it is a literary failure: "Very few [science fiction] works will endure because few of them reach the level of literature on literature's own terms" (253).

But Krim does allow for the possibility of a literary science fiction writer: "This is not to say that occasional science fiction stories by Ray

Bradbury or Fritz Leiber do not raise the point of view behind science fiction to something like literature" (253). The heavily qualified "compliment"—not the genre itself but the "point of view behind" it is "something like" literature—nonetheless conveys something of the elevated status Bradbury had attained by 1953 (six months before the publication of *Fahrenheit 451*), the status that the *New York Times* denied him in 2003. Further evidence of Bradbury's stature can be found in the fact that he was given space in *The Nation*, in an article titled "Day After Tomorrow: Why Science Fiction?," to make his own case for science fiction in May 1953, one month before the publication of Krim's review of Bretnor's volume. The confluence of events—Bretnor's volume, Krim's review, Bradbury's essay, all occurring months apart in 1953, all still a few months prior to the publication of *Fahrenheit 451*—suggests that this year was in a sense science fiction's coming-out, the moment when what was a relatively unknown subculture makes its presence felt in the more mainstream intellectual and commercial fields.

To the extent that *The Nation*, unlike *Commonweal*, allowed a science fiction insider to discuss the genre, Bradbury's essay was a victory for the genre; Bradbury was contacted specifically to defend it in response to criticisms from new detractors (Weller 206). In comparing it with Bretnor's essay, one finds clues as to why the literary mainstream was prepared to embrace Bradbury's brand of science fiction. Like Bretnor and Krim, Bradbury begins with a claim for the genre's contemporary relevance—science fiction is particularly important *now*, for a specific set of extra-literary reasons: "There are few literary fields, it seems to me, that deal so strikingly with themes that concern us all today . . . there are few more exciting genres, there are none fresher" (365)—and on roughly the same grounds (science fiction extrapolates and makes predictions based on scientific trends that are largely ignored by other writers but that are increasingly important in the lives of Americans).

But Bradbury, unlike many of the contributors to *Modern Science Fiction*, wants to do more than just make a case for his genre's timeliness; he wants to make a case for its timelessness as well, for its aesthetic or literary merits—a case that does not seem of much interest to Bretnor and Campbell and a case that Krim flatly rejects—and so he continues: "It is, after all, the fiction of ideas, the fiction where philosophy can be tinkered with, torn apart, and put back together again, the fiction of sociology and psychology and history compounded and squared by time" (365). Science fiction, in Bradbury's rewriting of its history, is not a genre with roots dating back to Gernsback's founding of *Amazing Stories* in 1926; it

the greatest writing in our past, from Plato and Lucian to Sir Thomas More and François Rabelais and on down through Jonathan Swift and Johannes Kepler to [Edgar Allan] Poe and Edward Bellamy and George Orwell" (365). Notably absent from this list are any of Bradbury's peers writing for the science fiction pulps—no Heinlein or Asimov, no one who actually calls himself or herself a science fiction writer. In these regards—the retroactive canon-formation, the overblown description of the genre's literary merits (science fiction in Bradbury's description encompasses not just the philosophical novel of ideas but also the fiction of sociology *and* psychology *and*, hardest of all to understand, perhaps, history), the effacement of pulp science fiction writers—Bradbury separates himself from his science fiction peers and bids on his own terms for symbolic capital for himself and the genre with which he was linked.

These specific grounds on which Bradbury bids are significant, and I will return to them shortly, but I want first to emphasize again that such a bid is made possible by the developing institutional structure for the dissemination of science fiction and that that structure was tied to the emergence of the paperback and thus to all of the demographic shifts and technological advancements that led to it, chief among them all the growth of the reading audience, the same growth that made the ABPC's and NBF's expanded promotional ventures possible. As Davis notes, Pocket Books had published the first science fiction paperback in 1943, Penguin published a similar volume in 1944, and Bantam published a collection in 1950 (166). But the genuine growth of science fiction in paperback form was still to come, a development predicted by Anthony Boucher in *Modern Science Fiction*: "More and more writers are looking with warm favor upon original paperbacks, priced at twenty-five cents or thirty-five cents and paying all the royalties unsplit, to the author" (28). The logic was simple: there was more money in book writing than in writing for pulps, and at the same time science fiction was far more likely to receive attention from paperback publishers than from traditional hardcover publishers. Boucher's prediction came to fruition quickly. By 1953, the paperback was enabling the genre's emergence as a viable commercial entity. Science fiction had a special thematic validity for the 1950s, but that validity is not the sole reason for its emergence.

Bradbury and Ballantine

The story of Bradbury's early career exemplifies this last point. As much as the success of *Fahrenheit 451*, a novel that draws on the possibility of atomic war and the predicted technological growth of mass culture, can be said to illustrate the "special validity" of science fiction in the 1950s, the story of Bradbury's career leading to that novel captures the importance of institutional shifts in the book trade and specifically the way the paperback transformed the science fiction genre. As what might be termed a second-generation science fiction writer, one, that is, who grew up reading science fiction pulps, Bradbury found his entry into the larger literary world through those pulps, publishing his first story with the help of Robert Heinlein in 1942. By 1951, when Bradbury published "The Fireman" in a relatively new pulp called *Galaxy* (it had previously been rejected by *Harper's* and *Esquire* [Weller 202]), he was already a major science fiction writer, having had *The Martian Chronicles*—made up, as almost all science fiction books then were, in large part of stories previously published in pulps—published by Doubleday, at the time the largest publisher of science fiction books. The positive reception accorded *The Martian Chronicles*, in particular a storied celebratory review from Christopher Isherwood made possible by a chance meeting between Bradbury and Isherwood in a bookstore, helped Bradbury make inroads into the literary mainstream. But without some fortuitously timed institutional changes, it is conceivable that he never would have become a full-fledged novelist. Certainly *Fahrenheit 451* itself is unthinkable outside the specific story of the relationship between science fiction and the paperback.

In May 1952, just a few months after Bradbury published "The Fireman," a young veteran of the paperback revolution, Ian Ballantine, formed Ballantine Books. Ballantine is the hero of the story of *Fahrenheit 451*. By the time he formed his own company, Ballantine was already something of a wunderkind of the book trade. Previously, he had been the point man for Penguin Books in its effort to compete with Pocket Books in the U.S. paperback market and he had later served as the first president of paperback upstart Bantam Books, a crucial second development (after Pocket Books) in the emergence of the paperback, as major players in the publishing world—not just risk takers like Simon & Schuster (which cofounded Pocket Books) and Random House but also more conservative houses like Scribner's—came to recognize its power.[19] As Davis tells the story, companies like Bantam and Pocket Books had cor-

tine turned to science fiction as a market with as yet untapped potential (this should not be a surprise: he had worked at Penguin when Penguin published its first science fiction paperback and at Bantam when the company published its, and Bantam had published reprint editions of Bradbury's *The Martian Chronicles* and *The Illustrated Man*). In this effort to push science fiction, Ballantine was not alone, which suggests, properly, that the emergence of science fiction was more a market-driven inevitability than the product of individual inspiration; as Bonn notes, New American Library, which published the paperback version of *The Wonderful World of Books*, also recognized science fiction's commercial potential (88). These two houses played the greatest role in making science fiction a staple of the book trade.

Although the increased production of science fiction books was inevitable, the specific strategy used by Ballantine, designed in part to help science fiction gain some literary cachet, was an innovation. Ballantine's idea was to publish simultaneous hardcover and paperback books, the same technique used to sell *Wonderful World*, and for many of the same reasons. The hardcover would get the book some respectability (perhaps a place in finer bookstores and review pages), and it was in this context that Ballantine called its science fiction books "adult science fiction," not to advertise the luridness of the stories (there was none, a key difference between science fiction and other mid-century literary genres) but to advertise their seriousness. The paperback, of course, sold on newsstands, at train stations, and in pharmacies at a low price, would generate sales. Ballantine perceived other benefits as well to this strategy: the mass production of the paperbacks would allow the hardcover to be sold at a slightly lower price, and to entice authors to publish works as original paperbacks he offered a higher royalty rate than any other company.[20] It is worth emphasizing that this was, in every sense, a business decision, and if the attention it received is any measure it was one that rattled the book trade.[21] Ballantine had been pondering such a system as far back as 1937 when, as a student at the London School of Economics, he studied an early (failed) version of this approach. The paper that resulted from this study was what led Allen Lane of Penguin Books to hire Ballantine for his first job in publishing, in 1939. Ballantine's very presence in the book world—the space, that is, for a student of business rather than a student of books—is, like the emergence of the National Book Awards, both an effect and a cause of the growth of the business.

Two versions exist of the story of how Ballantine and Ray Bradbury came to work together. In Bradbury's version, representatives from Ballantine Books, looking for original material to publish, contacted Bradbury's agent, Don Congdon, to ask him if Bradbury would have interest in expanding "The Fireman" into a full-length novel to be published in simultaneous hardcover and paperback editions ("Burning"). A slightly different version appears in Davis's history of the paperback; according to it the science fiction novel was Congdon's idea, and it was he who took the initiative in contacting Ballantine on Bradbury's behalf on hearing that the new company sought to publish original science fiction novels. Congdon had previously worked as an editor for Simon & Schuster, and Bradbury had hired him specifically for his knowledge of and connections to the mainstream literary world (his previous agent had ties only to the world of pulp publishing) (Weller 146–47).[22] However the deal was struck, *Fahrenheit 451*, published in October 1953, was the forty-first title in Ballantine's young catalog, and both Ballantine and Congdon were integral to its creation; behind both of them and behind the novel itself, enabling all of them, is the developing institutional structure for the production of science fiction books, itself a response to and reflection of the growth of the reading audience and the search for new ways to entice that audience.

Another Anti-Mass-Culture Paperback

When Bradbury tells the story of the writing of the novel, he emphasizes the difference between the process of composing "The Fireman" and that of expanding it into *Fahrenheit 451*. "The Fireman" was not commissioned; when Bradbury wrote it, he did not know who would publish it or even (he says) if it would be published at all, and he describes the writing process in terms of artistic inspiration: "I had been seized by an idea that started short but grew to wild size by day's end. The concept was so riveting I found it hard at sunset to flee the library basement and take the bus home to reality" ("Burning" 15). Later he claims that he did not write "The Fireman": "*It* wrote *me*" (15). These descriptions suggest a kind of possession, the artist seized by the art. The expansion process—that of transforming the short story into a novel—was altogether different: having contracted to write for Ballantine Books, as part of a specific effort on the part of the publisher to appeal to a growing demographic and after receiving an advance of $5,000, Bradbury had to produce on demand. Could he write this way? Bradbury asserts that he was unsure: "The best answer was to set a deadline and ask . . . my Ballantine edi-

down on me from the sky, I finished the last revised page in mid-August" (18–19).[23] Though it is not Bradbury's intention to paint it this way, the language of these descriptions suggest that while "The Fireman" was a product of romantic inspiration divorced from the machinery of literary production, *Fahrenheit 451* was a business opportunity and a collaborative effort enabled by the growth of the reading audience. Little wonder, then, that *Fahrenheit 451*, an attack on and a warning about mass culture, is dedicated to Don Congdon, Bradbury's literary agent, a symbol of the book trade's engagement with mass-culture institutions.[24]

None of this means that this anti-mass-culture novel—it is, I'll soon show, at least as hostile to mass culture as anything Dwight Macdonald ever wrote—is compromised by the author's engagement with what can fairly be called institutions of mass culture. Rather it sets into relief some of the ironies of this book about not just the impending death of the book but also about the impending death of the solitary, inspired, self-expressing author. In *Fahrenheit 451*, Montag's growing interest in the book is triggered by his realization that "a man was behind each one of the books. A man had to think them up. A man had to take a long time to put them down on paper" (52); it is this quality that makes the book special.[25] If it is true that the solitary author—"a man"—was becoming obsolete, Bradbury's story—the story, that is, of how he came to lament this fact in a novel—might be an ironic example of that process in action, even as the novel strenuously asserts the book's separateness from mass culture. In this sense, Bradbury's novel, so clearly the product of collaboration, demands to be understood not solely as the solitary author's lament but as, in addition, an example of mass culture's and book culture's commercial interest in disseminating this lament, the interest of the culture industry in depicting the horrors of the culture industry.

If the commercial strategy for science fiction belongs at least in part to Ballantine and the culture industry that he represents, the literary strategy bears Bradbury's stamp. Bradbury closes his 1979 "Coda" to *Fahrenheit 451*, one of numerous comments on the novel he has published since 1953, with a characteristic rhetorical flourish for the cause of art and the author: "All you umpires, back to the bleachers. Referees, hit the showers. It's my game. I pitch, I hit, I catch. I run the bases. At sunset I've won or lost. . . . And no one can help me. Not even you" (179). What is important, again, is not that Bradbury appears blind to the help he needed to become a "solitary" novelist who could claim complete control of his work (much in the way some contributors to *Wonderful World* appeared blind to the book's status as a commodity); what is important, because it is so characteristic a 1950s literary strategy, is the way Bradbury exploits the discourse of the solitary author to accrue symbolic capital to himself. By announcing his solitariness, Bradbury makes a case for the distinctive *literary* value of his work, and it is this effort more than any other that separates Bradbury from other science fiction writers. Bradbury's science fiction peers pointedly called their genre *modern* science fiction, but Bradbury's passionate celebration of the old-fashioned virtues of reading, in *Fahrenheit 451* as well as elsewhere throughout his career, is a willfully antimodern gesture. It is not surprising, in this context, that Bradbury's post-*Fahrenheit* unofficial anointment as spokesman for the science fiction genre was met with skepticism within the science fiction community. Whereas Bradbury's science fiction peers pointedly used fiction to make the case for the grandeur of science (which Campbell described in his contribution to *Modern Science Fiction* as "the magic that works" [15]), Bradbury used science—the dangers of science—to make the case for fiction.[26]

To the extent that Bradbury distanced himself from other science fiction writers, he implicitly linked himself to more obviously literary and otherwise quite different 1950s writers, like Bowles, like J. D. Salinger, like Jack Kerouac: all creators of characters who were outsiders, whose claim to heroism is marked by their refusal to engage with mass culture or mass society.[27] This is all done in the context of an overarching and coherent critique of mass culture; more than Bowles, for example, or many of the high-culture critics who bemoaned the rise of mass-produced forms of culture, Bradbury was interested in mass culture as not just a literary problem but a societal one, as the root of so many contemporary ills. Consider, for example, Clarisse's explanation in *Fahrenheit 451* for how she has come to be so different from other teenagers: "I'm afraid of children my own age. They kill each other. Did it always use to be that way? My uncle says no. Six of my friends have been shot in the last year alone. Ten of them died in car wrecks. . . . My uncle says his grandfather remembered when children didn't kill each other. But that was a long time ago when they had things different. They believed in responsibility, my uncle says. Do you know, I'm responsible. I was spanked when I needed it, years ago" (30).

Two issues—juvenile delinquency and child care—are here linked, and the subtext of both is mass culture. Fears of juvenile delinquency arose in the 1950s as the combined effects of the baby boom and the economic boom created a new youth culture. In *Seduction of the Innocent,*

the development of juvenile delinquency.[28] Comic books, of course, are also a target of Bradbury's in the novel—as Beatty, Montag's boss, notes, they are the only kind of book left and those in power are happy to let people continue to read them—and his vision of future juvenile delinquency comes one year before Wertham's book and two prior to Benjamin Fine's *1,000,000 Delinquents*. "Comic books," Wertham asserted in 1954, "are death on reading" (qtd. in Beaty 140). Bradbury agreed.

Equally notable is Clarisse's explanation in *Fahrenheit 451* for how she escaped the fate of other teens: "I'm responsible. I was spanked when I needed it, years ago" (30). Spanking as a means to instill discipline recalls the behaviorist child-rearing strategies propounded by John B. Watson, whose *Psychological Care of Infant and Child* (1928) demanded clockwork precision. These child-rearing practices held sway until the 1940s, when a less rigid, more permissive strategy took hold. The primary spokesman for this new set of child-rearing practices, though not its architect, was Dr. Benjamin M. Spock, whose *Common Sense Book of Baby and Child Care* was first published in June 1946. John Diggins sums up Spock's notion of child-rearing this way: "Before the child arrived at school he must be reared properly in an atmosphere of benevolent and systematic attention" (201). Spankings and punishments, tactics emphasized in an earlier age of behaviorist-styled child-rearing, fell out of fashion in the wake of Spock's more permissive approach.[29]

In many senses, Spock's book is the quintessential text of the paperback revolution (and, indeed, it was identified as such by Davis in his history of the paperback). The reasons go beyond the book's well-timed (for the baby boom) mass popularity. Mass culture, according to its critics, was bad because it coddled its audience rather than challenging it. As the editors of *Partisan Review* noted in 1952, it responded to market pressures and thus turned culture into a commodity, and so it told people what they wanted to hear rather than what they needed to hear. Critics of Spock's approach would assert that his famed paperback offers an analogous shift in parenting instruction. It told parents what they wanted to hear about child-rearing rather than the hard news that they presumably needed to hear about how to raise their child. Finally, not only was the advice congenial, the book itself had a good bedside manner. As Davis sums up, "He wrote a friendly book, speaking to new mothers with a voice of gentle reassurance rather than the condescendingly stern tones of medical authority" (7). That Bradbury takes aim at this approach shows that his critique of mass culture is more far-reaching than has been noted.

It is the "condescendingly stern tones" of cultural authority, however, far more than those of medical or child-rearing authority, that are Bradbury's famous focus in the novel. The fact that these authorities have been banished is presented as a tragedy, and it sets up the novel's curious ending. As Faber, the English professor, tells Montag, "There's lots of Harvard degrees on the tracks between here and Los Angeles" (132), critics, scholars, and teachers whose expertise has rendered them either dangerous or obsolete in a world dominated by mass culture. But how and why this process occurs is a vexed issue in the novel because Bradbury straddles the line between the humanist assertions of the book's importance favored by the NBF and the makers of *Wonderful World* on the one hand, and the more radical, exclusionary idea of culture favored by modernist intellectuals, the editors of *Partisan Review*, and James Laughlin on the other.

At the end of the novel, Montag listens in shock as Granger, a former college professor, explains that he and his associates, like the firemen whose job it is to destroy all books, "are book burners, too. We read the books and burnt them, afraid they'd be found" (152). "All we want to do," Granger explains, "is keep the knowledge we think we will need intact and safe. We're not out to incite or anger anyone yet" (152). The assumption that books have the power to "incite or anger" people is of course a commonplace that hardly needs to be defended, a crucial assumption for the book trade during the Cold War, central to the idea that the book was a Cold War weapon, a means to contain Communism, to promote individual thought and democratic action.

This idea of the value of the book, in short, matches the idea of the book as expressed in texts like *Wonderful World* and by organizations like the National Book Foundation. Not only are books important works of art, they also play an important role in society to the extent that they are read by the greatest number of people, for whom they hold the key to liberty and the survival of democracy; as Faber reminds Montag, in a remark that echoes the more portentous statements in *Wonderful World,* " 'If there were no war, if there was peace in the world, I'd say fine, *have* fun! But . . . all *isn't* well with the world' " (104), a fact that presumably makes the book more important than ever. It is not hard to see why the book trade would embrace a text that endorses this view: in this moment, at least, *Fahrenheit 451* is *Wonderful World of Books* as science fiction dystopia—albeit a much more effective version of it—both in the sense

atomic war and totalitarianism, as culture threatened by mass culture) but also that it is a product of the same economic forces (the expansion of the book trade) and thus implicated in the same set of ironies regarding the fact of its mass distribution and its representation of mass culture.

But Granger's notion that books might incite the public is at odds with much of the rest of the novel. In fact, most of *Fahrenheit 451* explicitly denies the book's (any book's) revolutionary political potential in the modern world. As Montag's two teachers, Beatty the fireman and Faber, tell it, books disappeared not because the totalitarian state feared their power to incite but rather because of what amounted to market concerns, because, finally, people preferred mass culture to literature. Faber explains to Montag , "The public itself stopped reading of its own accord" (87), suggesting quite clearly that books had lost their power to incite before the government deemed them illegal. Beatty, Montag's boss, offers a more nuanced, much quoted explanation of the decline of the book: "It didn't come from the Government down. There was no dictum, no declaration, no censorship, to start with, no! Technology, mass exploitation, and minority pressure carried the trick, thank God'" (58).[30] The emergence of profit-driven mass culture led to the decline in popularity of the book, which led to political support for the elimination of books that could be exploited by totalitarian institutions. The elimination of books was a process, an inevitability, it seems, in the context of the marriage of capitalism and scientific advancement, and not a matter of decree.

One reason this point is worth making is that it is at odds with what might be called the packaging of the novel. Everything about what Gerard Genette calls the "paratext" of *Fahrenheit 451*—the title ("the temperature at which books burn," according to the novel's tagline) and the focus on Montag the fireman and Beatty his boss, the famous front-cover illustration featuring pages aflame—suggest that book burning has great significance, that government-mandated censorship is a root cause of the decline of the book that the novel describes and laments.[31] But this is not the case: censorship in *Fahrenheit 451* is an effect, not a cause; the cause that produces the decline of the book and ultimately the censorship regime that is essentially an afterthought is simply mass culture, understood in the novel as a combination of large-scale, exploitative institutions and the growing (mass) public that had the time and (presumably) the money to consume their products and lacked the will, the desire, or both to resist them. That combination—made concrete in the novel by both the addictive television screens that fill all four walls of a room, the "seashells" that people forever keep in their ears, and people consumed by a desire to escape from a world gone bad—is the true target of Bradbury's ire in *Fahrenheit 451.*

All of which—the denial of the book's revolutionary power in the age of mass culture and the contempt for the masses implicit in such a denial—suggests that *Fahrenheit 451* has less to do with any humanist assertion of the cultural importance of the book (the kind we see in *Wonderful World*) than it does with the more exclusionary modernist idea of culture. "Today," Clement Greenberg asserts at the end of his seminal essay "Avant-Garde and Kitsch" (1939), "we look to socialism *simply* for the preservation of whatever living culture we have right now" (21). The implication is that capitalism is fatal to culture and, moreover, that the preservation of culture is less the means to a better world than it is the end in itself, the reason for trying to improve the world. *Fahrenheit 451* shares with Greenberg's essay the radical idea that civilization needs to change in order to save culture—and to the extent that Bradbury shares this view his idea of the value of the book is in fact the *reverse* of the NBF's idea, and his novel anything but an advertisement for a generalized notion of the cultural value of reading. The NBF, to put it slightly differently, suggests that culture will save civilization. In Bradbury's novel, culture cannot save civilization; civilization is doomed anyway, and its rejection of the book is a symptom of a larger problem rather than the cause of its problem. "'The whole culture's shot through,'" Faber tells Montag. "'The skeleton needs melting and reshaping'" (87). The problem in *Fahrenheit 451* is neither that the art produced by mass culture is not good enough nor that the oppressive government denied people the right to read; the problem is that the masses are not good enough to appreciate art, and so they sought out leaders who would ban books that the market could not support anyway.

Rather than asserting, as *Wonderful World* does, that the solution to the world's problems is mass reading, *Fahrenheit 451* looks back nostalgically to an age in which fewer people read: "'Once, books appealed to a few people, here, there everywhere. They could afford to be different. The world was roomy. But then the world got full of eyes and elbows and mouths. Double, triple, quadruple population'" (54). In bemoaning this fact, in bemoaning the spread of literacy, Bradbury has far more in common with Macdonald and Greenberg, both of whom connected the increase in the population of readers with a perceived decline in the

If anything, in fact, Bradbury's novel advocates a more radical position than the two critics. In another context entirely, historian Richard Wolin notes, "A distinct flirtation with nihilism was a corollary of the conviction that widespread destruction was required before anything of lasting value could be built" (8). *Fahrenheit 451* flirts openly with nihilism far more than it promotes a recognition of the social or civic value of the book; in 1939, at least, Greenberg might have seen socialism as culture's salvation (perhaps not so later), but as Bradbury describes a culture that can only be saved via its own destruction, his novel does not entertain this hope. The end of the novel, wherein a small community of educated readers, including Granger, read memorized books to each other, living in a world with no means to distribute texts to readers who presumably are incapable of understanding them anyway and who, furthermore, are about to be destroyed in an atomic war, is a kind of modernist fantasy—similar to Port Moresby's journey ever-deeper into the Sahara to find a place where writing is still possible—masquerading as book promotion. Maybe after nuclear annihilation, the novel suggests, the survivors and the new civilization they produce will appreciate books and they can be distributed widely. Until then, books should be left to the few. " 'Maybe,' " Montag muses early in the novel, before meeting Faber, " 'books can get us out of the cave. They just *might* stop us from making the same damn mistakes' " (74). By the end of the novel, this hope for the book has been dashed, and this is the true irony of Bradbury's novel's place as a promoter of the cultural and political importance of the book: Davis calls the postwar era that of the "paperback revolution," on the theory that the paperback was a revolutionary democratic force for culture (a rehearsal of the argument that some, like Chris Anderson, make today about the Internet). *Fahrenheit 451*, a creation of that earlier revolution, ends by imagining the antipaperback revolution, that which occurs only by not attempting to distribute books to the masses, by limiting distribution of books to a degree never imagined even by the most exclusionary modernists. The great divide was never harder to bridge than it is in this mass-produced paperback.

Timeless

One reason that the masquerade works, one reason that a novel ultimately hostile to the democratization of culture can be seen as an advertisement for it, is that the novel was and still is promoted as a humanist culture-as-savior text by commercial literary institutions; it is not surprising that the most radical antimodern, if not nihilistic, notions of the book are effaced in the efforts to market it. On the front cover of a reissue of *Fahrenheit 451*, from 1982, for example, were the following words: "The classic bestseller about censorship—more important now than ever before."

This copy has more to tell us about how books can be successfully marketed in the age of mass culture than it does about the text or context of *Fahrenheit 451* itself. Indeed, even if we accept the dubious proposition that this is a book about censorship, it is hard to understand why *Fahrenheit 451* would be more important in 1982 than it was in 1953, not just the height of McCarthyism but also a year rife with obscenity-based book bannings on a local level; and lest we strain to attribute the 1982 front cover copy to, say, the Reagan-era reemergence of Cold War tensions, it is worth noting that the blurb of the 1993 reissue of the novel—a hardcover, fortieth-anniversary edition—similarly proclaims, "The message of *Fahrenheit 451* is as relevant today as when it was first published."[32] The true lesson to be derived from this disingenuous front cover copy is not the importance or lack thereof of *Fahrenheit 451* at any time so much as it is the fact that in 1993, as in 1982, as in 1953, announcing the imperiled state of the book—whatever the reasons, whatever the lack of context—is a good way to sell books, a lesson borne out not just by the repeated use of the paratextual "books are threatened" motif to sell *Fahrenheit 451* but also by the frequent reissues themselves. *Fahrenheit 451*'s enduring popularity as an advertisement for the book—for this is how it is packaged—is the best evidence of the mass popularity of the culture-is-threatened motif.

This last point is made most ironically by the text on the same 1982 edition's back cover—"OVER 4 1/2 MILLION COPIES IN PRINT." One wonders if the book designers appreciated the particular irony that this paratextual advertisement so closely resembles the famed McDonald's announcements of how many billions of burgers they have served. McDonald's is, like *Fahrenheit 451* itself, another institution with roots dating back to the 1950s, dependent on both the technology and philosophy of mass production and the emergence of demographic shifts that could make that philosophy profitable. McDonalds is also, of course, the kind of institution for which Bradbury has the greatest ire.

The 1993 reissue of *Fahrenheit 451*, in contrast to the pocket-sized paperbacks, is a grand affair—a special hardcover edition produced to

prefaces and afterwords Bradbury had written over the years for a relatively short novel, and a new foreword as well for the occasion. The hardcover edition, surely meant to commemorate the novel's importance and achievement, is, like the 2000 NBF honor, a form of canonization. With over four million paperback copies of the book in print, it is difficult to imagine a large audience for this more expensive hardcover edition. It is a throwback, albeit a relatively inexpensive one, to an age of expensive "special editions" of books designed for a small audience, the sort of small audience imagined at the end of *Fahrenheit 451* as the preservers of the possibility of a nontotalitarian future. And it is appropriately blind to the irony of this effort.

Chapter 3
Synergy and the Novelist:
Simon & Schuster; Time, Inc.; and
The Man in the Gray Flannel Suit

Recent editions of *Fahrenheit 451* paratextually assert the work's ever increasing cultural and political relevance, if not its timelessness as a work of art. In contrast, Sloan Wilson's novel *The Man in the Gray Flannel Suit* (1955) is now billed with increasing frequency as a relic, an object out of the 1950s time capsule, both representative and little known. The novel, Jonathan Franzen says in his introduction to the most recent reissue, "will provide you with a pure fifties fix," and it is as a symbol of a bygone moment that the novel's profile has risen in recent years (v). The renewal of academic interest in the novel over the past two decades is another sign of this rising profile: it rates a mention in most recent cultural histories of the 1950s, again as a symbol of a certain lost aspect of postwar culture, and in recent years literary scholars have reexamined it as well as a sort of anti-road story, the antithesis to novels like *The Sheltering Sky* and *Fahrenheit 451* as well as the decade's most famous novels of nonconformity by Kerouac and Salinger, a quasi-sociological story of conventional, conformist middle-class, middle-management life from the decade famous for it.[1]

These scholars' assessments have generally been ambivalent: one scholar deems the novel "quintessentially middlebrow," while another calls it a "typical mid-fifties bestseller" (E. May 157).[2] According to these readings, the novel takes on the characteristics of the characters it purports to portray realistically. It is, in other words, doubly typical, not just a novel about a middle-class man with a middling job but also, aesthetically speaking, a middling novel, not just a novel about 1950s conformist culture but also, by virtue of its failure to sustain its critique of that culture,

Flannel Suit is a paradigmatic statement of unearned male middle-class angst and, beneath its happy ending, a depressing story of capitulation to the corporation, and this view of the novel is not all that different from its early negative reviews. The July 1955 *Commonweal* review of the novel asks, "What is the moral of the novel supposed to be anyway: the self-pitying shall inherit the earth?" Catherine Jurca makes a similar point in 2001: "He is above all the man for whom suburban-corporate existence is defined as endless suffering" (139).

How does a purportedly middling novel become so famous? The question entails consideration of more than just its supposed typicalness; it is one thing to be ordinary, but it is another to be famous for being ordinary. In fact, the story of *The Man in the Gray Flannel Suit*'s path to renown as a symbol of the 1950s illuminates little-discussed changes in literary production and promotion as the decade progressed, and perhaps the most important point to be made about it is that it is not a story of historical recovery, whereby contemporary historians look back to the 1950s and discover a novel that embodies the decade's peculiar qualities and concerns. On the contrary, the idea that *The Man in the Gray Flannel Suit* uniquely embodied its decade's concerns was a key element in the original, remarkably effective marketing campaign for the novel, and that campaign was enabled by specific changes to the book trade as the 1950s progressed: the emergence of new marketing tools and the emergence of a new network of corporate institutions—mass culture and otherwise—that collaborated in producing and promoting novels, in packaging them, in using them to market other cultural texts, and ultimately in marketing an interpretation of the 1950s itself. Wilson's novel is treated still as a symbol of a bygone moment, but this story of cross-promotional synergy, of witting collaboration among publishers and mass-media corporations, might have more contemporary relevance than anything in *Fahrenheit 451*. The collaboration that produced *The Sheltering Sky* was tentative and, in a sense, accidental; the collaboration that produced *The Man in the Gray Flannel Suit* was purposeful, a sign of the growth that had occurred in the decade since the end of World War II enabled the modernization and growth of the book trade.

From the outset, however, this collaboration did not serve the literary reputation of Wilson's novel; the novel is remembered, but not as an artistic achievement. Franzen notes in his introduction, "Nowadays, the novel is remembered mainly for its title, which, along with *The Lonely Crowd* and *The Organization Man*, became a watchword of fifties conformity" (v). Indeed, much of *The Man in the Gray Flannel Suit*'s reputation as *the* typical text is tied to its famous title, and even among those scholars who have brought the novel its recent, somewhat dubious renown, the title exerts an unusually strong influence on how it is understood. The title's enduring prominence is partially a historical accident, but even as such it is the byproduct of a specific and heretofore unexamined design, which is also to a large extent responsible for the novel's revived reputation as an ur-1950s text. The first part of this chapter reconsiders *The Man in the Gray Flannel Suit* in the context of an emergent network of powerful postwar institutions that produced and promoted it, examining, that is, the process by which an idiosyncratic unnamed manuscript was transformed into a "typical," critically derided novel and a wholly unlikely symbol of its historical moment. The title, which was instrumental in this transformation, is a good place to start.

There are two published versions of the story of how the book got its title and, although they differ in key respects that will be considered later, they converge on three points. First, the title was one of the last decisions made about the novel, well after the manuscript was completed and shortly before it went to print. Second, Wilson's original choice— "for some reason," he writes in his memoir (*What* 211)—was *A Candle at Midnight*, a lyrical title far removed from *The Man in the Gray Flannel Suit*.[3] Finally, in both versions of the story the decision ultimately rested not with Wilson but with Richard Simon, then the president of Simon & Schuster, Wilson's publisher. This is because Wilson had neither a literary nor commercial track record prior to the novel's publication, while Simon, a legendary figure of the book business nearing the end of a storied career, had for somewhat obscure reasons taken on the novel or, more precisely, the novelist, as a kind of pet project. Simon has yet to figure prominently in scholarly assessments of *The Man in the Gray Flannel Suit*, but more than anyone else he is the author of contemporary perceptions of it and thus an unlikely contributing author of an enduring interpretation of the decade that the novel has been said to embody; the distance between the titles *A Candle at Midnight* and *The Man in the Gray Flannel Suit* suggests something of the difference between Wilson's intentions for his novel and the lasting reading that Simon imposed on it and, in turn, something of the mid-century book trade's limited but developing power in the marketplace as it matured over the course of the 1950s.

To make this argument is at least momentarily to lift the novel out of its usual perceived thematic context of organization men and lonely crowds and to situate it instead in the context of the culture of the mid-century American book trade, though this is less of a shift than it might seem because the business of books in the 1950s was undergoing changes that were making it more like the conventional business culture that the novel purportedly describes. The novel is ultimately better understood as a product of those changes within the publishing world, and in the relations between that world and the more conventional corporate world, than as an attempt to represent the conventional corporate world itself, a subject about which Sloan Wilson, an aspiring writer almost from birth, knew next to nothing. Not only does Wilson's novel dramatize a version of his own atypical experience on the margins of corporate America as he struggled to forge a career as a professional writer but through the specific process by which the novel became "typical"—it was promoted by its publisher as such to capitalize on public interest in corporate culture and middle-class existence—it also exemplifies new strategies employed by the book trade to exploit its developing links to mass-culture institutions. Thematically *The Man in the Gray Flannel Suit* is reputed to fit squarely in the 1950s, but this reputation—and prior to it the novel's very existence—is partially a consequence of the fact that it was written, published, and promoted at a moment that fits squarely between two eras in American publishing history.

In his memoir, Jason Epstein deems the 1950s the last decade of publishing's golden age, when it was "still the small-scale, highly personal industry it had been since the 1920s" (8). In his multivolume history of American publishing, however, John Tebbel calls the 1950s the first decade *after* the golden age. Both authors mean the same thing by "golden age": the moment when publishing was, again quoting Epstein, "a cottage industry, decentralized, improvisational, personal . . . performed by small groups of like-minded people" (1), as opposed to what publishing would become—a "conventional business" (4). Epstein and Tebbel are nostalgic for the same moment in publishing's history, and it is the same moment for which Bowles and Bradbury, in *Fahrenheit 451*, are also nostalgic. Ultimately, their difference in periodization indicates that the 1950s were a transitional time for American publishers, a moment when they were caught between their previous incarnation as a group of growing but still relatively small, sometimes family-owned businesses, many formed in the 1920s, and the moment when they were consolidated into mass-media empires, as they would be in the 1960s and after. Michael Korda, whose career as an editor spans roughly the same period as Epstein's, suggests in his memoir that the perception of publishing as a cottage industry in the 1950s might have been wishful thinking: "Book publishers in those days like to refer to themselves with a certain pride as 'a cottage industry' . . . but the age of the cottage industry was already coming to an end" (44–45). As these attempts to characterize publishing in the 1950s suggest, modernization produced success but also, not surprisingly, a degree of ambivalence and anxiety about the impact that growth had on what made publishing special. *The Man in the Gray Flannel Suit* is one result of this awkward transitional moment, and anxiety about the price of growth is a subtext of it.

Simon & Schuster, which Simon cofounded with Max Schuster in 1924, had been one of those upstart companies of the golden age, and its story, and Simon's role in that story, captures the book business's transition perhaps better than that of any other publishing house.[4] More than a decade before Penguin hired Ian Ballantine out of the London School of Economics, it was Simon & Schuster that, as Tebbel puts it, introduced a new concept to the publishing world, "the businessman as publisher" (2: 156). The company enjoyed faster expansion than any other new company in American publishing history, and its growth is properly attributed not to high literary values (it achieved its early success by selling the first-ever crossword puzzle books) but to business innovations or, more precisely, to the fact that it brought a business sensibility to the publishing arena. The company used marketing techniques that were for its time sophisticated (among other things, it was the first house to test-market its books); invested more on advertising per book than any other house; and exploited the possibilities of the "house-generated idea," whereby editors conceived ideas for books in response to perceived demand and hired authors to write them, more than any other company.[5] This last idea is perhaps the best example of the book business's efforts to move from a producer-oriented—that is, an author-oriented—business to a more consumer-oriented one.[6]

In addition, Simon & Schuster was involved in the most significant efforts to bridge the gap between publishing houses and mass-culture institutions, the efforts that would help to lead American publishers out of their purported golden age and into the second half of the twentieth century, an ambivalent age of "synergistic" relationships with mass-media corporations. The most famous of these innovations is the company's

Davis calls "the paperbacking of America," the most consequential development in twentieth-century publishing and the one that did the most to give the book any kind of "mass" exposure. Simon & Schuster cemented its status as a symbol of twentieth-century publishing modernization in 1944 with a less celebrated but equally telling move, one that was indirectly crucial to the genesis of Wilson's novel. The company's two founders sold it, along with Pocket Books, to Field Enterprises, a relatively small multimedia conglomerate that also included four radio stations, a newspaper, and a textbook publishing company. At this point Simon, no longer the co-owner of the company he had founded, became its president. The merger, a harbinger rather than an immediate trendsetter, foreshadowed later multimedia conglomerations and reflected a belief on the part of all parties involved—later proven correct—that books in the postwar era would be a growth industry and that the making of books would help other aspects of a multifaceted business. Marshall Field himself was inspired to enter the publishing business by the chance sighting of Pocket Books on display at a Liggett's drugstore in Chicago. Field soon became convinced that "big business procedures had overtaken the old-fashioned book business, and . . . he wanted to be in on the ground floor" (Tebbel 3: 71).

Not surprisingly, the growth of the book business and the merger it enabled exacted a personal toll. By 1955, Simon was unhappy with the choice he had made to sell his company, though it had proven to be a profitable move. He missed the control he had had when Simon & Schuster was a smaller business that he could run with a co-owner's degree of autonomy, and he resented having to answer to others. Simon had risky ideas that he wanted to pursue, but the rest of the company, more conservative postmerger, was not receptive. Simon was a businessman, but he was not a 1950s businessman. He was an innovator and an entrepreneur, not an organization man, and so his unhappiness can be understood in the context of two distinct but related 1950s discourses: first, the critique of the modern corporation and its dehumanizing effect on the individual (the discourse of Riesman and Whyte) and, second, the nostalgia that many postwar novelists and publishers would come to feel for the earlier golden age of so-called gentlemanly publishing, the same nostalgia evoked by Paul Bowles in his descriptions of his move from Doubleday to New Directions and also by Epstein and Tebbel.[7] Unlike many of the others who partook of this nostalgia, Simon was in part responsible for the change he and they lamented. The story of Simon's unhappy later years—as a casualty of the modernization of the book trade—has itself become a staple of narratives of American publishing after World War II, a piece of a larger cautionary tale. When Simon died in 1960, Bennett Cerf wrote in a tribute in the *Saturday Review* that "the real Dick Simon . . . began to die in spirit way back in 1944, when he sold the control of his business to the late Marshall Field" (qtd. in Tebbel 3: 78). Simon & Schuster executive Leon Shimkin bought the company back from Marshall Field in 1957, but Simon, Korda reports, "was too ill and too depressed to join them." Simon "had become a rich man," Korda continues, "at the price of his own health, sanity, and vitality" (102). In his memoir, Wilson explains Simon's unhappiness in the mid-1950s: "Dick's problems stemmed mostly from the fact that he and Max Schuster had sold the publishing firm . . . gradually Dick had begun to learn that he was not the captain of his ship any more. For the first time he was answerable to a board of directors, . . . Worst of all, the words 'published by Simon and Schuster' were printed on several books which Dick Simon personally loathed" (*What* 248).

Simon's solution to the problem of his newly corporatized publishing house—and, apparently, the rest of Simon & Schuster's solution as well—was to set up an imprint all his own within the company to publish his pet projects. This imprint was called New Ventures, and Simon's idea was that it would function like the old, premerger Simon & Schuster, a point emphasized in Peter Schwed's account of the company's history: "Simon was allocated a separate budget to create his own private undertakings . . . essentially the two Dicks [Simon and his protégé Dick Grossman] had to make New Ventures work on their own" (193).[8] For Simon, this was in a sense a return to the 1920s, when he and Schuster alone ran the company, took risks, and almost literally made something out of nothing: the company had begun with an office, a budget of $8,000, and no books to publish. Predictably, New Ventures was a short-lived idea—the golden age had passed and, by the time books that originated with New Ventures were published, the imprint had already been folded back into the rest of Simon & Schuster—but it was crucial in the production of a few notable successes.[9] *The Man in the Gray Flannel Suit* was one of the first (Schwed 194).

For a variety of reasons, *The Man in the Gray Flannel Suit* is unthinkable outside the context of this chain of events. For one thing, no other publisher was willing to give Sloan Wilson an advance large enough to allow him to support his family while he wrote his novel simply because, as noted earlier, Wilson had no track record on which a publisher's

not show interest in Wilson because he was an unsafe investment, and a small house, which might be more willing to take a chance on an unsung writer, would lack the money needed to support Wilson, his wife, and their three children for any stretch of time. A maverick with money was required to give Wilson a chance to write his novel. This suggests one of a few ways in which *The Man in the Gray Flannel Suit* is a distinctly old-fashioned Simon & Schuster success story produced in what was in many respects a new era. Now considered a novel quintessentially of its time, *The Man in the Gray Flannel Suit* is in this sense not just an anomaly but also something of an anachronism.

This back story helps to explain Wilson's preface to the first edition of his novel, which includes the following: "During dark hours when there was no realistic reason to suppose that the manuscript was ever going to get finished, Richard L. Simon, my publisher, administered miraculous transfusions of skill and courage. He emboldened me to have a try at this book in the first place, and now that the work is done, leaves me feeling as though he had fought at my side through a long war. There is no greater friendship." As expressions of thanks go, this one is unusually effusive, the language probably more melodramatic than anything in the novel itself; comparing the process of writing a novel to the experience of going to war is probably not an unusual analogy for the 1950s, but figuring the publisher as a miracle worker, wartime comrade-in-arms, and the novelist's greatest possible friend is more than unusual. In a peculiar way, it transgresses postwar literary ideology and in doing so it offers an indirect clue to the novel's middling reception.

Pierre Bourdieu has described the relationship between writer and publisher as one of "adversaries in collusion" ("Production" 79). Though this description reflects Bourdieu's own investment in a modernist ideology of art that perhaps no longer obtains, the concept is useful for putting into context Wilson's novel and its reception.[10] In Bourdieu's account, the relationship is collusive rather than openly collaborative in order to perpetuate the idea of the solitary artist, divorced from the business concerns that would be the first priority for a mainstream publishing house like Simon & Schuster. The notion that the publisher-writer relationship is adversarial is one of the means by which artists and literary institutions produce belief in the value of art (Wilson's comparison of the writing process to war might be construed as another means to this end), one of the ways, that is, in which the institutions that produce and receive literature make the case that the novel is something more than a mere commodity. In the short term, the author accrues symbolic capital. The long-term effect of belief, the reason, that is, that commercial publishers as well as authors might have an interest in this adversarial relationship, is that it can help to sell books to an audience that itself seeks cultural distinction.

Just as Paul Bowles's apologies for his agent become comprehensible in the context of the story of his rejection by Doubleday and his early relationship with James Laughlin, Wilson's praise for his publisher—and his insistent flouting of a belief-producing strategy—points in part to a genuinely close relationship that Simon and Wilson developed during the time Wilson wrote his novel, and that relationship must be understood as a function of New Ventures' unusual attempt to recreate an older model of book publishing within a modernized corporation. A telling indicator of New Ventures' distance from the conventional publishing world is that Wilson trusted Simon enough to fire his literary agent, that postwar symbol of the author-as-businessperson, and negotiate directly with his publisher: "Friends," Wilson writes in his memoir, "who thought they knew a lot about the literary marketplace told me I was a fool to deal with a publisher without an agent, but Dick was as good as his word. He made many deals for me, but never one I had any reason to regret" (*What* 215).[11] Wilson had the direct, "gentlemanly" relationship with his publisher that in different ways Bowles and Bradbury eulogized, implicitly and explicitly, in and out of their novels.

That Wilson's preface implicitly rejects a strategy for accruing prestige is consequential only in an indirect way. The preface, after all, is not what critics have responded to in finding fault with the novel. But the preface reproduces what I will later discuss as the novel's supposed literary sin, representing big business as benevolent enabler of the individual rather than as a stifling force, the enemy against which individuals must fight. And the connection between the attitude expressed in the preface and the novel's depiction of the corporation is neither incidental nor accidental: the story told in the novel, in which a man's fealty to the corporation is justified by the corporation's remarkably—and, to many readers, implausibly—good treatment of him, draws on and fictionalizes Wilson's atypically "gentlemanly" postwar relationship with his publisher. It is one of several autobiographical sources for *The Man in the Gray Flannel Suit*. In ways that have yet to be appreciated, the novel fictionalizes the unusual circumstances of its own production, far more than it illuminates the conventional corporate world.

Before pursuing this point, there is one final way in which the novel

to flex his selling muscle. It can even be said that this publisher-author relationship, with the emphasis on the publisher, was *structured* to allow Simon to sell. At the time he offered Wilson a book deal, the novel did not exist even as an idea (thus allowing for the possibility that the plot could be based partly on the story of the novel's path to publication) and Simon, moreover, had never read a word Wilson had written. As I will discuss in some detail later, Wilson had been recommended to Simon by a friend, and Simon professed to be uninterested in Wilson's writing ability: "'Generally,'" Wilson remembers Simon telling him, "'I tend to deal more in men than in manuscripts'" (*What* 196). Simon was, as Tebbel says, a "super-salesman"; he had started his career in publishing as a salesman for Boni & Liveright, the storied publisher of high modernist texts. Part of the legend of Simon & Schuster's early years stems from the fact that it was formed before it had books to publish; the content of the books mattered less than the ability to sell them. The principle was the same in 1955. Whatever Wilson produced, Simon likely believed he could sell it, and for him the central question surrounding Wilson's manuscript called *A Candle at Midnight* was not "what is this book about?" but "what is the best way to sell it?" The starting point was the title.

The Title

The official version of the story of the title appears in two places. The first is the jacket copy of the first edition of the novel, at the end of the author biography: "And to this his publisher wishes to add that it was Mrs. Wilson who so ably summarized the theme of her husband's book by suggesting the title *The Man in the Gray Flannel Suit*." In his memoir, Wilson elaborates. In February 1955, after the manuscript was finished and four months before the book arrived in bookstores, Elise Wilson convinced her husband that *The Man in the Gray Flannel Suit* was a better choice than *A Candle at Midnight*, but Simon resisted at first, on the grounds that it was too similar to Mary McCarthy's short story "The Man in the Brooks Brothers Shirt" and to the movie *The Man in the White Suit*.[12] Wilson records Simon's explanation for his fateful change of heart as follows: "On the train going to work today I counted more than eighty men wearing gray flannel suits," he said. "*Eighty*, and I walked through only a few cars. It's a uniform for a certain kind of man, and I think it will make a great title for the book. We'll go to press as soon as we can" (qtd. in *What* 212).

Why did Simon come to like the title so much? The broad answer is clear enough and it helps us to understand *The Man in the Gray Flannel Suit* as an old-fashioned publishing triumph that was marketed to exploit a set of contemporary concerns. "By the middle of the 1950s," Thomas Frank writes, "talk of conformity, of consumerism . . . were routine elements of middle-class American life" (11). It was this talk, this media interest, that Simon sought to exploit. He saw in the title the basis for a marketing campaign, according to which the subject of the novel would be not merely one man in one suit but a group of men who wear the same kind of suit. Thus Tom Rath, Wilson's protagonist, would be made to represent the new "everyman": one of the growing class of middle-class, middle-management suburban commuters, a group that had already received attention as a postwar phenomenon from sociologists Riesman and C. Wright Mills and also in the mainstream press. Recent readers have rightly criticized the very notion that the middle-management, suburban white male's experience was in any way "typical," but it is important to note that the decision to market the novel this way was made by the publisher, and it was made, I'll soon argue, with little attention to the text itself.[13]

Regardless, the novel's commercial success validated Simon's idea: the fact that *The Man in the Gray Flannel Suit* was one of the top-selling books in 1955 is just one aspect of this validation. The long-term effects, surely unanticipated by Simon but surely the product of his marketing efforts, are equally notable. The novel's title has entered the vernacular even as the novel has drifted from public consciousness, and now the novel, despite never achieving great literary acclaim, is back in print, studied as an artifact of a bygone era. Fifteen years after his novel was published, Wilson was as effusive about his publisher's marketing achievement as he had been about his publisher's friendship in the preface: "No one," he writes with characteristic gratitude in his memoir, "ever did a better job of advance publicity on a novel than Dick Simon did with my book" (*What* 224).

As the preface to *The Man in the Gray Flannel Suit* indicates, Wilson was given to overstatement regarding Simon, but it is possible that in this case Wilson actually understates Simon's achievement; in changing *A Candle at Midnight* to *The Man in the Gray Flannel Suit*, Simon did more than just promote a single novel and publicize a catchphrase, and it is this fact that both casts doubt on Wilson's version of the story of the title and points, as well, to what may be the paradigmatic significance of *The Man in the Gray Flannel Suit*. Wilson's account, whereby Simon's random train ride triggers his embrace of the title, presents Simon's embrace as

train ride was required to make Simon aware of the phenomenon of men in gray flannel suits is implausible. For one thing, as already noted, middle-class conformity was a topic of mainstream media attention throughout the first half of the decade. It was a theme of Riesman's *The Lonely Crowd* (1950), and Whyte had discussed the problem of corporate conformity in *Is Anybody Listening?*, which Simon & Schuster published in 1952.[14] During the first half of the 1950s, Whyte continued to explore the subject in *Fortune* magazine, and the articles were later expanded into Whyte's next book, *The Organization Man* (1956), a critical study of the effect of modern life—particularly modern corporate and suburban life—on old-fashioned American individuality, published to great critical and also popular acclaim one year after Wilson's novel.[15]

The relationship between *The Man in the Gray Flannel Suit* and *The Organization Man* is an unusual one. Although Whyte's book includes a fairly mocking assessment of Wilson's novel—in fact, its criticism sets the tone for decades of criticism that followed—typically, in both literary studies of the novel and histories of the era, Wilson's text is seen as the novelistic complement to Whyte's work of popular sociology, and both are understood as crucial contributors to the discourse on middle-management, middle-class existence. It is difficult to find a recent study that mentions Wilson's novel that does not link it with *The Organization Man*; what these studies rarely mention is that both texts were published by Simon & Schuster, one year apart.[16] Both books, in fact, originated under Simon's short-lived New Ventures imprint, which invites speculation that one of Simon's motivations for promoting Wilson's novel as he did was his realization that it would help him promote another of his books, soon to be published (Schwed 194). Unlike Wilson, who as I will discuss later was selected by Simon at the essentially blind recommendation of a friend, Whyte was a known commodity, an editor and writer for a Time, Inc., publication who had already published a high-profile book for Simon & Schuster. All of which suggests that the title of Wilson's novel figured in not one but two marketing efforts; there seems little doubt that *The Man in the Gray Flannel Suit* functioned as a kind of novelistic advertisement for *The Organization Man*, a contribution to a cultural conversation that would in some way amplify the value of Whyte's text. Possibly Simon intended it that way.

That, at least, is one way to interpret the unofficial, revisionist version of the story of the title, which comes from Schwed's history of Simon & Schuster: "Nobody [at Simon & Schuster] was very happy about the tentative title, *A Candle at Midnight*. Wilson was talking to Simon . . . about how the book idea had first occurred to him: 'I went crazy on that commuters' train each morning, seeing all those guys in gray flannel suits—' He was interrupted by Dick Simon's shout of jubilation: 'That's it!' Some book titles are born, some are achieved, and some are thrust on us, and *The Man in the Gray Flannel Suit* falls into the third category" (194). Schwed, regrettably, makes no mention of the discrepancy between his account of the title and the official one. Regardless, his conclusion is dubious. The title was not thrust on Simon; rather it was an opportunity recognized and seized.

How that opportunity was seized is best seen in the ways that the paratext was put to work to promote a particular reading of the novel. Everything about the physical, material first edition of *The Man in the Gray Flannel Suit* outside the text of the novel itself—every part, that is, designed not by Wilson but by Simon & Schuster—announces its putative subject as the typical middle-class man and along with it announces Simon's marketing wizardry. The front-cover illustration, for example, was a faceless, gray, silhouetted man standing beside the title, a fairly obvious attempt to communicate the title character's loss of individuality in the corporate world. In fact, the silhouette says more about the corporate world than is immediately apparent. A deal for a movie version of the novel was struck before the first edition was in bookstores; the silhouette was designed specifically to evoke Gregory Peck, its star. Simon & Schuster's original plan was to use Peck's actual picture on the front cover instead of the silhouette, figuring that his fame would help sell the book and also drum up interest in the movie that would appear soon after—corporate synergy at work. The plan, though, was ultimately rejected on the grounds of taste and marketing; the publisher decided that it would be unseemly to promote a movie so blatantly on the cover of a novel, a concession to old-fashioned literary values made easier by the realization that the very facelessness of the cover illustration functioned as a comment on the novel's purported subject matter (Schwed 194–95). All told, then, the cover figures in three marketing campaigns. Used to help promote the novel itself, *The Organization Man*, and the movie version of the novel, the cover conveys *The Man in the Gray Flannel Suit*'s participation in the new world of cross-promotion, the developing "synergistic" relationship between the publishing industry and the institutions of mass culture that mergers like that of Simon & Schuster into Field Enterprises were designed to exploit. Written and published only because Simon briefly created an "old" version of Simon & Schuster

lished, would become an example of the marketing possibilities for the book in the age of mass culture, connecting the novel's publisher with both Time, Inc. (Whyte's employer), and Twentieth Century Fox, which produced the movie.

If the cover illustration is the clearest visual symbol of the novel's purported subject, the oft-quoted original jacket copy was the most explicit aspect of Simon's marketing effort, and it imposed an interpretation on the novel that it has yet to shake. "This is a novel about the man in the gray flannel suit," it begins. "In these particular pages, the man's name is Thomas Rath. He happens to work at Rockefeller Center in New York City, and his home happens to be in a near-by Connecticut suburb." The use of first "these particular pages" and then the repetition of the "happens to" construction suggest that Rath could have any name, could live anywhere, and could work anywhere. In fact, Rath was deliberately named to suggest an angry character: "Tom Rath was of course a very angry man," Wilson writes in his 1983 preface to the novel (reprinted as an afterword to the 2002 reissue). "When I named him 'Rath' I thought I might be criticized for making this too obvious" (279). And although Rockefeller Center may seem to be a random workplace location, its selection by Wilson was likely not random: it was the address of Simon & Schuster's offices, suggesting again the novel's autobiographical subtext. The jacket copy asserts that Rath is but one of many just like him. In so doing, it does to him what in the 1950s the corporation was said to do its employees: it denies Tom Rath his individuality, his distinctiveness as a literary character, by asserting that he could be anyone, anywhere. By shifting the focus away from what is unusual about him, it renders him faceless.

This point is soon made explicit: "Although this novel is about the Rath family, the man in the gray flannel suit is a fairly universal figure in mid-twentieth-century America. The gray flannel suit is the uniform of the man with a briefcase who leaves his home each morning to make his living as an executive in the near-by city." The unusual "although" at the start has the effect of further diminishing the importance of the Raths themselves. The real story here, the jacket copy suggests, is not the Raths themselves but a sociological phenomenon. The rest of the jacket copy is similarly devoted to effacing whatever might be unusual or contingent about the experiences that the novel describes, and to the extent that it strains to do this it suggests what is obscured by treating the novel as a kind of sociological case study: "Though most men do not fall in love with girls in Rome and don't, even in the course of war, kill seventeen men, each man has his own problems about which the world knows very little. These men are all over America wearing gray flannel." This is a fairly extraordinary sentence in that even as it suggests other ways that Wilson's novel might have been marketed by Simon & Schuster and interpreted by readers—as a romance, a story of lost love (the reading suggested by Wilson's original title, *A Candle at Midnight*), or as a war story or a postwar story, or all of these choices—it does so only to dismiss those ways and thus dismiss even the most extraordinary experiences as sociologically irrelevant and thus irrelevant to the novel.

The jacket copy's interpretation of the novel has proven influential. It is telling, for example, that several studies of *The Man in the Gray Flannel Suit* quote at least part of this text, which of course Wilson did not write. This pattern of citing the jacket copy also begins with Whyte's *The Organization Man.* "As the dust jacket says," Whyte notes, "Rath is a true product of his times" (131). And Jurca writes aptly that the "protagonist of *The Man in the Gray Flannel Suit* was billed, preposterously, as 'a fairly universal figure in mid-twentieth-century America'" (139). The novel's paratextual claim about Tom Rath's universality does merit debunking, but it is important to acknowledge that it is not Wilson but the publisher making this claim and that the claim was made in the service of objectives that go far beyond the marketing of a single novel. To put it slightly differently, the story of the novel's genesis and promotion might matter less were the novel actually about the stereotypical man in the gray flannel suit. That it plainly is not is a fact that has been lost to literary history, obscured in part by Simon and Whyte and in part by certain choices Wilson made in fictionalizing his experience.

Rath's Rebellion

If we assume that Wilson conceived of the experience of the returning veteran seeking work in a large corporation as a paradigmatic 1950s experience—and there is some reason to support this view—then the novel's aim is sociological for about the first ten pages. In this time, Rath, with some reservations, but with the prospect of a higher salary too good to resist, decides to apply for a public-relations job at the United Broadcasting Company (UBC). "'I've never thought of you as a public-relations man'" (6), his wife Betsy says to him when he tells her about it, and we are given to understand that public relations is a particularly demeaning enterprise.[17] At the job interview, Mr. Walker, the personnel

yourself to me," Walker says. "Tell me what kind of person you are. Explain why we should hire you'" (11). Rath is free to write whatever he wants, Walker explains, but the last sentence should begin this way: "The most significant fact about me is . . . "

At this point, the novel strays from the typical and rebels against the sociological. Burdened by painful memories of his hellish World War II service, Rath finds himself both perplexed and offended by the autobiography requirement. One's life cannot be summed up in an hour, particularly when one killed seventeen men during a war and then returned home to a placid suburban life. The war experience seems at once too essential to be left out of an honest autobiography and too *real* to be included in a superficial job interview, an exercise in self-promotion and therefore, presumably, as suspect as the public-relations job itself. The autobiography request seems to Rath both inappropriate and impossible to carry out honestly, an example of the kind of degrading conformist dishonesty that the corporate world demands, exactly what he had feared when he decided to apply for a job at UBC. What is most interesting about this reaction is how over-the-top it seems to be, how exaggerated Rath's discontent seems to be at a fairly innocuous request: Rath's initial response to Walker's request is this: "Son of a bitch . . . I guess the laws of cruel and unusual punishment don't apply to personnel men" (11–12). But how bad is it, really? An autobiography is merely another way of talking about oneself, which is what one does at a job interview. Among other things, the fact that somehow being asked to *write* about himself in a dishonest, self-promoting way is worse than being asked to talk about himself in such a way lends Rath's frustration a literary cast. It is a writer's frustration and, in the throes of it, Rath imagines an angry response: "The most significant fact about me is that I detest the United Broadcasting Corporation, with all its soap operas, commercials, and yammering studio audiences, and the only reason I'm willing to spend my life in such a ridiculous enterprise is that I want to buy a more expensive house and a better brand of gin" (13).

As he will throughout the novel, Rath here flirts with cynicism even as he idealistically condemns the emergent mass culture that his prospective employer represents and produces. Rath's previous job had been with a foundation established by an "elderly millionaire . . . to help finance scientific research and the arts" (3), a patron, in short, and as such an example of a precapitalist approach to producing art that modernist writers looked back to longingly and sought to reproduce when possible.[18] Rath's move from foundation to UBC, prompted by his felt need to earn more money—to the extent that his experience is seen as paradigmatic—is yet another modernist parable about the ever increasing reach of mass culture and the demise of superior culture at the hands of capitalism. Rath's attack on mass culture, moreover, is consonant with those of postwar intellectuals who decried its impact on high culture, just as his and his wife's general suspicion of corporate public-relations work is consonant with 1950s representations of corporate conformity. These moments link the novel with prevailing 1950s discourses, with Greenberg as much as with Whyte, but what proves to be characteristic of the novel is the way it ultimately sidesteps these discourses rather than participating in them. Rath's job turns out to have little to do with the mass culture he here purports to abhor, and he always works outside the corporate culture he fears and disdains. What is striking about the novel is not its typicalness but the way it seems to work so hard, often to the point of implausibility, to elude the typical.

Although Rath characteristically opts to forgo his imagined outright rebellion (in fact he never seriously entertains it), he does so not in favor of conformity or capitulation to a corporation he claims to detest but instead in favor of an understated, polite rebellion; after several abortive attempts at the kind of autobiography he thinks Walker wants, Rath chooses not to write one at all. Instead, using little of the time allotted to him, Rath writes a paragraph that includes only the most basic information about him before concluding this way: "After considerable thought, I have decided that I do not wish to attempt an autobiography as part of an application for a job" (17). "'I've written all I think is necessary,'" Rath tells a surprised Walker when he turns in his paper a full fifteen minutes before his allotted hour runs out.

Literary history, with assists from Simon and Whyte, has tended to remember Rath as, in Wilson's words, "the squarest guy in the world . . . a guy who would never go on the road with Jack Kerouac or rock around the clock with anybody" and Wilson as either an apologist for conformity or a failed critic of it (Afterword 278). But this episode seems to have all the elements needed to make Rath and Wilson heroes to the literary counterculture: a refusal to write on demand; a refusal to write dishonestly; in the act of giving up the job, a self-sabotage in the name of principle; an attack on the cultural bankruptcy of a mass-culture institution; and, finally, in Rath's recognition of the impossibility of assimilating his war experiences into his postwar suburban life, postwar alienation. The main thing, it seems, that prevents the character from attaining the sta-

that Rath gets the job, apparently though not explicitly in part because of his quiet rebellion. After Rath turns in his nonautobiography, Walker tells him he will hear from UBC in about a week; the letter offering a second interview arrives only three days later, suggesting, implausibly, that his quasi-literary refusal to follow orders has been rewarded by the mass-culture institution. All this happens without satisfactory explanation from UBC and without even any remark by narrator or character on its strangeness. No one ever tells Rath or the reader that the corporation admired Rath's refusal to write an autobiography, but it is difficult to draw any other conclusion about his hiring. The seeming strangeness of the novel is embodied in this episode. The stereotypical organization man would have written his autobiography; the stereotypical organization would have rejected him for not doing so.

This strange moment is made stranger by the fact that similar episodes recur throughout the novel; these are the moments that have given the novel its reputation as "middlebrow" and these are the moments that led Whyte to assert that in the world of the novel there is no longer any reason to be rebellious (*Organization* 251). Repeatedly, Rath finds himself faced with what appears to be a situation with two choices—either lie in order to succeed or tell the truth, maintain honor, and fail. Each time, after wavering, Tom chooses truth, and each time (always to his surprise—he chooses truth with the fatalistic attitude he developed jumping out of planes during World War II) the truth leads to success, exactly the kind of success that he thought required lying. The novel's central, prolonged workplace drama involves Rath's wavering over whether he should tell his boss, Ralph Hopkins, his honest opinion of a speech Hopkins plans to deliver. After much handwringing, Rath decides to give his honest opinion ("'I'm afraid I just don't think it's a very good speech'" [222]), and of course he is rewarded for his candor ("'You've helped me cut through a lot of fog on this . . . can't thank you enough!'" [223]).[19] And in the novel's infamous ending, Rath fears that telling Hopkins that he is not happy as his personal assistant will cost him everything. He confesses to Hopkins and is rewarded with an even better job outside the corporate "rat race." This is surely a Hollywood ending, but it is not apologia for conformity. Rath never gives in to the organization or conforms for the sake of it, and what is odd is that the organization never asks him to do so; rather, the organization rewards him for his polite refusal to conform and is, moreover, the site of and the enabler of his honesty. In Whyte's terms, Rath seems to have found the postwar corporation at which the protestant ethic has not been replaced by the social ethic. (It should be noted that Wilson applies this plot device—rewarding Rath's honesty—not just to his participation in the corporate institution but also to his marriage. Rath decides to tell his wife that he fathered a child while in Italy during the war and that he wants to send money to Italy to support his son; she eventually agrees: " 'I'm sorry I acted like a child. . . . You're right about helping the boy in Italy. Of course we should do all we can' " [271].)

Although the implausibility of Rath's good fortune—working for the organization that does not demand that he conform—is one of the novel's literary sins, the grounds for viewing the novel as a kind of corporate propaganda, on a plot level, Rath's situation is not difficult to explain: *The Man in the Gray Flannel Suit* is the story of a man with an unusual job. Walker begins Rath's second interview by saying as much: "I think I should begin by saying that this isn't just an ordinary job in the public-relations department we're considering . . . as a matter of fact, this position wouldn't really be with United Broadcasting at all, except in a purely technical sense . . . you would be working directly for Mr. Hopkins on an outside project completely unrelated to the company" (24). The job turns out to be a campaign to raise public awareness about mental health issues, which for obscure reasons is of great importance to Hopkins. The unusualness of Rath's situation is made more explicit when he tells his friend Hawthorne, who also works for UBC, that he will be meeting Hopkins. " 'Hell . . . I've been working for this damn outfit for four years, and I've never laid eyes on the guy' " (29). Rath's corporate experience is unusual but that unusual quality is acknowledged in the novel; the novel is not blind to it. The circumstances that surround Rath's hiring are strange because the job is strange; the job is strange because it is unrelated to the business of the corporation. Contrary to the jacket copy and much of the critical reception, this is not a novel about corporate life.

The Cold War

But if *The Man in the Gray Flannel Suit* is not a novel about corporate life, then what is it about? Why does it veer so close to the typical corporate experience only to sidestep it? One way of approaching these questions is to consider the degree to which the work-related plots of the novel fictionalize various aspects of Wilson's own professional experience. Prior to writing *The Man in the Gray Flannel Suit*, Wilson worked as an assistant director of a nonprofit corporation called the National Citizens Com-

This was no ordinary advocacy group. Established in 1949, and partially funded with a grant from the Carnegie Corporation, the implicit rationale of Better Schools was that the need to improve public education was particularly urgent because of the threat of Communism. The commission was the brainchild of then-Harvard president James B. Conant, who had been instrumental in the creation of the atomic bomb and the Scholastic Aptitude Test, both of which were seen as weapons in the national effort to contain Communism.[20] The responsibility for organizing it was passed on to Harvard alumnus and president of Time, Inc., Roy Larsen. Better Schools is thus an example of the mobilization of powerful U.S. institutions in the effort to contain Communism; the stated goal of the commission was "to help Americans realize how important our public schools are to our expanding democracy" (qtd. in Corbally and Seeger 142). Members included such luminaries as Walter Lippmann and George Gallup among other corporate and labor leaders. One executive, Neil McElroy, then the president of Procter & Gamble, used his presence on the commission as a springboard into public service. He was appointed secretary of defense under President Dwight D. Eisenhower just days after the Soviet Union launched Sputnik in 1957, an event that paved the way for the National Defense Education Act of 1958, a massive federal investment in education that serves as the clearest link between federal education policy and the Cold War.[21] In another bit of effective cross-promotion, *Time* quoted Conant's judgment on the work of the commission: "Potentially the most important move for the advancement of public education taken in the past 50 years" ("By and For" 80).

Despite this high praise, Better Schools barely rates as a historical footnote, and Wilson believed that it accomplished little: "To my knowledge," he writes mockingly in his memoir, "no one seriously criticized the . . . Commission . . . for spending several million dollars of Ford, Carnegie and Rockefeller money for such meager results" (*What* 178). But Better Schools does merit a small place in 1950s literary history because Wilson's experience there is the basis for the work he describes in the novel. Wilson's work for Better Schools entailed ghostwriting speeches—Rath's major task when he starts working for UBC—and meeting with corporate executives and other leaders to impress on them the importance of public education, which (along with Simon) no doubt informed Rath's representation of benevolent bosses Ralph Hopkins and Dick Haver, head of his first employer, the Schanenhauser Foundation.

More important, awareness of Wilson's Better Schools experience helps us locate some of the strangeness of the novel's corporate story line in the fact that Wilson divorced it from the very specific experience on which it is based. Instead of an explicit Cold War theme, Wilson has Hopkins develop a campaign to foster awareness of mental health issues, "something," Walker explains, "which would do for mental disease what the March of Dimes has done for Polio" (25). Mental health is a suggestive choice with respect to Rath, who struggles to adjust to postwar life after a harrowing experience during the war. Giving this work a connection to Rath's personal struggles has the effect, moreover, of distancing the novel's urban-suburban middle-class story line from the larger geopolitical context, and this too might be an effect Wilson intended. When the Cold War is mentioned in the novel, it is to emphasize the distance between Rath's tame but real concerns about work and family in suburbia, on the one hand, and the terrifying possibility of World War III, on the other. While Tom talks to Mr. Walker early, he "heard a fire engine, deprived of its siren because of the need to reserve sirens for air raid warnings" (24). Shortly thereafter, Rath rides the commuter train home from work: "All up and down the aisle men were sitting, motionless and voiceless, reading their papers. Tom opened his and read a long story about negotiations in Korea. A columnist debated the question of when Russia would have hydrogen bombs to drop on the United States. Tom folded his paper and stared at the suburban stations gliding by" (67).

Wilson here develops a theme noted earlier in the novel, the chasm that divides the domestic from the professional, the domestic and professional from the political, and the present from the past. At the start of the novel, Tom reflects, "There were really four unrelated worlds in which he lived": work; childhood memory; "best-not-remembered" wartime memory; and "the entirely separate world" of his wife and children, "the only one of the four worlds worth a damn" (22). The geopolitical arena dominated by the Cold War is an unnamed fifth world; perhaps Wilson emphasizes its distance from Rath's life in part to point out his privileging of the private or domestic sphere. When the theme of education does show up in a subplot near the end of *The Man in the Gray Flannel Suit*, after Rath's children complain about the condition of the public school, the novel makes no attempt to link the Raths' efforts to improve the schools to larger cultural or political concerns. Rather, the aim appears to be to connect Rath's fight to improve the school—a public issue, to be sure, but one that matters in the novel to the extent that it affects Rath's family—to his insistence on separating himself from Hopkins's consuming professional world.[22]

Although the political context of Wilson's work for Better Schools is absent from the novel, the story of how he came to work for Better Schools is not. In the same way that Tom Rath found himself working on a civic-minded project without intending to, Wilson had come to Better Schools by accident. Like many other mid-century writers and aspiring writers and like Whyte, he went to work for Time, Inc., prior to writing his book. Time was a frequent target of postwar intellectuals, even as it hired them and, at the moment Wilson was hired, in the late 1940s, the company was getting worse in this regard. Allen Ginsberg writes in "America" (1956), published months after *The Man in the Gray Flannel Suit*: "I'm addressing you / Are you going to let your emotional life be run by Time Magazine?" (40). Macdonald, who like Whyte once worked for Time-owned *Fortune*, famously remarked in *Against the American Grain* that *Time* "gives Americans something to read when they aren't thinking" (401).

James L. Baughman describes the environment at *Time* as follows: "Those joining *Time* as writers in the late 1940s and early 1950s . . . accepted the new regimen. Old timers could see it coming. The magazine no longer hired so many class poets, touched by radicalism, accepting Luce's paychecks for a few years before leaving to write the American *Iliad*. Now 'careerists,' still male, filled the office. Although usually Democrats, they acquiesced to the magazine's editing routine. They were *Time*'s 'organization men'" (*Henry* 166). Wilson, a Democrat and not a radical, knew the company's reputation. As he describes it in his memoir, his decision to work for Time, Inc. was distinctly that of a writer by necessity selling out his literary ideals to support his family: "In those days I was still young enough to think in melodramatic terms. The question obviously was whether I would sell my soul to the devil. The answer came to me unhesitatingly: yes! The devil would undoubtedly prove to be a difficult employer, but no problem he could offer would be worse than trying to raise two children on fifty dollars a week" (15). Wilson's father was a poet and journalism professor, and his mother a journalist and women's rights activist. Wilson was raised to be a writer, and he never considered doing anything else; the misgivings that Tom Rath felt about leaving a charitable foundation to work for a television network are the misgivings Wilson had about selling his literary soul to Luce. Like Rath, Wilson took the job because it paid more than his previous job (as a newspaper reporter in Providence, Rhode Island). Thus the start of the novel, in which Rath decides to leave his job for corporate America, is modeled on an aspiring writer's paradigmatic postwar experience; if it is typical, it is only because, as noted earlier, the world of literary production was in the process of becoming more like conventional organization society.

Wilson found Time, Inc., even worse than he had feared. He was assigned stultifying work for its in-house organ, *FYI*—worse even than writing for *Time*, Wilson was initially assigned to write pro-Luce propaganda for an audience of *Time* employees. "The bright-eyed eagerness of *FYI* about all the workings on *Time* would not be easy for me to contrive," Wilson writes, "no matter how anxious I was, as the saying went, 'to sell out' for money" (*What* 173); earlier he notes that "writing for *Time* had seemed a definite downward step which was necessary for financial reasons, but being assigned to *Time*'s house organ seemed to place me about as low as a writer could go" (172). This might be the work of the prototypical man in the gray flannel suit, and it is tempting to say that if Wilson had stayed at *FYI* he might actually have written the protest against conformity, of the man stifled by the demands of corporate life, that social and literary critics craved. But to say this is to misunderstand the process by which the novel was produced, specifically to ignore the institutional network that created the novel; in light of the story of Wilson's path to publication, recounted in the next section, it is probably more apt to say that if Wilson had continued writing for Time's house organ, he would not have written a novel at all. In any event, Wilson did not stay long at *FYI*. Almost immediately after being assigned, he was summoned to Roy Larsen's office and offered the opportunity to work for what would become Better Schools, Inc. It was, in one sense, an incredibly lucky moment for Wilson; in another sense, it was not luck at all.

Connections

Nicholas Lemann describes American culture in 1945 as follows: "High-Protestant men of the Eastern seaboard occupy the White House, all of the great university presidencies, the captaincies of finance and the professions, and many other leading positions, and each has rough access to the others" (4). Wilson, himself a Protestant man of the Eastern seaboard, benefited immensely from this network of relations; his career testifies to its power. Wilson was asked to work directly for Larsen on the Better Schools project for the same reason he was hired by Time, Inc., in the first place: a recommendation from a famed, well-connected Harvard professor (non-Protestant but still powerful Paul Sachs, whose family cofounded Goldman Sachs), who happened to know Roy Larsen well and whose daughter happened to have married into Wilson's wife's family. "In principle," Wilson writes in his memoir, "I disapproved of the practice of using a family connection to get jobs, but in practice I employed it as much as possible" (*What* 154). Wilson was lucky enough to know the right people, and not for the last time.

Wilson's connections and good fortune implicate him in a classic postwar irony. Better Schools' campaign was founded on the idea that public education was fundamentally democratic and thus useful in a battle against a totalitarian ideology. Public education, it was believed, would ensure that the best and brightest of students would have the opportunity to rise: the goal was to make the US more of a meritocracy. Merit and not ideology or economics or class would determine one's ability to succeed. As Lemann summarizes: "Conant's central cause . . . was creating a new American elite, drawn from every region and background, and disabling the current, suffocatingly narrow one," dominated by that homogenous group from the Eastern seaboard (44). What is perhaps most important about the irony that Wilson was appointed to a commission promoting the importance of meritocracy not because of his merits but because of where he had gone to college and who he had known there—"This was a job," Wilson writes, "for which I had absolutely *no* qualifications" (175)—is that it is altogether typical and not at all surprising.

In any event, Wilson did want to rise on his literary merits. After two years at Better Schools, he quit his comfortable job to pursue again his literary ambitions, a fairly reckless decision. But he found himself in the same circumstance that prompted him to work for Time, Inc., in the first place; with a family to support, he needed a sizable advance in order to begin writing in earnest. With his limited literary and commercial track record (he had published one little noted and commercially unsuccessful novel and several *New Yorker* magazine stories), he had to face the realities of the postwar book business and the vocation of writing: no publisher was willing to give him what he needed. "In the early 1950s," he later wrote, "it was not easy for a young man who had only one slender novel . . . to get much of an advance" (*What* 195). Wilson began looking for other jobs, and he was immensely surprised when Simon contacted him and offered him as much money and as much time as he needed to complete a novel. Not only had Simon never read a word Wilson had written, Wilson had never contacted Simon to even ask for an advance. With no literary or commercial track record, he considered Simon & Schuster out of his league. In a world where publishing houses were less and less likely to read an unsolicited manuscript, an unsolicited offer to publish from one of America's largest and most successful publishers was an extraordinary event. So what prompted the offer? The answer is mundane but telling. Simon's offer was the result of a recommendation made on Wilson's behalf but unknown to him by Roy Larsen, his former boss at Time, Inc. As Wilson recounts Simon's words: " 'I haven't read anything you've written, . . . but Roy Larsen says you're a person who might do something someday, and Roy has good judgment' " (196). Wilson's ability to write the novel that would become *The Man in the Gray Flannel Suit* is a product of his small place in a network of powerful postwar institutions. The links between first Harvard and Time and then Time and Simon & Schuster (and the company's place amid these major institutions in and of itself says something about the growth of the book business) are essential but hidden aspects of the genesis of Wilson's novel, just as the links between the novel, the movie version of the novel, and *The Organization Man* are essential but hidden aspects of its reputation.

"The union of bosses" Wilson writes in the novel, "is the most powerful union in the world" (25), and apparently the sentiment appealed to him because he repeats it a few pages later, with a key addendum: "The union of bosses is powerful, but, within its self-prescribed limits, marvelously scrupulous" (37). As noted earlier, from Whyte's review to the present, Wilson's portrayal of the corporate world as benevolent has been cited as a problem. But given Wilson's own set of experiences leading to the writing of his novel, it is not surprising that he represents bosses as marvelously scrupulous. Wilson's novel contains within it a fictionalized and transformed story of the growth of the book business and a fictionalized and transformed story of a Cold War public-relations effort. What is most interesting about it is how it alters what actually happened to him: as Richard Simon's marketing campaign has obscured Wilson's intentions for his novel, Wilson's transformation of his own experience in the novel obscures his debts to the institutions and privilege that got him a publishing deal. In the novel, Rath rises not by connections but by virtue of an inner-directed honesty—refusing to trivialize his war experience by writing an autobiography for a job interview, telling Hopkins the truth about his speech. Rath does not "sell out" to the corporation, and the corporation does not demand that he do so; in this regard, the novel is faithful to Wilson's own experience. But the novel does suggest that one can be rewarded for refusing to conform, and in this regard it diverges from the story of Wilson's rise.

Artists and Gray Flannel

The literary problem with Rath—what makes him purportedly typical—is that, as Frank writes, he "can imagine no alternative to the corporation and the commute" (38). Unlike other, more celebrated novels of the era, *The Man in the Gray Flannel Suit* seems to lack an "artist" character—a character who separates himself or herself from conventional life, who refuses to play by typical rules, and who is made to suffer for this refusal. But one artist who does appear in the novel briefly is Rath's uncompromising five-year-old daughter, Janey: "She did everything hard: she screamed when she cried. . . . upon deciding that she wanted to play with ink, she carefully poured ink over both her hands and made neat imprints in the wallpaper, from the floor to as high as she could reach. Betsy was so angry she slapped both her hands and Janey, feeling she had been interrupted in the midst of an artistic endeavor, lay on the bed for an hour sobbing and rubbing her hands and eyes until her whole face was covered with ink" (2). This scene might be said to include much of what is wrong with the Raths and 1950s culture because it seems to link their desire for a comfortable middle-class existence, represented by their suburban home—as Jurca shows, the greatest symbol of that existence—with the need to stifle their daughter's artistic expression.[23] Janey's commitment to her art recurs a bit later, when she insists again on her need to create when she is supposed to be in bed, recovering from the chicken pox: ("You're not very well. . . . You're supposed to be in bed," Tom says, and Janey replies, "indignantly, 'We're *painting*!'" (31).

As has been well recorded in recent studies of postwar literary culture, a still-celebrated canon of 1950s novels themselves celebrate characters like Janey, outsiders who refuse to live according to the dictates of whatever organization it was that was trying to impose rules on them, "liberated," as Schaub says, "from both social convention and aesthetic orthodoxy" (70).[24] Augie March, the Invisible Man, Holden Caulfield, and Sal Paradise are the classic examples: the creators of these characters, as was the case with Bowles's portrayal of Port and Bradbury's of Clarisse and Montag, gain symbolic capital from the characters they represented, though the authors themselves, as shown throughout this book, could only gain their opportunity to advertise this vision of artistic freedom by linking themselves to institutions of commercial artistic production that were large and growing larger. As argued in this chapter, something of this need to connect to larger institutions is in evidence in the plot of *The Man in the Gray Flannel Suit*, in which Rath only gets to be his honest self because his employer allows it. The clearest and perhaps most unusual way the novel shows the growing interconnectedness of the corporate and literary fields, ultimately, is through its other artist character, Ralph Hopkins. Given that he is the corporate boss, in charge of the organization—the art-stifling mass-culture organization, no less—that supposedly demands conformity, Hopkins's benevolence has been a target of critics; he is no doubt based in part on Roy Larsen and in part on Richard Simon. His hiring of Rath suggests again the connectedness of what would elsewhere be described as separate spheres; Walker explains, "One reason we think you might be suited for the job is that you would be working quite closely with the foundations" (24).

The oddest thing about Hopkins, however, is not his sincere interest in the cause of mental health awareness; it is that, in a novel that seems to have no place for the suffering, belief-producing artist, it is Hopkins himself who assumes that role. Hopkins's job requires all of the suffering, the detachment, the avoidance of family that artist-characters of other postwar novels—not just Holden Caulfield and Sal Paradise but also Bowles's Port (dead in the Sahara), Bradbury's Clarisse (killed by the government)—exhibit; Wilson devotes much of the novel to the deterioration of his family life, his shattered relationship with his wife, his inability to connect with his daughter. Dick Haver, Rath's boss at the foundation, calls Hopkins "one of the few authentic business geniuses in New York today" (36), and Rath explains to his wife, "Why do you think Hopkins is great? Mainly, it's because he never thinks about anything but his work, day and night, seven days a week, three hundred and sixty-five days a year. All geniuses are like that—there's no mystery about it. The great painters, the great composers, the great scientists, and the great businessmen—they all have the same capacity for total absorption in their work" (250). Like the artist-characters in Bradbury and Bowles's novels, Hopkins pays for his passion; we are led to believe that he is on the verge of a fatal heart attack. The fruits of Hopkins's labor—the money—seem hardly to matter to him. His pleasure comes from the work. Certainly, the last thing one would expect Hopkins to do is actually watch television for entertainment. If there is any way in which *The Man in the Gray Flannel Suit* is subversive, this is it. Because it positions the corporate, mass-culture giant as a great artist at the historical moment at which fears of mass culture were at their apex—because, that is, it refuses throughout to instantiate a rigid distinction between the arenas of business and the arts, the businessman and the artist—the novel can be read as an unwitting challenge to the conventional highbrow wisdom about the relationship between art and corporate culture and the notion of a "great divide" separating distinct spheres of culture, ideas crucial to the prewar modernist moment and to the plots of celebrated 1950s novels.

In this regard, moreover, Wilson's novel is prescient, if unwittingly so. As the rest of this book explores, by the end of the 1950s, that conventional highbrow wisdom about the relationship between literary culture and the business world generally was itself discredited. Publishing itself became a high-profile business, as larger houses purchased smaller ones and then were absorbed into larger multimedia corporations. These kinds of relationships among media companies were anticipated by Simon's efforts in promoting *The Man in the Gray Flannel Suit.* The misreading of the novel as apologia for conformity—the novel's status as a symbol of the 1950s, as complement to the work of Riesman and Whyte—and indeed the endurance of that image of the 1950s as a decade dominated by men in gray flannel, is an unlikely register of the success of that promotion.

Chapter 4
From Novel to Blockbuster:
Peyton Place and the
Narrative of Cultural Decline

Peyton Place (1956), Grace Metalious's scandalous first novel, was an immediate and unprecedented commercial success. At a time when first novels typically sold a total of 2,000 copies, it sold 60,000 copies in the first ten days of its official release and 104,000 copies in its first month. It was the second-best-selling novel of 1956 despite not arriving in bookstores until September 24 of that year, and it went on to be the best-selling novel of 1957 as well, spending a total of 59 weeks at the top of the *New York Times* best-seller list. That this is, in a sense, only the first part of the story of *Peyton Place*—it was soon followed by various multimedia attempts to capitalize on its fame that make the marketing of *The Man in the Gray Flannel Suit* seem quaint and that, in terms of audience, dwarfed the success of the novel itself—should not obscure the extent of this initial popularity. *Peyton Place* became, in its time, the best-selling novel of the twentieth century (Cameron viii).

In the decade in which American publishing grew out of its beginnings as a cottage industry, *Peyton Place* became a kind of cottage industry unto itself, and it produced two sets of offshoots. One is the series of multimedia exploitations (movies, a literary sequel, two prime-time television series, and several television movies), which seem to fulfill the commercial promise of corporate synergy that the story of *The Man in the Gray Flannel Suit* anticipates. The second set, to which much of this chapter will be devoted, has been produced not by the "culture industry" but by the culture-analyzing industry: the novel's unprecedented success brought with it inevitable and almost immediate efforts to interpret that success. And in the 1950s, culture critics did not have to look far for an interpretation of the *Peyton Place* phenomenon. This was, as this book has shown throughout, a golden age for narratives of cultural decline. The form of these narratives varied—essays by Macdonald and others of the *Partisan Review* set, and novels by the likes of Bradbury and Bowles—and so too did the terminology—"kitsch," "masscult," and the "culture in-dustry" all being variants of the same phenomenon—but the essential story of superior culture for the few threatened by encroaching culture for the masses remained unchanged. Even *The Man in the Gray Flannel Suit*, distinguished by its refusal to demonize the corporation, includes a version of this narrative, as the promise of more money leads Tom Rath to consider leaving his job with the Schanenhauser Foundation for one at a television network. Such narratives of decline were not new to the 1950s: as Patrick Brantlinger shows, laments about the spread of culture date back at least as far as the Roman Empire. But in the context of Cold War fears of totalitarianism and the rise of television, on the one hand, and the increase in college-educated consumers and the rise of the Eng-lish Department (the growth, that is, of the audience for predictions of culture's demise), on the other, these narratives increased in number, urgency, and theoretical sophistication.

It was probably inevitable that *Peyton Place*, with its combination of scandal and unprecedented sales totals, its luridness ripe for accusa-tions that it coarsened culture, would come to be seen in the context of those predictions, particularly in light of the gendered subtext of much of the modernist disdain for mass culture. As Andreas Huyssen has ar-gued, critics of mass culture dating back to the mid-nineteenth cen-tury frequently posited it as feminine, in opposition to superior (male) modernist culture: "Connotations of mass culture as essentially femi-nine . . . remain central to understanding the historical and rhetorical determinations of the modernism/mass culture dichotomy" (48). This gendering has taken multiple forms; in some cases, it is the masses themselves that are associated with femininity, and in others it is the producers and arbiters of a culture deemed inferior that are linked to a notion of femininity that in and of itself connotes artistic inferiority. In whatever way mass culture has been linked to femininity, *Peyton Place* seems to fit: not only was the novel authored by a woman and largely about women and presumably read by women, it was also produced in hardcover and paperback by what were at the time the only two Ameri-can publishing houses headed by women. Thus the gendered subtext of the modernism and mass-culture debates seems particularly relevant to a discussion of the novel's reception and the novel itself seems an obvious symbol of the problem that a feminized mass culture represented to postwar intellectuals.

Indeed, though intellectuals of the *Partisan Review* set had little to say about *Peyton Place*—an important aspect of the novel's reception that has itself been lost in the recent critical discussion about it—the novel's reception, not just its literary reputation but also the interpretation of its success as a historical and cultural event and the apparently felt need to interpret that success, is in part a function of the fact that it achieved its mass popularity at the historical moment when anxiety about this kind of popularity was at its zenith. And this has proven a barrier to grasping the story of *Peyton Place*'s commercial success, to appreciating what it has to tell us about American novels and their relation to mass culture in the 1950s. Narratives of mid-century cultural decline of the kind this book has described throughout are themselves, like *Peyton Place*'s unprecedented success, the products of a specific set of historical and cultural circumstances, incomprehensible outside the context of technological growth, demographic change, and the Cold War among other factors. But almost from the moment Metalious's novel was published, these narratives have been used as though they were self-evident, transhistorical lenses through which the *Peyton Place* phenomenon could be interpreted. This is regrettable: as this chapter argues, the story of the making, marketing, and reception of *Peyton Place* does have a great deal to tell us about literary culture over the course of the twentieth century, about changes in American publishing and the reading public, but highbrow narratives of decline have gotten in the way.

The first aim of this chapter is to reconsider *Peyton Place* and its receptions specifically in order to examine the multiple ways in which the novel has figured in and been refigured by various retellings of the narrative of cultural decline. Both the original dismissal of *Peyton Place*, which happened shortly after the novel was published, and its eventual revival as a novel of literary merit, which did not occur until the 1990s, have relied in different ways on the notion that Metalious's novel either causes or exemplifies a seismic shift in American culture, that it is somehow essential to the supposed usurpation of literary culture by mass culture. The second aim is to use the often told but in important respects unexamined story of the publication and promotion of *Peyton Place*, in relation to other stories of postwar literary promotion, as an occasion to revisit and reassess the novel's place in American cultural history and along with it an entire approach to talking about cultural change in the twentieth century. *Peyton Place*'s substantial but neglected connections to publishing's purported golden age of the 1920s—that "gentlemanly" age celebrated or longed-for in different ways by Bowles, Bradbury, Wilson, and Simon, and by chroniclers of publishing Tebbel and Epstein—and to the institutions that produced some of that decade's most celebrated literary texts constitute a challenge to the idea that the novel was produced by institutions of some new and threatening mass culture. Neither a symbol of Huyssen's "great divide" between high art and mass culture nor the "first blockbuster," as recent, sympathetic accounts of the novel characterize it, *Peyton Place* is an unlikely symbol of institutional continuity, and the story of its success, typically used to validate narratives of postwar cultural rupture and decline, argue in favor of casting those narratives aside.

Cultural Decline

How inescapable was the narrative of cultural decline in the 1950s? So much so that a version of it can be found in *Peyton Place* itself. Chapter 19 of Book Two of *Peyton Place* describes the town's annual carnival, "The Show of 1000 Laffs." The original owner of the carnival, Metalious tells us, was a "true 'carny'" named Jesse Witcher, and although Metalious never does explain what it is that makes a carny true, Witcher's authenticity seems to be tied to one of the few details that Metalious does tell us about him, the fact that he "liked his whiskey and woman . . . a helluva lot more than he enjoyed paying his bills" (257). As a carny, Witcher was an indifferent businessman, his authenticity signified at least in part by his inability or refusal to turn his carnival into a viable commodity. By the time the carnival is described in the novel, September 1939, the bank had foreclosed on it. Mill owner and bank chairman Leslie Harrington, Witcher's supremely inauthentic opposite, assumed ownership, eager to turn his employees into paying customers on their state-mandated day off.

When Harrington's friends question his decision to buy the carnival, he presents it as a kind of lark, the driven businessman's lone nonbusiness pleasure: " 'God damn it . . . I got a right to have something just for the hell of it, don't I? With some men it's electric trains or postage stamps. With me it's carnivals' " (257). Ownership of the carnival is just a hobby, the capitalist's form of leisure—in the same way that attending a carnival would be a form of leisure for working people—and it is for this reason, Harrington explains, that he chooses to stage the carnival in his hometown of Peyton Place on Labor Day, when he could easily make more money staging the carnival in a more populous location. Harrington's purchase and unstrategic use of the carnival might be seen as a humanizing moment for the novel's central villain, if not for the more sinister private motive: by staging the event in Peyton Place on a mandated day off for workers, Labor Day no less, Harrington makes back from his mill workers some of the money he pays out to them in salary. Harrington is willing to sacrifice the extra profits he would make by staging the carnival elsewhere to enjoy this irony, which is all the richer because traveling carnivals, even when not owned by big business leaders, as they typically were not during their pre–World War II heyday, were noted for their scams and frauds.[1] If anything, Harrington's purchase ups the ante on this trickery; his hobby, such as it is, is less the carnival than it is the exploitation of his employees. For those employees, the carnival itself becomes less an escape from work—on the one day off that is meant to honor them for their work—than an example of the insidious degree to which the work, and the employer, dominates their lives. Harrington is, in short, an untrue carny, and the results of this inauthenticity are both dire and aptly grotesque: Kathy Ellsworth, Allison MacKenzie's friend and the daughter of one of Harrington's mill workers, loses her arm in a fun-house accident that is the result of Harrington's negligence.

Compared to the novel's more salacious moments, the carnival episode is tame, but the story of Kathy's injury resonates in the context of old and new efforts to locate the novel's place in cultural history and in the history of the American book trade that have dominated the intermittent critical conversation about *Peyton Place* almost from the moment it was published. The brief description of the shift in the carnival's ownership captures in miniature something of an inevitable shift in the ownership of entertainment in the twentieth century, the movement of what might seem to be a genuine form of popular culture toward something like what Kammen calls "proto-mass culture," now owned not by the people but by larger businesses with commercial interests.[2] Kathy's injury can be seen as a sign of what is lost with this shift in ownership and, when she loses her lawsuit against Harrington despite his plain culpability, the sinister degree to which Peyton Place's nascent culture industry is in league with the larger power structure—the breadth, that is, of Harrington's power—is revealed. "It would have been impossible," Metalious explains, "to find twelve people in Peyton Place who neither worked at the mills nor owed money on mortgaged property at the Citizens' National Bank where Leslie Harrington was chairman of the board of trustees" (287).

Harrington is, to put him in terms appropriate to the 1950s, the most powerful of the town's power elite (he owns not just the carnival but also the field in Peyton Place on which the carnival is held, which might supply another ulterior motive for staging the carnival in town), and the novel's carnival episode functions as an unlikely allegory of the commodification—and thus the decline—of a form of "authentic" culture. The problem with commodified, mass culture, Macdonald explained in 1953, is that it is "imposed from above. It is fabricated by technicians hired by businessmen" ("Theory" 60). As Peyton Place's chief businessman, Leslie Harrington is ideally suited to the role of the owner who ruins what had been a cultural activity, fabricating, to use Macdonald's term, a carnival that was, when owned by Witcher, "true."

It is appropriate in several ways that Metalious's date for the carnival, where the negative consequences of the shift in ownership are made concrete in Kathy's injury, is 1939, not just the year that war breaks out in Europe (Labor Day in 1939 was September 4, three days after Germany invaded Poland, an event that the novel does not mention), but also the year, and the season, that *Partisan Review* published Greenberg's "Avant-Garde and Kitsch," perhaps the most influential of all the narratives of cultural decline written in the twentieth century. Greenberg's essay is famous for its attack on what he calls kitsch for its role in the prophesied destruction of high art: "The avant-garde itself, already sensing the danger, is becoming more and more timid every day that passes. Academicism and commercialism are appearing in the strangest places" (9). It might seem too great a leap to link the decline of Metalious's carnival to the decline of Greenberg's avant-garde art. But Greenberg's essay, to be mimicked by numerous similarly styled narratives of cultural decline in the 1950s, tells not one but two inseparable stories of cultural decline, not just the decline of high culture at the hands of kitsch but also, in a more direct way, the erasure of what Greenberg calls folk culture, which falls victim to the same phenomenon: "Kitsch . . . has flowed out to the countryside, wiping out folk culture" (12). The stories are inseparable because in Greenberg's account the participants in what had been a strictly regional folk culture are transformed by the creation and dissemination of kitsch into the passive, impersonal market for mass-produced culture, and it is the emergence of this market that threatens high art. In Greenberg's essay, as in the novel, once-prevalent cultural forms are declining if not disappearing, casualties of capitalism.[3]

In fact, Metalious's carnival episode combines elements of Greenberg's two stories. The carnival itself is akin to, though not the same as, what Greenberg considered folk culture, but what happens to it is similar to what culture critics of the 1950s said was happening to high culture: it was commodified, in this case by Harrington, and therefore ruined. In depicting this decline, Metalious drew on the real, typically unlamented decline of the traveling carnival over the course of the first half of the twentieth century. Carnivals came to American life in the 1890s on the back end of industrialization—along with circuses, dime museums, and amusement parks, "part of the burgeoning world of the 'popular amusement' industry" (Bogdan 69).[4] They were far from mass culture, of course, in that they were distinctly regional and played to small crowds whose participation was essential; at the same time, though, their flourishing was a product and byproduct of industrialization and advances in infrastructure: the emergence of train lines made the traveling carnival economically feasible, and the carnival rides themselves required technological advancement.

The birth of the traveling carnival is usually traced to the World's Columbian Exposition in Chicago in 1893, a monument to American progress at which visitors flocked to the famed Midway Plaisance, which was set up for amusements specifically so that the fair could turn a profit. It was there that the world saw, for the first time, the Ferris Wheel, an engineering marvel. The success of the entertainment exhibitions at the fair convinced entrepreneurs of the possibility of a successful traveling carnival.[5] The resulting growth of the carnival is easy to quantify: by 1902, there were 17 traveling carnivals in the United States; in 1905, there were 46; and, in 1937, there were close to 300 (Bogdan 59). A new form of culture, like television and every other such new form that was the result of a combination of technological and demographic change, had emerged. But as *Peyton Place* suggests, what began in 1893 was in decline by 1939, in large part because of the emergence of more mass-produced forms of culture of the kind that Greenberg describes. Carnivals are an intermediate step on the road to a culture that earns the label of "mass," not only because they helped to replace folk culture but also because they too were eventually replaced by more technologically advanced forms of culture that could more easily reach large numbers of people, with which regional, participatory carnivals could not compete. By the time they were fading away, replaced by something more technological and less participatory, a kind of nostalgia for carnivals was discernible; Metalious, who set the decline of the "Show of 1000 Laffs" at the historical moment when the American carnival industry was irreversibly losing ground, draws on this nostalgia in her description of the shift in the carnival's ownership, from authentic Witcher to villainous, fraudulent Harrington.

According to Greenberg and other contemporary theorists of cultural decline, a prime offender in the demise of both high and folk cultures was the combination of industrialization and mass literacy: "Kitsch is a product of the industrial revolution which . . . established what is called universal literacy" (9). In 1939, the year of the ruin of the Peyton Place carnival, Pocket Books was formed by Robert De Graff and Simon & Schuster, fulfilling the promise (or, for Greenberg and others, the cultural threat) of the mass availability of the book. As discussed earlier, Pocket Books was not the first effort to sell paperbacks, but the scale of its success in America dwarfed that of previous efforts, which suggests that the paperback had found its historical moment: technology (the ability to cheaply mass-produce and distribute books) and demographics (the emergence of a mass audience for those books) combined to spread books farther and wider than had ever happened before.[6] It is this combination of mass production and mass demand that the institutions that produced and promoted *Peyton Place* would exploit, with greater success than had ever been done before, in 1956. In scholarship on *Peyton Place* and in some of the early attacks on the book, the story of the novel's unprecedented success marks 1956 as a year like 1893 and 1939, a moment when culture shifts profoundly because of a critical mass of technological and demographic change.

From Novel to Sensation

One of the earliest assessments of *Peyton Place* as a marker of a profound cultural shift came in January 1957, a little more than three months after the book arrived in bookstores, when it was written that "the decline and fall of the American novel predicted by the pessimists had one corroboration in the sensation of the year, Grace Metalious's *Peyton Place*" (Butcher 35). Given the well-documented pervasiveness of narratives of cultural decline in the fifteen years after World War II, the sentiment is not surprising. Perhaps it is surprising, however, that the comment appeared not in *Partisan Review* or even in the *New Yorker* (which had little to say about *Peyton Place* for decades after it was published)—publications that were to varying extents in the business of culture, ensconced in what Bourdieu calls the "field of cultural production" within the larger field of economic production—but in *Publishers Weekly*, a trade magazine that at the time did not even regularly review novels and that was, as the very idea of a "trade magazine" suggests, in the business of business, entrenched in the larger economic world.[7] This is one reason that this assessment merits attention.

Another reason is the sly way in which this assessment implicates the novel in its own unlikely version of a narrative of cultural decline. Strictly speaking, *Publishers Weekly*'s assessment is not a book review; the badness of *Peyton Place* is only implicit (as though so obvious that it does not need to be elaborated) in the idea that it corroborates a far-reaching and unspecified decline of the novel. The idea that a single bad novel could be evidence of a decline in the quality of all novels is, of course, specious: novels deemed bad are written every year, and even assuming that an objective rating of novels were possible, the only evidence for such a decline would be the absence of good novels rather than the presence of bad ones, much less the existence of a single bad one. But it is notable that *Peyton Place* is, in fact, not specifically identified as a novel in *Publishers Weekly*'s assessment, a designation that would in itself signal an aesthetic achievement. Instead it is called a "sensation," a term that not only denies the novel its status as such but also insists on viewing it in the context of its popularity, as a kind of constructed media event, the product of a hype machine. The problem that *Peyton Place* represents is found, in other words, in the relationship between its apparently self-evident badness and its astounding popularity, the number of people willing to spend their time and money on something so bad. James Baldwin noted in the symposium eventually published as *Culture for the Millions*, another seminal document of the debate over mass culture, that he was "less appalled by the fact that *Gunsmoke* is produced than . . . by the fact that so many people want to see it" (121). Something similar is at play in *Publishers Weekly*'s designation of *Peyton Place* as a sensation rather than a novel, and although *Publishers Weekly* does distance itself from the narrative of the novel's decline that it alludes to by attributing it to unnamed "pessimists," the fact that it concurs with those pessimists regarding the quality of *Peyton Place* suggests some degree of assent with the narrative in which they situate it; it seems unlikely that Butcher intended to suggest that the novel corroborates a nonexistent decline.[8]

One might argue that it is a mistake to make so much of a cultural assessment that appears in a source so rarely given to evaluating or theorizing about culture, a source with little credibility or authority as a voice of criticism. But in an age in which narratives of culture's fall are inescapable, the magazine's absence of cultural authority is precisely what matters. *Publishers Weekly* was founded in 1872 by Henry Holt, Frederick Leypoldt (a cofounder of Henry Holt and Co.), and Rogers Bowker, as a periodical devoted specifically to the book as commodity, as a chronicle of the book *trade*—it's original name was *The Publishers' and Stationers'*

Weekly Trade Circular—and its existence and growth demands to be understood as at once a contribution to that trade and a sign of its development and modernization. Given *Publishers Weekly*'s clear interest in the financial well-being of the book trade and, given the fact that its audience comprised people—publishers, booksellers, literary agents—with a clear interest in that economic well-being, it seems plausible to expect that the mass success of *Peyton Place* or any novel would have been cause for *Publishers Weekly*'s celebration.

The fact that, at least in this case, it was not, and the fact that the narrative of cultural decline, here figured specifically as the decline of the novel, had filtered down from avowedly highbrow sources not just to mainstream middlebrow periodicals but also to a magazine explicitly devoted not to literary culture but to the commerce of book production, illustrates some of the paradoxes of the postwar culture wars; it might reveal as much about 1950s culture as does the success of *Peyton Place* itself. More than any high-culture or middlebrow attack on *Peyton Place*, *Publishers Weekly*'s condemnation of the novel-as-sensation suggests again the complicated, always overlapping relationship between a novel's status as work of art and its status as commodity, and it suggests, again, how mixed the artistic and commercial fields were at the moment when critics were trying their hardest to reinforce distinctions between them. The emergence of the art-house cinema and the surprising profitability of James Laughlin's New Directions publishing house show the salability of culture marketed as "art" after World War II. *Publishers Weekly*'s condemnation of *Peyton Place*, and the specific grounds of that condemnation, is the sort of complementary opposite of this phenomenon: not only were avant-garde publishers collaborating with show-business agencies, developing sophisticated advertisements, and turning profits, but trade magazines were assuming the roles of high-culture critics, complete with their own version of the cultural jeremiad.

One way to appreciate how completely and how swiftly the novel's popularity transformed perceptions of it is to consider how far removed the dismissal of the novel is from the fairly good reviews *Peyton Place* received when it was published just three months earlier. As Emily Toth, Metalious's biographer, has documented, although *Peyton Place* did not receive rave reviews, it was not unkindly reviewed in such mainstream publications as the *New York Times*, the *Chicago Tribune*, *Time* magazine, and the *San Francisco Chronicle*. "She has humor, heart, vigor, a feeling for irony," wrote Phyllis Hogan in the *San Francisco Chronicle* (qtd. in Toth 135). "When authoress Metalious is not flustered by sex, she captures a real sense of the temper, texture, and tensions in the social anatomy of a small town," according to *Time*, adding that "her ear for local speech is unflinching down to the last four-letter word" ("Outsiders" 100). "The pace is swift, for Mrs. Metalious has great narrative skill," said Edmund Fuller in the *Chicago Sunday Tribune*, in a review headlined "New Hampshire: Activities for Strong Stomachs" (B7).

Publishers Weekly's own original capsule description of the novel is notably different from what it would write just three months later: "Another very promising first novelist has written a rather grim but powerful study of a small town in New Hampshire in which there is considerable illicit sex, murder, and suicide. Before the final page, however, most of the characters are happy and properly married. Messner plans a $10,000 advertising campaign" (Edes 916). The description of Metalious as a "very promising first novelist" is particularly telling, all the more because it is an idea that was echoed even in critical moments of other reviews.[9] After hailing Metalious as literary kin to revolt-from-the-village luminaries like Sherwood Anderson and Sinclair Lewis, for example, Carlos Baker, a Princeton professor and later Ernest Hemingway's biographer, concluded in the *New York Times Book Review* in late September 1956 that "Metalious is a pretty fair writer for a first novelist . . . if Mrs. Metalious can turn her emancipated talents to less lurid purposes, her future as a novelist is a good bet" (4).[10] What is surprising about these passages, in retrospect, at least, if hardly so in context, is how Metalious's output is described in terms of possibility and potential; her career is considered a literary one and it is on those grounds that she succeeds or fails. As *Publishers Weekly*'s January 1957 dismissal indicates, however, within months and well before the novel gave way to a movie, a plainly inferior literary sequel and a television show, the subjects of Baker's review and Hogan's and Fuller's—*Peyton Place* as novel and Metalious as novelist—and, in a sense, Baker's review itself and the rest of the novel's immediate critical reception had already been erased from the cultural memory. As early as January 1957, *Peyton Place* already was what it has remained in most critical conversations to this day, not so much a novel, good or bad, that could be talked about in terms of literary success or failure, but instead something nebulous and indefinable called a "sensation," and as such a symbol in an often-told narrative of decline.

The reissue of the novel in 1999 by Northeastern University Press, after it had spent years out of print, was an attempt to remedy this, to restore attention to *Peyton Place* as a novel. In that sense, it constitutes a challenge to the sort of assessment the novel received (or the absence of an assessment) in *Publishers Weekly* in 1957; Cameron's introduction makes a persuasive case that the rejection of the novel by the male literary establishment is tied to its defiant representation of independent women and its focus on "female sexual agency, hypocrisy, social inequities, and class privilege" (Cameron x). In another important sense, however, *Publishers Weekly*'s reassessment of the novel in 1957—its dismissal of it as a novel—challenges an assertion made by Cameron about the novel's place in American cultural history. Cameron argues that the erasure of the novel in the historical memory is a consequence of the damage done to it by the movie versions, the literary sequel, and especially the television show, which, as Cameron asserts, "aggressively relocated [*Peyton Place*] within a narrative more in tune with the conservative politics of domesticity, social consensus, sexual conformity, and male privilege" (xvii). Cameron rightly notes that the television audience for the original *Peyton Place* television show far exceeded that of the novel and, although it is no doubt true that the spin-offs have altered our understanding and memory of the original and, more specifically, that the television show intentionally replaced the novel's overt sexuality and unsentimental exposé of hypocrisy with conformity and conventional morality, the *Publishers Weekly* dismissal suggests that the process of erasure began well before the movie—the first spin-off—arrived in theaters.

Blockbuster

The recent reevaluation of the novel is a welcome development. Both Toth and Cameron argue convincingly that *Peyton Place* is a novel of neglected literary merit and that that merit has been missed in part because of the entrenched sexism of the literary establishment and in part because of that establishment's knee-jerk disdain for the popular, the tendency toward what Cameron aptly calls "the conflation of well-liked with badly written, of pop with trash" (xvii). What has not been addressed is the way this reevaluation of the novel as literature necessarily alters our understanding of the novel's place in book history and indeed our understanding of the development of the book trade in the second half of the twentieth century. If *Peyton Place* is a novel of literary merit, then the narrative of decline in which it has previously figured needs either to find a new symbol or to be revised. If it is a novel of literary merit, its claim to an important place in the history of the book trade is suddenly ambiguous. (The fact that the best-selling novel of the 1950s has literary merit is grounds for rethinking the 1950s-centered narratives of decline that we keep telling.) As *Peyton Place* gains in literary status, its claim to an important place in the history of the book trade becomes tenuous, and the narrative we tell about the postwar book trade loses a central plot element.

Some of this difficulty is encapsulated in the designation Cameron uses to fix the novel's place in book history. Citing its massive sales, she calls it "the first 'blockbuster' " (viii). But "blockbuster" is undefined and its usefulness is an open question. The term *blockbuster* is itself an ambiguous product of the postwar emergence of mass culture. Its origins date back to World War II, to the emergence of megaton bombs that were said, literally, to destroy entire blocks. As early as the 1940s, apparently, the term was used in movie advertisements and the like to connote an enormous popular success (and some trace its origins to lines forming around the block for a popular movie or play).[11] But the term receives its widest usage to describe developments in American movies during the 1970s and 1980s, and the recent use of it to describe *Peyton Place* is in that sense anachronistic.[12] In any event, the term has a double-sided quality— used by advertisers to describe commercial success that was meant to engender still more commercial success, but soon to be used by critics to signify the problem of commercial success—that reflects the cultural field's unusual relationship with the larger economic field.

Given the scale of its success, to call *Peyton Place* a blockbuster is not controversial; the idea that it is the *first* blockbuster, however, is something different, because it suggests that the novel either occurs after or triggers (this appears to be Cameron's intention) a break in cultural history, after which things were not the same as they were before. Otherwise, why would Margaret Mitchell's *Gone with the Wind* (1936), the best-selling novel prior to *Peyton Place* and one that has also become something of a cottage industry, not be considered the first blockbuster? Why not Harriet Beecher Stowe's *Uncle Tom's Cabin* (1852), another astonishing commercial success, the cultural and political impact of which dwarfs that of *Peyton Place?* If not these earlier novels, why not Jacqueline Susann's *Valley of the Dolls* (1966), with which *Peyton Place* is often linked, or Mario Puzo's *The Godfather* (1969), which supplanted *Peyton Place* as the top-selling novel and which seems an even stronger example of lasting corporate synergy? Some, though not all, of these novels are famously lurid. Some are dismissed as trash while others are not. What distinguishes *Peyton Place?*

For that matter, what distinguishes *Peyton Place* from what is arguably its truer forebear, in terms of the kind of controversy it engendered, if not in terms of literary style, Kathleen Winsor's similarly scandalous *Forever Amber* (1944)? Winsor's novel sold more copies than any other American novel of the 1940s, and it provoked outrage comparable to that of *Peyton Place* for its overt sexuality (the Massachusetts attorney general banned it), and it has since prompted recollections of the experience of reading it that are themselves similar to the recollections of reading *Peyton Place* that Cameron records in her introduction. "In 1952, when I was 11," Elaine Showalter writes in an essay that celebrates Winsor's "special brand of feminine genius," "I discovered the graying and mildewed hardcover stashed away in the cupboard of our beach cottage. I knew immediately it was contraband and I should keep my find a secret." Her memory is hard to distinguish from the memories that Cameron records ("'It was the kind of book,'" one reader remembers, that "'mothers would hide under the bed during the day'" [vii]) and so raises the question, again, of what distinguishes Metalious's novel from earlier or later enormous successes.

Cameron implicitly addresses the question of *Peyton Place*'s specialness—the distinctiveness that makes it the first blockbuster—by asserting its importance in the history of the book trade. The novel, she writes, "remapped writing's publics" (viii) and "helped create . . . the modern reading public" (ix) and its success "transformed the publishing industry" (vi). And, while little is offered to flesh out these broad claims, in the context of them the designation "first blockbuster" suggests connections between Cameron's conception of cultural history and Thomas Whiteside's in his study *The Blockbuster Complex* (1981), which gives the term its fullest treatment. What Whiteside calls a blockbuster is the product of, among other things, the postwar expansion and consolidation of the book trade and its developing links to mass-culture institutions. He argues that "drastic changes" befell the book trade starting in the late-1950s (these changes and their implications are discussed in some detail in Chapter 5) and the moment he cites as the trigger of these changes is Random House's decision to sell 30 percent of its stock to the public in 1957 (the sale did not actually happen until 1959), followed quickly by Random House's purchase of Alfred A. Knopf and Pantheon Books, which was itself soon followed by RCA's takeover of Random House, the sequence of events figuring in Whiteside's narrative as one example of widespread concentration within the publishing industry that has had a deleterious effect on the quality of literature produced.[13]

"The upshot" of this consolidation, Whiteside writes, "is that the entire economy of trade-book publishing seems to have become focused on the pursuit of 'the big book'—the so-called blockbuster" (19). In this formulation, with its emphasis not just on success but on the pursuit of that success, blockbusters are not merely books that happen to prove enormously popular; rather, they are books designed to be popular, the product, that is, of the publishing industry's recognition of the possibility of a certain level of mass commercial success and of the possibility that that success can to some extent be engineered. The possibility of success, moreover, includes not just book sales but also movie and maybe even television-show tie-ins, the likelihood—if not, as was and is often the case, the certainty—of which are built into the decision to publish the book in the first place.[14] Whiteside warns that as a result, "The trade-book business seems on the way to becoming nothing more than the component of the conglomerate communications-entertainment complex which happens to deal primarily with books" (22). To call a novel a blockbuster in Whiteside's sense of the term is both to make a negative literary judgment—the badness of the work a fait accompli given the circumstances of its production—and to observe a new set of institutional relationships between publishers, Hollywood studios, and television networks; it is, moreover, to cite the latter as the cause of the former in what amounts to a familiar, if more concrete and dispassionate, narrative of cultural decline, not unlike the narrative of the decline of the Peyton Place carnival. When big business enters the picture, the culture suffers.[15]

Peyton Place and the Bible

Whether big business causes culture to suffer is perhaps an open question, but *Peyton Place* is not the right text with which to test this claim. To clarify *Peyton Place*'s place in the history of the book trade, the first point that needs to be made is that in crucial ways it does not fit Whiteside's definition of the blockbuster; old and new literary judgments aside, it fails the institutional test. Metalious's novel was not the product of anything approaching multimedia corporate calculation. As Cameron and Toth emphasize in their retellings of the story of the novel's publication, the scale of the novel's success was a surprise to most everyone associated with it, and its origins can be traced not to the high-powered marketing campaign of a mass-media corporation but rather to the efforts of a modest publishing house called Julian Messner, Inc. The novel's original advertising budget of $10,000 was not extravagant even by Messner's modest standards; that same year, Messner budgeted $25,000 for a new novel by Francis Parkinson Keyes, who had been to that point Messner's most commercially successful novelist.

One way to highlight the relative modesty of Messner's original, $10,000 campaign for *Peyton Place* is to contrast it with another such campaign that shows the kind of power the postwar book trade could have in collaboration with other extra-literary institutions. Four years prior to the publication of *Peyton Place*, Thomas Nelson and Sons had spent an unprecedented $500,000 (fifty times what was spent on *Peyton Place*) to market the Revised Standard Version of the Old Testament (RSV) ("Summary 1952" 271). The RSV, moreover, was always a commercial endeavor on a scale much grander than anything that Messner imagined for *Peyton Place*. Research on it began only after Thomas Nelson shrewdly agreed, in 1937, to provide $35,000 for translators' expenses in exchange for exclusive rights to publish. Metalious's publisher did not expect an "enormous profit" from *Peyton Place* (Toth 117); in contrast, the enormous success of the RSV—it sold 1.6 million copies in its first eight weeks, far more than *Peyton Place*, and was America's best-selling nonfiction book in 1952 and 1953—was anticipated fifteen years before it was published.

That success has been understood in the context of a rise in Cold War religiosity, arguably the flip side of *Peyton Place*'s revelatory luridness, and for good reason.[16] This was the era of Hollywood biblical epics and the addition of "under God" to the Pledge of Allegiance. The nonfiction book that the RSV replaced in the top spot on the bestseller list was Whittaker Chambers's seminal Cold War tract *Witness*, which memorably presented the Cold War as a struggle between religious America and the godless Soviet Union. "The crisis of the Western world," Chambers wrote, "exists to the degree in which it is indifferent to God" (17). But the RSV's success is also a consequence of a formidable promotional machine. The "Greatest Bible News in 341 Years," was the way an advertisement in *Life* magazine described it, and that ad was itself featured in a two-page advertisement placed by Thomas Nelson in the August 30, 1952, issue of *Publishers Weekly*, designed to showcase its impressive promotional campaign: "A full page in Life plus a full page in The American Weekly plus a full page in Parade plus SPREADS (yes, 2-page spreads!) IN SUNDAY BOOK-REVIEW SECTIONS . . . full pages in Household and independent Sunday supplements . . . and spreads and full pages in more than 30 leading religious publications PLUS RADIO and TV. All of this makes the advertising of the Revised Standard Version of the Bible unprecedented in publishing history."

If any text deserves the title of "first blockbuster" according to White-side's criteria, it is this one.

The promotion of the RSV, moreover, epitomizes the kind of postwar institutional collaboration that it was the aim of the American Book Publishers Council to foment: in this case, the book trade partnered with an organization called the National Council of the Churches of Christ (NCC), founded in 1950. The NCC represented the coming together of twenty-nine Protestant and Eastern Orthodox denominations, with a combined membership of 33 million. It was decidedly ecumenical, aiming to unite Protestant factions in pursuit of common interests, just as the ABPC aimed to do for institutions of the book trade, a consensus approach well suited to the 1950s and to the era of emergent mass culture, when, as the advertising of the RSV suggests, the opportunity to reach a mass audience was never greater. Like other postwar attempts to engender consensus and like other attempts to reach the widest possible audience, it produced both success and controversy. Drawing on its network of state and local councils, the NCC aimed to turn the publication of the RSV into an "epoch-making" event that resembles recent Hollywood studio efforts to ensure the commercial success of the opening weekend of a big-budget film (Thuesen 91); such an event here was needed to drive sales of the RSV's initial printing of 925,000 copies, which as Thomas Nelson's triumphant ad proclaimed in the October 4, 1952, issue of *Publishers Weekly*, was "the biggest first printing of any book in publishing history." To that end, the NCC arranged more than 3,000 religious services, attended by roughly 2 million people and officially called "Services of Dedication and Thanksgiving," held simultaneously across the nation to celebrate publication. As a final touch, the NCC arranged for Luther Weigle, chairperson of the RSV committee, to publicly give a copy of the RSV to President Harry S Truman (Thuesen 90).[17]

Thus the RSV, with its enormous advertising budget and its collaboration between the book trade and outside institutions, its success engineered from the outset, anticipates far better than *Peyton Place* the postconsolidation "blockbuster" that Whiteside describes, and it does so three years before Metalious's novel was published. The promotion of the RSV also sets into relief some of the cultural pitfalls of marketing a book so aggressively, of reaching for the widest possible audience, at this historical moment. In the middle of RSV mania, Frederic Melcher, always sensitive to the need of the book trade to maintain literary dignity and who had criticized the inaugural National Book Awards ceremony for being too glitzy, commented revealingly in *Publishers Weekly* on the developing, lucrative relationship between books, religion, and commerce: "True, it may seem almost embarrassing to consider Bible distribution in terms of production and sales when the importance of the Bible must ever rest upon its widened reading and appreciation, and not upon the speed of sale or the variety of editions. However, the extent of the sales is observed with pleasure by the churches...so that...the book trade— publishers and booksellers—can promote Bible sales in this busy year with unlimited enthusiasm" ("Melcher, Bibles Seeking" 698). Though the apparently felt need for this quasi-apology for the unabashed marketing of the Bible might suggest otherwise, Melcher asserts that because the Bible's transcendent value, its value beyond its status as a mere commodity, was self-evident and was in this case authorized by the churches, it could be marketed without shame, which is to say it could be treated unabashedly as a commodity without losing its stature as something that transcends commerce.[18]

And so it might have seemed, at least, at the time, but the RSV itself was soon enmeshed in its own set of controversies, one of which (the lesser of the two) was the cultural controversy prompted by the translation committee, Thomas Nelson, and the NCC's collective efforts to make the RSV pleasing to the widest possible contemporary audience.[19] In 1953, Macdonald attacked the RSV in the *New Yorker* for being essentially middlebrow, for having sacrificed the poetry of the King James Version for 1950s readability; citing the translators' aim to produce a Bible in "the life and language of our day," Macdonald writes that "the closer the Bible is brought to the . . . sort of . . . writing the American masses are now accustomed to, the farther it must depart from the language of Shakespeare and Milton" (*Against* 272). The King James Version, Macdonald adds, is high art; he specifically compares it to *Ulysses* and *The Waste Land* (283). The RSV was designed to be for the masses, and that design compromises it aesthetically; its prose is "flat, insipid, and mediocre" (273). Pound, he notes, might have done a better job of translation than the translation committee. It is, in fact, hard to imagine a better example of what Macdonald deemed "middlebrow" than this. For Macdonald, to the extent that the RSV aimed at mass success, to the extent that it aimed to please the largest number of readers, it was a cultural problem, "bland, flavorless mediocrity" (285).

What is of interest about this controversy is how different it is from the kind of controversies in which *Peyton Place* would become enmeshed a few years later. Although *Peyton Place* was attacked by many, by and large it was *not* attacked by self-styled protectors of highbrow culture like Macdonald; the aspects of it that made it a cultural scandal were distinctly different from those aspects that made the RSV a cultural scandal. In fact, *Peyton Place* scandalized social conservatives in much the same way that novels celebrated by the New York intellectuals—novels by Vladimir Nabokov or D. H. Lawrence—scandalized them, and one thing for which Macdonald attacked the RSV was for watering down the sexier language of the King James Version (282).[20] Toth notes that "small-town reviewers were more hostile" to the novel, whereas "big-city reviewers often saw some virtues in the book, or at least some promise" (135); as noted earlier, some of these reviewers praised it specifically for its connections to earlier, famous exposés of small-town life by writers like Sherwood Anderson. The novel was banned in Fort Wayne, Indiana, and in Rhode Island, and libraries in towns such as Beverly, Massachusetts, refused to carry it (Toth 131). Toth quotes a letter to the editor from a woman from Laconia, New Hampshire, one of the towns on which Peyton Place is said to be based: " 'Perhaps there is some virtue in living in a small town,' " which in Toth's paraphrase "teaches basic goodness . . . as opposed to what 'the cigarette butts of the gutter' teach in a place like New York.' " Though *Peyton Place* has come to be seen in some accounts as a casualty of the "great divide," separating high culture from mass culture, in the 1950s it was not attacked as bad literature by the guardians of high culture. Its attackers, rather, were guardians of morality.

Genealogy

If the story of the RSV helps to clarify that *Peyton Place* was not a blockbuster by Whiteside's definition, it leaves open the question of how to understand what it was and how to understand its place in postwar cultural history. The institutional origins of cultural products have been essential to prevailing narratives of cultural decline; thus the question of what Messner was, if not a multimedia conglomerate, if not a maker of blockbusters, is crucial to the effort to locate the novel in cultural history. As noted earlier, both Toth and Cameron emphasize the fact that at the time *Peyton Place* was published, Messner was run by Julian Messner's ex-wife, Kitty Messner, then one of only two women in America in charge of a publishing house.[21] The other, both note, was Helen Meyer at Dell, which published the paperback edition of *Peyton Place*, having purchased the rights to it for $11,000 before it had been published in hardcover form (Dahlin 54). This emphasis, however, is designed not to establish the novel's place in book history but to help reframe it as a feminist text, the value of which was seen by the independent women who ran these two houses but not by the otherwise male literary establishment. According to Cameron, *Peyton Place* and its readers rebel not just against a notion of "high culture" traditionally gendered as male but also against guardians of a relatively new form of middlebrow culture that, as Radway shows in *A Feeling for Books*, were repeatedly gendered as female by their critics.[22] To read *Peyton Place* in the repressed 1950s, Cameron argues, was to "traverse the borders of middlebrow culture and taste" (vii), and the novel's institutional origins with Messner and Dell are used to support a reading of it as "a powerful political commentary on gender relations and class privilege" (xiii), appreciated by women and rejected by the male literary establishment.

My aim is neither to deny the salience of the fact that Messner and Meyer, unlike their male counterparts in publishing, recognized *Peyton Place*'s merits nor to take issue with Cameron's altogether persuasive reading of the novel as a feminist text. However, Cameron's interpretation of the story of the novel's publication risks reinforcing the notion that the novel was produced in a sphere of culture separate and apart from the sphere that produced high culture (or middlebrow culture), on the other side, as it were, of a cultural divide. This perspective obscures Messner's and thus the novel's significant connections to American publishing's past, and it is these connections that illuminate the novel's otherwise murky place in cultural history and challenge the narrative of decline in which the novel has long been said to figure. To recover these links, we need to reconsider Messner from a genealogical perspective, from which *Peyton Place* is best seen not as the first blockbuster—not as something new, not as something that follows or causes an unseen break or rupture in cultural history—but rather as an end, a culmination of a distinctly commercial success story that dates back to the early twentieth century.

That story properly begins in New York City's Greenwich Village, and it might be said to start with the founding of the Washington Square Book Shop in 1911. The shop was founded by two brothers, Albert and Charles Boni, and it quickly became a meeting place for Greenwich Village artists and activists, including John Reed, Emma Goldman, Edna St. Vincent Millay, and Max Eastman. The Boni brothers, like Witcher, Metalious's "true carny" in *Peyton Place*, were true believers in art but poor businessmen. Their bookstore failed to turn a profit while they were running it—in part because they loaned rather than sold books to their friends and neighbors—and their stated reason for entering the publishing business was not to turn a profit but to overcome "the philistine attitude of the American public toward the arts" (Satterfield 17); they were, according to Harry Scherman, their friend and later the founder of the Book-of-the-Month Club, "bitten by the idea of being publishers of *avant garde* things" (qtd. in Satterfield, 17). Their first publishing venture was the Little Leather Library, which they cofounded with Scherman in 1915, low-cost reprints of short classics and abridgments of longer ones, including works by Shakespeare, English romantic poets, Shaw, Ibsen, and Tolstoy. The Little Leather Library proved to be a commercial success, but the Bonis never enjoyed it: financial problems at the bookstore forced them to sell their share of the Library before it hit its stride.

In 1915, after he had sold his share in the Washington Square Book Shop, Albert Boni met Horace Liveright and together they developed the idea of the Modern Library: inexpensive reprints of the best modern literature. Liveright had socialist sympathies and capital to invest; Boni was the artistic soul with a passion for avant-garde books. Early Modern Library authors included Strindberg and Ibsen, Nietzsche and Schopenhauer. As Satterfield describes it in his study of the Modern Library, Boni and Liveright initially aimed for "titles that exuded a scandalous air" that would appeal to an audience of bohemians (20). This is a recipe for commercial success that, in a way, would be repeated with the publication of *Peyton Place*, and the connections between the two are more than analogous.

The Modern Library's success having proven the existence of an audience for literature advertised as "modern" and "avant-garde," Boni and Liveright soon founded a publishing house, called Boni & Liveright, that would produce original books (Boni left the company less than a year later). This house, which published Eugene O'Neill, William Faulkner, e.e cummings, and Sherwood Anderson, among others, is forever associated with the Greenwich Village art scene of the 1920s, with modernism and a golden age of American literature; but notwithstanding its deservedly privileged place as a disseminator of American modernism, Boni & Liveright's legacy is as much commercial as it is literary. The company functioned as a training ground for some of the most successful American publishers of the twentieth century; one-time Boni & Liveright salesmen Richard Simon and Bennett Cerf went on to found Simon & Schuster and Random House, respectively. More important, as much recent scholarship has discussed, some of the most savvy and most sophisticated marketing efforts of the early twentieth century were for modernist novels.[23]

There is, moreover, a clear but as yet unnoted line connecting the marketing of those novels and the eventual marketing of the scandalous *Peyton Place*. When Cerf and Simon worked in Boni & Liveright's sales department, their manager was Julian Messner. Messner's role at Boni & Liveright was considerable. In addition to managing the sales department, Messner was, Tom Dardis notes in his biography of Liveright, the company's "general factotum" who Liveright intended would assume the role in the company held by the Boni brothers after they left in July 1918 (67). It is said that when Cerf bought the Modern Library from Liveright (who was, in his storied profligacy, also not unlike Witcher, the carny), Messner pleaded with Liveright to reconsider.[24] Messner remained loyal to Liveright after the sale, which, along with his drinking, triggered Liveright's demise, and Messner was at Liveright's bedside when he died in 1933. The company Messner formed that same year when he set out on his own was to remain considerably smaller than Random House and Simon & Schuster: in 1956, for example, Messner published 45 books to Random House's 146 and Simon & Schuster's 180. (The company was purchased by Simon & Schuster in 1966, part of the intense concentration of the publishing industry in the 1960s). Toth suggests that the company's 1950s-era modesty was intentional: Julian and Kitty Messner "wanted to publish books that most interested them, including juvenile books; their adult list would be small, so they could give each book individual attention. . . . For the first few years, Kitty and Julian did everything. He was president and in charge of sales; she was secretary, treasurer and all-around clerk . . . Both did editorial work, and except for the advertising—handled by Aaron Sussman from the start—Kitty could do any job in the publishing firm" (101).

Aaron Sussman, the advertiser, is rarely more than a footnote in accounts of *Peyton Place*, but he might be the unlikely key to its place in American book history. Among other things, Sussman is credited with rejecting Metalious's original title for her novel, *The Tree and the Blossom*, and suggesting *Peyton Place* as an alternative (Toth 96). But what Sussman did for the novel matters less than where he came from. Prior to working for Messner, Sussman had been in charge of advertising for Boni & Liveright; he later established his own agency, with Franklin Spier, that specialized in advertising for publishers (Turner 205), which continued to handle advertising for the Modern Library after Cerf took over—he was instrumental in the development of the Modern Library's low-key marketing strategy—and Random House from the start (Satterfield 47–48).[25] Among many other ads, Sussman wrote the famous "How to Enjoy

James Joyce's Great Novel *Ulysses*" ad for Random House in 1934, which originally appeared in the *Saturday Review*, hailed then and now as a landmark in the marketing of modernism to the general reading public (Turner 205–9).[26] Almost unknown to twentieth-century literary history, Sussman has the unique distinction of helping to sell both the most celebrated literary novel published in English in the twentieth century, the acknowledged high point of high modernism and high culture, and one of the most reviled, the purported symbol of that culture's decline.

The connections between *Peyton Place* and *Ulysses* go beyond the fact of Sussman's involvement. In the attempt to revive interest in *Peyton Place* as a novel of literary merit, it has been common to note thematic similarities between it and more celebrated literary novels.[27] However, as the story of Sussman's involvement suggests, another, perhaps more fruitful, set of connections can be found by comparing the marketing of *Peyton Place* to that of more celebrated literary novels. This requires rethinking *Ulysses* more than it does rethinking *Peyton Place*; we are not accustomed to thinking of James Joyce's novel as a great commercial success, but that is just what it was (and, needless to say, what it continues to be): in his memoir, Cerf, who knew better than anyone, notably and accurately described *Ulysses* as "a big commercial book" (94), "our first really important trade publication" that was not a reprint (94), "a great best seller" (95). The advertisement Sussman designed was no small part of that success: a coupon attached to it was redeemed for purchase of the novel 25,000 times (Turner 210). Like *Peyton Place*, moreover, and like early Modern Library texts, *Ulysses* sold in large part on the basis of scandal. Another advertisement for it, placed in the *Saturday Review of Literature* in 1934, called it "the novel America was forbidden to read!" (Turner 202). In this respect, again, *Peyton Place* has more in common with modernist scandal than with anything associated with safe, chaste "mass culture" as that term was understood in the 1950s.

In fact, two things link *Ulysses* to *Peyton Place*: the exploitation of a scandal that preceded publication, and Aaron Sussman. *Ulysses*' scandal was more or less genuine—the novel had famously been banned in America for obscenity. *Peyton Place*'s prepublication scandal, however, was a contrivance—marketers exploited a perhaps untrue story that Metalious's husband was fired from his job because of the novel about to be published.[28] But this suggests, more than anything, perhaps, that over the course of the century, lessons about the value of scandal had been learned from previous marketing triumphs. There are, in fact, reasons to think that those lessons were learned from *Ulysses* itself: as Turner argues in *Marketing Modernism*, well before Random House published *Ulysses* Sylvia Beach had made the scandal surrounding *Ulysses* the center of her marketing campaign for the limited-edition version of the book (180).[29] Scandal, and the potential of that scandal to lead to strong sales, was no doubt part of the reason Cerf wanted to publish *Ulysses* in the first place.[30] When he announced that Random House was going to publish it, an advertising agent wrote to him that the novel was "the most talked about book since the bible" (qtd. in Turner 175). Prior even to publication, in short, the novel was what *Peyton Place* would be twenty-three years later: a sensation. Cerf, moreover, was not under the illusion that *Ulysses* sold solely on the basis of literary merit: "Perhaps," he wrote, "many did read the last part to see the dirty words; in 1934 that sort of thing was shocking to the general public" (95). This speculation again bears comparison to the reactions of shocked readers to *Peyton Place* in 1956, which Cameron documents.[31]

The links between *Ulysses* and *Peyton Place* are institutional rather than literary, and they suggest that the commercial success of the one is not that different from the commercial success of the other, a truth obscured in the prevalent narratives of cultural decline of the 1950s that have dominated discussions of *Peyton Place*'s place in book history. Those narratives of decline notwithstanding, no great institutional divide and, just as important, no cultural-historical rupture separate *Ulysses* from *Peyton Place*; they are products of the same book trade. Both novels were commodities marketed to great success by some of the same people, using the same strategies. Though typically viewed as a lamentable sign of things to come, when viewed in its institutional context *Peyton Place* has more to tell us about the marketing of literary novels that preceded it— that they were marketed with great savvy, their dual status as both works of art and commodities—and about the impressive growth and modernization of America's publishing industry and the growth of the audience of educated consumers in the first half of the twentieth century than it does about postwar cultural decline, the consolidation of the book trade, and the literary value (or lack thereof) of the blockbusters that followed.

Greenwich Village and Peyton Place

Boni & Liveright's Greenwich Village makes an unlikely appearance in Metalious's novel, which is, among other things, a portrait of the artist— Allison MacKenzie—as a young woman. Until the moment Allison leaves Peyton Place for New York City, New York City functions for her in a way familiar to those versed in the story of Boni & Liveright and the Washington Square Book Shop. It is a kind of ideal escape from the combination of hypocrisy and conventional morality that characterizes Peyton Place, and it is a symbol of artistic and personal freedom, bound up in Allison's twin desires to become a writer and to avoid conventional married life. Midway through the novel, speaking to Kathy Ellsworth, who wanted to marry and have babies and was soon to be a victim of Harrington's carnival, Allison says, " 'I'm going to move away . . . as fast as ever I can after I finish high school . . . to New York City' " (222). Later, she notes: "New York . . . that's where all the writers go to get famous," and Kathy replies: "Maybe we could go together and be bachelor girls in an apartment in Greenwich Village, like those two girls in that book we read" (213). In Allison's imagination, which Metalious frequently reminds us is naïve, New York City is the anti–Peyton Place, a haven of authenticity and artistic freedom. Allison's decision to leave Peyton Place for New York is in part motivated by her unhappiness after Kathy's injury at the corrupt carnival.[32]

The events in New York City, told in a flashback after Allison returns home to Peyton Place for Selena's trial, like the carnival episode, are noteworthy in the context of attempts to locate the novel in both literary history and the history of the book trade. When Allison arrives in New York City in the early 1940s, she finds that the literary world is not what she thought it was. It is an unforgiving business in which concepts like literary merit are complicated by the presence of intermediaries and the need to sell books. This fallen, compromised world is embodied in the love triangle in which Allison becomes enmeshed. On one side of it is David Noyes, an ambitious writer of the sort, presumably, that would have been at home at the Bonis' bookstore: "David was twenty-five," Metalious writes, "and had been hailed as a brilliant new talent by the critics on the publication of his first novel. He wanted to reform the world" (356). On the other side is Allison's literary agent, Brad Holmes, a married man who seduces her and whom, Allison quickly learns, she needs in order to get published. Noyes is an artist, but Holmes, the unscrupulous businessman, is necessary for a career: "She never would have begun to be successful without Holmes" (353). This portrayal of the 1940s book trade aptly suggests that changes to that trade that have been attributed to the emergence of postwar mass culture and to the success of *Peyton Place* itself in fact predate that success; if literary culture was in decline in 1956, it was not because of *Peyton Place*.

Chapter 5
1959 and Beyond:
Mergers, Acquisitions, and Norman Mailer

Television is the greatest thing that's happened to kids since the discovery of mother's milk.

—*Bennett Cerf, co-founder of Random House,*
in 1960 (qtd. in Tolchin 13)

The way to save your work and reach more readers is to advertise yourself.
—*Norman Mailer, "First Advertisement for Myself"*
(1959) (Advertisements 21)

If the wild success of *Peyton Place* did not transform American culture, then what did? It is inarguable that, as Whiteside and others show in their histories of American publishing, the economics of book production, relations among publishers, and the relationships between publishing and other industries changed at the close of the 1950s as publishing companies merged with each other and then were merged into mass-media corporations.[1] Moreover, as the quotes from Cerf and Mailer, two literary figures from the preconsolidation age, might suggest, the zeitgeist itself seemed to shift at about this time; in cultural and historical accounts of the 1960s, the rigid distinctions that obtained in the 1950s and before, between art and commerce, between high and low culture, between fiction and nonfiction—distinctions that had been crucial to the institutional effort to carve a cultural and an economic space for the novel in the age of mass culture—were challenged and subverted.[2] Why then? What, in particular, caused the idea of a categorical distinction between high art and mass culture, between art and commerce, to lose at least some of its currency when it did?

These are difficult questions in the way that all questions about the passage from one seemingly synchronous historical moment to another are difficult. As Louis Menand writes of historical change in general, "The world just rolls over, without anyone noticing exactly when, and a new set of circumstances is put in place" (x). Still, it is not hard to list various, interrelated demographic and institutional causes for this particular rolling over, some of which have already been suggested in this study and some of which will be suggested in this chapter and the Epilogue. New relationships among publishing houses, Wall Street, and mass-media corporations that made it harder to support the claim that literature was not commerce; the end of truly *mass* culture and the incipient hierarchization of mass-produced media such as television, film, and popular music, along with the emergence of audiences that take those forms seriously; and the growth of the college-educated population: these developments together helped to shift the cultural and economic ground beneath the novel. This chapter describes the moment in which these changes first were felt, looks back on what caused them, and shines a light on one forward-looking effort to reconceive the novel in the light of them.

It was just as these neglected institutional changes began to take hold that Mailer's early, unorthodox career retrospective, *Advertisements for Myself,* was published in 1959, and it is in the context of them—as a response to and register of the modernization of the American book trade—that *Advertisements* demands to be read. It was likely inevitable that changes in the ways that publishers did business in the late 1950s and changes in the space publishers occupied in the cultural and economic fields would engender new strategies of authorial self-construction; much as novelists such as Bowles and Bradbury participated in the articulation of the earlier "great divide" discourse at the moment the threat of mass culture seemed greatest, later novelists—avatars of the postmodern such as Thomas Pynchon and John Barth, who emerged at about this time— would similarly collaborate in the articulation of its demise. My interest, however, is less in situating Mailer in relation to the theoretical project of postmodernism and the vexed question of its origins than it is in examining his work in the light of the concrete but not always well-understood institutional developments that coincided with the dawn of the postmodern age, as an early attempt to rearticulate the novelist's place in American culture for what was suddenly recognized as a new era.[3]

Advertisements collects previously published and unpublished essays, short stories, and excerpts from novels, and it includes along with them "advertisements" for those collected pieces, brief discussions of them and of the circumstances in which they were written. That it is an act of self-construction, of authorial reconstruction, is well known: "I was trying," Mailer said in 1985, "also to end a certain part of my literary life and begin anew" (qtd. in Dickstein, *Leopards* 152). Typically this reconstruction or rebirth is seen, aptly but narrowly, as a response to Mailer's private, often-told literary struggles, the critical and commercial failures of his second and third novels, but the form of Mailer's literary rebirth only makes sense in a larger context that has yet to be sketched: that of the swift and surprising transformation of the American book trade in the late 1950s, which culminated a decade of modernization, and which functions in *Advertisements* as both cause and symbol.[4] In responding to personal literary failure and to a series of shifts in American literary culture, *Advertisements* contributes to an emergent, little-noted extra-literary discourse about the book as a commodity and in relation to other commodities, a discourse that as discussed throughout this study had been notably absent earlier in the decade. *Advertisements* happens to have been published at the exact moment when American publishers began selling shares of their companies on the stock exchange, when publishers began to merge with each other and then were merged into larger multimedia corporations, when articles about the business of books appeared in *Variety* and *Fortune*; it was published at the moment when it became impossible to deny what the book trade had been denying for decades and most loudly throughout the 1950s: that books were a business, that publishing was a trade, that novels were commerce.

The first part of this chapter traces the emergence of this discourse about the book as commerce and describes *Advertisements*' relation to it: at the moment the book trade went public, as it were, *Advertisements* announced that a certain set of ideas about culture that were prevalent in the 1950s, a certain ideology of art and along with it a certain strategy for achieving literary distinction, were no longer tenable. These were the ideas implicit in the novels of Bowles and Bradbury and in the marketing strategies of New Directions and Ballantine among other publishing companies, and this was the ideology of art implicit in critiques of *The Man in the Gray Flannel Suit* and *Peyton Place*—in short, the very ideas and ideology that this book has described as a paradoxical consequence of the modernization of the book trade in the age of mass culture's emergence. *Advertisements* did not enact change any more than *Peyton Place* did, but because it shines a light on the trade's modernization, because it articulates the fact of modernization, it is a part of the constellation of late 1950s and early 1960s events that constitute the change, the rolling over from one cultural moment to another. For his own reasons, connected to his personal literary struggles but unthinkable apart from the larger context of the transformation of the literary field throughout the 1950s, Mailer, along with the Wall Streeters who bought and sold stock in publishing houses and the mass media and technology corporations that purchased the houses outright, participates in the project of naming, of reifying, of establishing the modernization of the book trade as an event.

1959 and Beyond

In the same month that *Advertisements* was published, October 1959, Random House sold 30 percent of its shares to the public, kicking off the wave of mergers and stock sales that would dominate the publishing world throughout the succeeding decade and beyond. This end-of-the-fifties moment—another part of the rolling over from one moment to the next—signifies what Tebbel describes as publishing's "traditional pattern toward more anonymous corporate organization" (4: 181), and of course it testifies both to the marketplace successes of American publishing houses throughout the 1950s and to the widespread belief that that success would continue. Months later, Random House used the money raised from the sale to buy Knopf, a smaller, even more venerable house. The following year, Random House purchased another smaller house, Pantheon Books; some people, Random House co-owner Bennett Cerf records in his memoir, thought Random House paid too much for the press, but almost on its own the sales of one Pantheon book, Boris Pasternak's *Dr. Zhivago*, strengthened by the release of the film version four years later, returned to Random House much of the money it had paid for the entire house (283).[5]

Mergers among publishers occurred for specific reasons tied to the relative strengths and shortcomings of the publishing business. The industry's low barriers to entry—which made it possible for small, underfunded companies to produce books and prevented publishing from becoming an oligopoly like television in the 1950s or Hollywood in the 1930s—also led to "numerous undercapitalized small firms," which would benefit from the pooling of resources (Powell, "Competition" 89). Larger corporations bought publishers to diversify, by investing in a separate business; to create synergistic relationships among publishers and movie and television producers; or to exploit education markets with new technologies. In 1966, for example, Random House was purchased by RCA, which was also the owner of NBC, for $38 million, the ultimate signal of the wedding of the book trade to mass culture. (Nine years earlier, CBS had negotiated to buy Random House for "a few million," the company's increase in value yet another sign of the recognition of the financial health of the book trade. Eventually CBS purchased Holt, Rinehart & Winston instead (seven years after Holt purchased Rinehart and Winston, another high-profile publishing merger, and not long after RCA took control of Random House [Tebbel 3: 187, 169].)[6]

It is advisable to be cautious in ascribing consequences to Random House's stock sale and to the mergers that followed. Although the consolidation of the publishing industry provoked understandable fears that the diversity of literary voices would be limited, sociological studies of concentration in media argue against these dire results—or at least they argue that it is difficult to draw firm conclusions about how consolidation affected the production of specifically literary texts.[7] As Powell explained in 1980, "The low capital entry costs and the availability of freelance services . . . have mitigated against trends toward oligopoly that are prevalent in most other communications industries" ("Competition" 89). Moreover, Powell notes, throughout the 1960s and 1970s, the rational response to the circumstances of the book trade—that combination of low barriers to entry and uncertain demand for specific titles—continued to be overproduction, producing more books than the market will bear either in the search for the elusive best seller or to reach various small groups of readers. As the industry consolidated in the 1960s, the number of titles published grew at a higher rate than they had in the 1950s or before; between 1958 and 1976, annual output increased by 210 percent (90). This is not to suggest that the consolidation of the publishing business had no effect. As Whiteside documents, it was a boon for star authors, and certainly individual houses changed as they were absorbed by larger corporations, as this chapter discusses a bit later. But there is little evidence beyond the anecdotal suggesting that the concentration of the publishing industry produced major effects on the production of literary novels or books generally. Nor can the heyday of consolidation and incorporation be said to mark the moment when novels became mere commodities. Publishing had always been a business, and novels, whether published by avant-garde New Directions or incorporated Simon & Schuster, always commodities.

What can be said about the Random House stock sale, however, is that it is one development among many in the late 1950s that rendered attempts to deny that publishing was a business, to disavow, ever less credible. Some of this shift is evident in Cerf's description of his reaction to the stock sale: "I nearly fainted when I saw the check that I got—over a million dollars. [Co-owner] Donald [Klopfer] and I had always said that by going into the publishing business we had deliberately passed up real wealth . . . and suddenly we were rich in spite of ourselves" (*At Random* 278). Wall Street's interest in Random House bears this out: shares sold for $11.25 on its first day, then rose to $14, and then, as Wall Street's interest in publishing generally grew, hit a high of $45. This was good news for investors and for the book business, but it was questionable news for anyone invested in the notion that literature transcended or was separate from commerce, for anyone invested in making the case for the novel's importance by presenting it as an alternative to what the "culture industry" produced. The grounds for producing belief in the novel's singular value would perhaps have to shift accordingly.

More evidence that publishing had been "outed," as it were, can be found in a lengthy *Fortune* feature about Henry Holt & Co. that appeared in December 1959, just two months after the publication of *Advertisements* and the Random House stock sale. Tebbel notes that the article "may have been the first full-length examination of a publishing house in a business magazine, reflecting Wall Street's new interest in the industry" (4: 170). The specific focus of the feature was Holt president Edgar T. Rigg and his move "from Wall Street to books"—he previously had been president of Standard & Poor's (Lubar 104). The broader subject is the modernization of American publishing, which had been "the industry capitalism forgot": "Before a Texas oil millionaire [Clint Murchison] got a Wall Street analyst to head Henry Holt, this old firm was run 'like a literary tea party' [Rigg's phrase]. Now it is being run like a business, and its financial reports make dandy reading" (104). Holt had indeed become a success over the course of the 1950s and, as the article notes, that success could be measured in various ways: "Holt's sales [in 1959] will amount to around $23 million, up $3,600,000 or 18.5 percent over 1958 and more than seven times what they were in 1950. . . . Even more gratifying, from Murchison's standpoint as an investor, has been the spectacular performance of Holt common, now selling at around 30 on the American Stock Exchange" (Lubar 105).

The *Fortune* article apparently went to press shortly before Henry Holt made its biggest business move yet, what Tebbel calls Riggs's "crowning achievement," the aforementioned purchase of Rinehart & Winston in December 1959, again only two months after Random House's stock sale and the publication of *Advertisements* (4: 167). (Rinehart, as I will discuss in some detail later in this chapter, had published Mailer's first two novels before refusing to publish his third, *The Deer Park*—all of this prior to its merger with Henry Holt.) By the time of the merger, in any event, ten years into Rigg's tenure at Henry Holt, Holt had already been transformed from a struggling house to a major success; the combination of Holt and Rinehart, which had been founded, like Simon & Schuster and Random House, in the 1920s, built on that success to make Holt the most complete educational publishing company in the country, well-positioned to exploit college education's golden age and, especially, the Sputnik-inspired federal investment in education.

The series of events in late 1959 and 1960—the Random House stock sale and acquisitions of Knopf (which was front-page news in the *New York Times*—the article was by Gay Talese) and Pantheon, the *Fortune* article, Holt's purchase of Rinehart and Winston—suggests that, as a business, American publishing was indeed changing, but in interpreting these changes it is important to remember that Rigg had been hired by Henry Holt in 1949. In 1959, publishing's status as a business went public; however, publishing had been in the process of becoming modern at least since the end of World War II and the founding of the ABPC in 1946. That process becomes visible in its early stages in the indirect, almost accidental collaboration among the William Morris Agency, Doubleday, and New Directions to produce *The Sheltering Sky*, in the continued rise of the paperback and the emergence of the trade paperback early in the 1950s, and in the sophisticated multimedia exploitations of novels written by Wilson and Metalious later in the decade. The events of 1959 mark a culmination, or an acceleration of a process long in place, but not a revolution.

The story of Random House amplifies this point. One reason its October 1959 stock sale fits particularly well into the narratives of corporatization and decline that the previous chapter explores—it is, as noted earlier, the starting point of Whiteside's account of the blockbuster—is that it has as its main character Bennett Cerf, the company's cofounder and an interesting counterpoint to both Edgar T. Rigg and Norman Mailer.[8] Cerf, who had started his career in publishing working for Boni & Liveright, was the publisher of *Ulysses* in America and thus a modernist hero; he was the owner of the Modern Library, which had demonstrated the market for specifically literary works; he was also, according to Tebbel, something of a throwback to publishing's more "gentlemanly" past, "the most personal of personal publishers . . . in the nineteenth century manner" (4: 181). But well before he sold Random House to the public or to RCA, Cerf embodied many of the paradoxes of the 1950s book trade. His gift for promotion belies any attempt to posit a strict opposition between literary and mass culture, and not only because he was an accomplished businessman; as a panelist on the television show *What's My Line?* from 1951 to 1968, Cerf was also a television celebrity, like Mailer a performer in the literary field, who claimed, at least, that he used his appearances to improve his company's name recognition. As he remarks in his memoir, "Though some around our office felt that playing a game on television wasn't exactly appropriate for a dignified publisher . . . I thought it was fun and a good way to make our firm known to a wide audience" (*At Random* 213). Ensconced in the literary field at the moment that institutions of that field set mass culture up as a cultural and political bogeyman, Cerf, the brave publisher of high modernist classics, nonetheless exploited the opportunities that mass culture presented to sell books. "Even the doubtful people at the office," he writes in his memoir, "had to admit that I made 'Random House' a household name" (214). This advertisement for the company brand, rather than for the individual products, may not have helped Random House sell books (it likely did help Cerf sell his own humor books, though many of them were published by Simon & Schuster), but it could not have hurt the company's successful stock offering.

Among literary figures and publishers with roots in the 1920s, moreover, Cerf is distinguished by his refusal to demonize mass culture and by his own ability to adapt to the corporatization of the book trade. Unlike Simon, his friend, fellow entrepreneur, and former colleague at Boni & Liveright, who grew unhappy about his own decision to sell his company to a corporation and has been figured in publishing histories as a casualty of the book trade's modernization, Cerf was outspoken about how and why big business would not result in the downfall of the book trade. As Tebbel describes him, "Cerf from the beginning welcomed the prospect of placing Random House among U.S. Steel and other giants on the 'Big Board'" (4: 187). In April 1960, years before the RCA takeover and only weeks after the Knopf merger, Cerf participated in a panel at Columbia University, where he argued that "television is the greatest thing that's happened to kids since the discovery of mother's milk" (qtd. in Tolchin 13). Cerf's thesis was not necessarily that television is edifying in and of itself; rather, it was that television promotes literacy: "the sale of good children's books has multiplied tenfold since the advent of television" because, he said, it whets viewers' appetites for information on subjects that they could read about in books. (It is noteworthy that Cerf's claim is not just that television promotes book-buying but that it promotes the buying of quality ["good"] books.) "Even television Westerns," Cerf continued, "gave children something of the background of American history, and a hankering for more" (qtd. in Tolchin 13). This specific claim is hard to support, and the article notes no evidence that Cerf offered for it, but the increased book sales he cites nonetheless refute the claim that mass culture was fatal to literacy or ultimately to literature and strengthen the argument for collaborations that connect literary culture to mass culture.

Two years later, still well before RCA bought Random House, Cerf wrote a revealing article in *Variety* (the distance between *Variety* and *Publishers Weekly* again suggests how the book trade had changed since the end of World War II) titled "Publishing Stocks Today." The subject is "Wall Street's sudden interest in publishing"; unlike Rigg, an outsider with no ties to the heyday of literary modernism, Cerf is again concerned that the incorporation of publishing houses will affect the quality of books produced.[9] But he argues from the outset, in terms that accord with later sociological studies of the publishing industry, that this will not happen: " 'Big Business' neither will diminish the number of genuinely good books being produced, nor will it dampen the ardor of any honest publisher to discover same. Furthermore, should the big companies ever become too 'commercial,' as some doubting Thomases have predicted, there will always be idealistic newcomers ready to snatch the good manuscripts they turn down" (18). Years later, at the time of the sale to RCA, Cerf said the takeover reflected his "conviction that publishing and electronics are natural partners for the incredible expansion immediately ahead for every phase of education in our country" (qtd. in Whiteside 8). Not only were literature and television not categorically distinct, they worked best in tandem.

Advertisements for Himself

About the same time, Mailer arrived at a similar conclusion, though his route to it is circuitous. Like Cerf and *Fortune* and Wall Street's buyers and sellers, Mailer in 1959 announced to the reading public that books, including literary novels, were a business like any other. And, as Cerf had been at least since the early 1950s, Mailer in 1959 became a performer who unabashedly marketed himself in order to sell his literary output. Given their respective positions in the literary field, however, to say nothing of their differing temperaments, it is not surprising that their attitudes toward the shifting circumstances of literary production differed. Cerf was at peace with modernity, and specifically with the modernization of the book trade, the process that culminated in these mergers and stock sales of 1959 and beyond. Mailer was not, and *Advertisements for Myself,* which was something of a stopgap release in advance of a much-delayed, never-completed major novel, and which anticipates and attacks developments like the Random House mergers in much the same way that novelists of the 1950s and literary institutions generally attacked mass culture, constitutes his protest. But at least as much as it is a protest, *Advertisements,* like the Random House mergers, is also, crucially, an adjustment to the modernized book trade. To the extent that it articulates outrage about or disdain for changes to literary culture, to the extent, that is, that its rhetoric positions Mailer against and outside the book trade in an explicit effort to revive his flagging literary career, it embodies an authorial strategy for working within that trade.

The paradoxes of this effort are embedded deep in the text. As its title indicates, *Advertisements* insists on foregrounding what was only buried subtext in the other novels discussed in this book, in the promotional materials produced by the ABPC, in the highbrow attacks on mass culture, and indeed in some of Mailer's own earlier work, particularly his 1955 novel *The Deer Park*: the idea that literature—all literature—is a commodity that needs to be and in fact is marketed; that writers compete with other writers for cultural and economic rewards, in the forms of prestige and money; that, in Bourdieu's terms, the cultural field is indeed a subset of the larger economic field, albeit one governed by its own peculiar set of rules.[10] If readers believed what *Advertisements* was telling them about novels in 1959, they could not believe much of the belief-producing ideology articulated by literary institutions throughout the decade. To the extent that the work as a whole thus discredited a cultural worldview, it is because *Advertisements,* once stripped of the metaphysical, existential, and sexual concerns that to date have dominated discussions of it, tells a story of the American book trade's commercial rise and thus explicitly, again, of cultural decline—of its coming of age, that is, into corrupt maturity.

The starting point is the work's curiously neglected but crucial foregrounding of the advertisement. One of the oddities of this choice—of the decision to use "advertisement" to describe what he is doing in his text—is that none of Mailer's advertisements are recognizable as such; if they were not so labeled, they would be seen as unusually confessional prologues (which leads some readers to point to Fitzgerald's "The Crack-Up" as an influence, which in turn suggests how little these prologues have in common with conventional advertisements). Of an early story, Mailer writes, "I'm embarrassed to read the story today" (*Advertisements* 70). Of the disastrously received *Barbary Shore*: "I was obviously trying for something which was at the very end of my reach, and then beyond it" (94). Of "The Homosexual Villain": "It is without a doubt the worst article I have ever written, conventional, empty, pious, the quintessence of the Square. Its intellectual level would place it properly in the pages of the *Reader's Digest*" (221). All of which suggests that the decision to name these introductions "advertisements" was motivated by something other than accuracy. To appreciate that something, it is necessary to look more closely at how and in what context Mailer discusses advertising throughout.

Literary studies of *Advertisements*, of which there are few, have not done this. They tend to focus on individual pieces of the work that are collected, most of which had been published previously, rather than the whole as a whole or on the text of the advertisements themselves. Readers who do focus on the entirety of the work rightly see it as the start of Mailer's project of creating "the persona of the perpetually embattled writer" (Poirier 4), the character, named Mailer, who would remain center stage in much of his later journalistic work.[11] Mailer theorizes his embattlement in his much-quoted contribution, included in *Advertisements*, to the *Partisan Review*'s "Our Country and Our Culture" symposium from 1952: "The writer does not need to be integrated into his society, and often works best in opposition to it" (*Advertisements* 188). He elaborates in his advertisement for his tenure as editor of *The Village Voice* in 1955: "I was at the time an actor looking for a rare role. . . . At heart, I wanted a war, and the Village was already glimpsed as the field for battle" (277). Not surprisingly, the *Voice*'s cofounders did not share his ambitions; as Mailer advertises, they "wanted it to be successful; I wanted it to be outrageous" (278), and so his tenure as editor was brief. Still, Mailer would become a columnist, and he would keep his military metaphors. His column represented to him "the declaration of . . . private war on American journalism, mass communications, and the totalitarianism of the totally pleasant personality" (278).

It is in the service of this effort to mythologize his embattlement that, in his first advertisement, Mailer asserts his need to advertise himself, asserts that his text is an advertisement, and asserts that all literary writers (all of whom are, by definition, also embattled) need to be advertised: "The way to save your work and reach more readers," he writes, "is to advertise yourself" (21). Advertising—however Mailer defines it—is a tactic required for literary survival and so a tactic required for literature's survival. And it is because he is already embattled that, he says, no one besides himself can advertise him: "Perhaps I should hire a public relations man to grease my career, but I do not know if I can afford him (with the size of the job he would have to do for me), and . . . I would be obliged sooner or later to spoil his work" (22). Mailer is advertising himself because no one else can or will, in part because he will purposely sabotage any such effort and in part because, outlaw that he is, he is so unsuited to being advertised or otherwise promoted by literary institutions or by what Mailer calls "the snobs, the arbiters, managers and conforming maniacs who manipulate most of the world of letters" (22), an early instance of the text's vitriol toward critics and publishers.

Mailer's embrace of advertising comes at a moment of explosive growth for the advertising industry. In 1946, the total advertising dollar volume in the United States was 1.6 percent of the gross national product; by 1956, it had risen to 2.4 percent (Bauer 13).[12] And it was not just the amount of money poured into advertising that was new; the emergence of market research after World War II professionalized advertising. Lizabeth Cohen describes the change this way: "Over the course of the 1950s and 1960s, sociological categories of analysis—'social class' and 'status hierarchies,' 'reference groups' and 'subcultures'— . . . entered the world of marketing" (299).[13] These advances, and the rise of advertising generally, generated a great deal of public anxiety on the part of American intellectuals, and it is characteristic of *Advertisements* that it participates in the expression of this anxiety about the political and cultural ills of advertising in extreme terms ("Talk of pornography," he writes about another of his frequent targets, "ought to begin at the modern root: *advertising*" [431]), even as it insists on the novelist's own need to "advertise" himself. It is further characteristic that it makes no effort to resolve this apparent contradiction: if advertising is such a bad thing, then why is he insisting on doing it?

Some of Mailer's attacks on advertising collected in *Advertisements* were published in the early 1950s and thus anticipate Vance Packard's enormous best seller *The Hidden Persuaders* (1957), which famously presented modern advertising as a sign of the coming totalitarianism, a "portent," Packard writes, "of what may be ahead on a more intensive and effective scale for us all" (3). That Mailer concurred is evident when, in a work originally published in 1952 and collected in *Advertisements*, he critiques Riesman's own critique of advertising for not going far enough: "Nowhere in this work does Riesman seem to have the faintest idea that there is an unconscious direction to society as well as to the individual, and that . . . a particular man or as easily all Americans can believe consciously they are superior to advertising while in fact they suffer an unconscious slavery which influences them considerably. One feels almost embarrassed to remind Riesman of something so basic as this" (197). Mailer might be referring here, as Packard later would in *The Hidden Persuaders*, to the emergence of "motivation research," a supposed innovation in advertising that, as historian Stephen Fox describes, "replaced the older statistical techniques of polling and counting with esoteric methods . . . especially depth psychology and psychoanalysis. Instead of treating consumers as rational beings who knew what they wanted and why . . . [motivation research] delved into the subconscious, nonrational levels of motivation" (183). In Fox's judgment, Packard was, ironically, himself the victim of advertisers' inflated claims about the possibilities of subliminal advertising.[14] But in another sense, Packard and Mailer both exploited fears of motivation research to carve their own niches in the culture and of course to sell books; Mailer could hardly be perpetually embattled without a great enemy to fight.

With respect to his critique of advertising, in any event, Mailer invites the appearance of contradiction when he does not need to; he does not need to call what he is doing "advertising" in the same work that he attacks advertising, but he insists on doing so. In a similar gesture toward purposeful and explicit contradiction, Mailer transgresses specifically literary ideology—the ideology of disavowal of the commercial, practiced in different ways by Bowles, Laughlin, and Bradbury, that was such an important part of postwar literary promotion—by imploring novelists to advertise while at the same time insisting that the novel remains utterly divorced from consumer culture. Why invite these contradictions? In part, of course, the aim is to tweak the literary establishment that Mailer felt had mistreated him. And in this light it is perhaps plausible to connect Mailer's embrace of advertising to the playful postmodern conflation of art and commerce that would become a staple of post-1950s literature and culture, of Warhol and postmodern architecture. But this should only be done with caution: although Mailer seems to enjoy the transgression of embracing the language of advertising, few novelists have ever been as candid about their old-school, antimodern ambitions, and about their concomitant belief in the cultural importance of the novel, as Mailer is in his introduction to *Advertisements*, where he famously proclaims his aim to make "a revolution in the consciousness of our time" (17), and announces himself as one who believes in a "Reality whose existence may depend on the honest life of [a writer's] work" (24).

That Mailer's embrace of marketing sits uneasily alongside his announced theme in *Advertisements*—"the shits are killing us, even as they kill themselves—each day a few more lies eat into the seed with which we are born, little institutional lies from the print of newspapers, the shock waves of television, and the sentimental cheats of the movie screen" (23)—is again an apparent contradiction his text makes no effort to resolve; resolving contradictions is in itself contrary to the antimodern, antiscience tenor of the work. Later, when reminiscing about the start of the Korean War, Mailer describes mass culture as follows: "Anybody who worked and wrote for newspapers, magazines, television, movies, and *advertising* was discovering . . . that the natural work of his pen was to hasten our return to chastity, regularity, pomposity and the worship of the lifeless, the senseless, and the safe" (105, emphasis added). Advertising is a piece of the larger problem that mass culture represents, in other words, and totalitarianism is coming: Mailer felt as strongly about this as any other writer of his time. What could save us from it? Mailer concludes, "It would have taken a good novel to overcome that bad time" (105). The paradoxes of the work are encapsulated here: the novel is presented as the heroic antithesis of the advertisement, which stands for the coming totalitarianism, and as the only thing that could possibly save American culture. But however bad it may be, the advertisement is nonetheless needed to save the novel. *Advertisements for Myself* is animated by the tension between its attacks on advertising, mass culture, and consumer culture generally—which are as fierce as anyone else's in this decade of attacks—and its assertion of the utter necessity of advertising, of the novelist's overt participation in the economic field. And the contradictory argument for advertising, the exhortation that novelists participate in the economic field, is motivated by the realization that the book trade has become precisely what Cerf and *Fortune* claimed it to be in 1959: a business like any other, partner of the mass-media machine.

Song of Experience

How Mailer arrived at this realization—at the same time as did *Fortune* and Wall Street—is the story told in the various advertisements throughout *Advertisements*. To tell this story, of course, is to puncture a myth about the book trade's separateness from ordinary business; that Mailer himself had once believed devoutly in that myth is what gives *Advertisements* whatever pathos to which it might lay claim. He writes in an early advertisement of his reaction after winning a short-story contest at the age of eighteen, in 1941: "The far-away, all-powerful and fabulous world of New York publishing—which, of course, I saw through Thomas Wolfe's eyes—had said 'yes' to me" (70). Mailer paints himself as a cliché of the wide-eyed young writer. His attitude matches that of Allison Mackenzie in *Peyton Place* when she first travels to New York to become a writer, like Mailer after winning a short-story contest as a teenager. Tom Makris, Allison's stepfather, comments: " 'Allison really believed that she had burst into the top literary circles when that story won the prize' " (272). Like Mailer, Allison would soon learn from her unfortunate relationship with her literary agent that the book trade was not what she had imagined it to be, that it was an unforgiving business that demanded compromise.

For Mailer, that realization begins after the disastrous reception of his second novel, *Barbary Shore*. He writes that he "thought dispiritedly of attempting to make some sort of interim career as a writer of short stories—a New York career, so to speak, I would get myself published in the *New Yorker*, in *Harper's Bazaar, Mademoiselle*" (107). Failure leads Mailer to scale down his ambitions by abandoning the novel, a literary form viewed, as already noted, with reverence. But, he notes, sheepishly it seems, in his "Advertisement for 'The Man Who Studied Yoga,' " that his short stories "didn't do too well" (153). After one called "The Paper House" (1951) is rejected by a "woman's fashion magazine," Mailer writes of his disappointment with himself for being so naïve about the literary world: "Any agent," he writes, invoking that persistent symbol of the modernization of the book trade at mid-century, "could have told" him that the magazine world would not embrace his brand of truth (153).[15] The rejection, he says, prompts him to renounce his efforts to collaborate with literary-commercial institutions, at least those involved with the making of short stories: "That evening was the end of many dead months for me. I was done with short stories and markets and editors and agents" (154), done, that is, with the commercial world that short-story writing represents. Mailer instead takes up a large-scale project, an eight-part novel inspired by a dream (the story of this inspiration is fictionalized in "The Man Who Studied Yoga," which is included in *Advertisements* and which was intended as a prologue for that novel). Mailer associates the short story with commerce and magazine editors and the novel, at least in this retrospective telling, still exists for him in that separate, noncommercial sphere. This too would change.

That this planned multipart novel never came to pass is well known. In

Mailer's version of the story, "The deeper I pushed into the first draft . . . the more I knew that this first of the eight novels was going to die . . . unless I gave way to the simpler novel which was coming forward from my characters" (155). That simpler novel is *The Deer Park* (1955), and Mailer's advertisement for it, "Fourth Advertisement for Myself: The Last Draft of *The Deer Park*," comes midway through *Advertisements* and functions as the dramatic climax of its portrait of the novelist at mid-century. Crucially, it was published on its own in the November 1959 issue of *Esquire*, simultaneous with the publication of *Advertisements*, under the title "The Mind of an Outlaw." This marked the beginning of a long relationship between Mailer and the magazine that marked the post-*Advertisements* phase of his career and helped to shape the rise of what would come to be called New Journalism, soon to emerge in the 1960s as competition with the novel for symbolic capital.[16] It is also yet another example, along with *Fortune*'s article on Rigg and news coverage of the Random House stock sale, of the dissemination of the new realities of the modernized book trade late in 1959, because it is in the fourth advertisement that Mailer makes his most explicit attack on the modernized book trade and makes most clear how, in his eyes, the book trade has degenerated.

Much of the advertisement retells the story of Mailer's struggle to get *The Deer Park* published. In the wake of the critical and commercial failures of *Barbary Shore*, he found publishers, in a censorious cultural moment, unwilling to take a chance on a difficult, sexually candid novel that few saw as a masterpiece anyway (the novel's description of oral sex had prompted Mailer's original publisher, Rinehart, to stop publication shortly before it was to arrive in bookstores). Random House was the first company after Rinehart to reject Mailer's manuscript, and it is here the postwar stories of Mailer and Cerf converge. But the details of the convergence are elusive because there exist two conflicting accounts of Random House's rejection. According to *Advertisements*, Random House editor Hiram Haydn recommended against publishing the novel, simply on the grounds that he did not think it was a strong novel and not because of its explicitness (230). Mailer's source for this account, he says, is Haydn himself. In Haydn's memoir, *Words and Faces*, he tells more or less the same story, that it was his decision to reject the novel and that he told Mailer that it was his decision shortly after (263). While Haydn asserts that the decision was his, he notes that Mailer wrongly blamed Cerf for it. *Advertisements* quotes Cerf as saying that *The Deer Park* would "set publishing back twenty years," though it does not indicate when Cerf might have said this (229).[17]

However, according to Hilary Mills, Mailer's biographer, the decision to reject was indeed Cerf's, not Haydn's, and the fact that Mailer continued to blame Cerf suggests that this is the case. Cerf's involvement in the manuscript's travails, moreover, did not end with Random House's decision not to publish. Knopf was another of the companies to whom Mailer had submitted the novel (this was several years before Random House purchased Knopf) and, according to Mills, Blanche Knopf and the company's senior editors wanted to publish the novel. An agreement was almost reached when Cerf intervened, calling Alfred Knopf, who was unaware of the negotiations with Mailer, and warning him against publishing *The Deer Park*. Alfred Knopf took his friend's advice, and his company passed. (In *Advertisements*, Mailer quotes an alleged comment from Knopf to one of his company's editors: "Is this your idea of the kind of book which should bear a Borzoi imprint?" [229].)

It is not clear why Cerf went so far out of his way to stop publication of Mailer's novel, but fears of government censorship, of the impact of that censorship on the publishing industry as a whole, appear to have been a driving concern. Even after G. P. Putnam's Sons agreed to publish the novel, Cerf called Walter Minton, the son of the company's president and the driving force behind the decision to publish *The Deer Park*, to warn him against it. "Cerf said that once again we would draw down the shade of censorship upon the book industry," Minton said. Referring to Cerf's daring decision to publish *Ulysses* in the face of government censorship two decades earlier, Minton continues, "'I asked him if he had heard from Mr. Joyce's shade recently'" (qtd. in Mills 154). Cerf's attempts to stop publication of *The Deer Park* suggest that something about American publishing had indeed changed for Cerf over the course of two decades, though the reasons for that change—a different political or historical context, changes in Cerf's own view of the book trade, the growth and modernization of it—are again elusive. However, the fact that Minton, the son of one of Cerf's contemporaries who had only recently assumed a management position at Putnam, had emerged to publish *The Deer Park* among other controversial works (most famously, Nabokov's *Lolita*), suggests that whatever the cause of his apparent work to stop publication of *The Deer Park*, Cerf was right when he wrote in *Variety* that new publishers would emerge to publish challenging books that more conservative publishers, newly aligned with big business, might deem unsafe.[18] In assessing changes to publishing in the 1950s and beyond, the existence of companies like Putnam with Minton at the helm needs to be factored in alongside whatever decline in daring is shown by newly incorporated houses like Random House. Indeed, the existence of a house like Putnam is one factor that Mailer seems to bracket out of his harsh assessment of American publishing.

Mailer would go on to publish four more books with Putnam, and it was a fruitful if unlikely collaboration. Minton's father, who was ailing at the time Minton requested the manuscript, was Putnam's president and had been the first president of the ABPC, and the younger Minton was the company's advertising manager at the time he heard about Mailer's novel. As such, Walter Minton recognized the commercial value of literary scandal and he looked for opportunities to exploit it. Before agreeing to publish *The Deer Park*, Minton had embraced the controversy surrounding a British novel, *The Image and the Search*, by Walter Baxter. The novel had been withdrawn from bookstores by its English publisher, Heinemann, after the *Sunday Express* attacked its overt sexuality (Tebbel 4: 216). Thus Minton's motivations were not entirely literary; as Mailer recounts, Minton told him that he "'was ready to take *The Deer Park* without even reading it'" because he believed that Mailer's name would justify the investment and generate sales, and he believed, wrongly, it turns out, that at some point in the future Mailer would "write another book like *The Naked and the Dead*" (231), a novel Minton loved. It seems just as likely, though, that it was the controversy itself surrounding *The Deer Park*, and the potential for more, that motivated Minton not just to agree to publish the novel but to offer Putnam's largest ever advance to Mailer for it.

That Mailer found a willing collaborator among mainstream American publishers suggests some of the ways in which American publishing had not changed between the 1920s and the 1950s, but Mailer did not allow that fact to alter the larger view he takes of American publishing in the fourth advertisement. Mailer praises Minton as "the only publisher I ever met who would make a good general" (231), a military metaphor that recalls Sloan Wilson's lavish praise of Richard Simon in the preface to *The Man in the Gray Flannel Suit*. But unlike Wilson, Mailer did not allow his praise for his publisher to cause him to relinquish Bourdieu's notion of the publisher-in-general as adversary of the literary writer. Above all, this decision reflects Mailer's keen sense of the literary field, in a work that was explicitly devoted, after all, to positioning himself as the ultimate, embattled outsider.

In the fourth advertisement, Mailer accomplishes this task specifically by distancing himself from the business of books. "People in publishing," Mailer writes of the lessons learned from his experience with *The*

Deer Park, "were not as good as they used to be, and . . . the day of Maxwell Perkins was a day which was gone, really gone, gone as Greta Garbo and Scott Fitzgerald . . . now were left only the cliques, fashions, vogues, snobs, snots, and fools" (233). The nostalgia is for the same bygone era of publishing that Paul Bowles and New Directions evoked in marketing *The Sheltering Sky*, that Wilson and Simon briefly recreated in making *The Man in the Gray Flannel Suit*, that Epstein and Tebbel both retrospectively celebrate. And again, the irony is rich, for it was the *older* guard of American publishing, the generation that came of age in the early decades of the twentieth century, that rejected *The Deer Park*—led by Cerf and Knopf—and it was a representative of the newer generation of businesspeople, embodied by Walter Minton, that embraced the opportunity to publish it and other controversial novels.[19] But Mailer is understandably less interested in making this point than he is in presenting himself and the literary novelist as endangered. Largely because of the decline in American publishing, Mailer laments, there was no longer any room "for the old literary idea of oneself as a major writer, a figure in the landscape" (233). This is, again, standard-issue nostalgia for a culture that respects literature and the novelist more, except, in this case, unlike earlier in the decade, the enemy is not mass culture but the institutions of book culture, the fallen literary world. Mailer no longer claims that the novelist provides the solution to a massive cultural problem; rather, he says that the modernized book trade is now complicit in the cultural problem and has erased the space in the culture that the novelist could once occupy.

This shift constitutes Mailer's coming of age. At the start, he is as naïve as he was when he won his first short-story contest. "I was amateur agent," he writes of his efforts to get *The Deer Park* published, drawing again on the agent as symbol of the professionalization of the book trade, "Fool of the five o'clock drinks, I was learning the publishing business in a hurry, and I made a hundred mistakes and paid for each one" (232). The harsh initiation prompts a seemingly harsh self-assessment: "I realized in some bottom of myself that for years I had been the sort of comic figure I would have cooked to a burn in one of my books, a radical who had the nineteenth-century naïveté to believe that the people with whom he did business were . . . gentlemen" (232–33). But Mailer's target is not himself. He realizes on finding out the book trade is a business like other businesses that "my fine America which I had been at pains to criticize for so many years was in fact a real country which did real things and ugly things to the characters of more people than just the characters of my books" (233). Even as Mailer confesses his naïveté, his negative experience with the book trade confirms the stories told in his novels and thus in a sense validates them (it is, after all, an advertisement). Not only does the book trade not stand apart from the rest of America, Mailer suggests, the book trade now *is* America and vice-versa. This was, as noted, good news for *Fortune* and Wall Street, and now that the word had gotten out, it was bad news for partisans of the great divide.

Based on this perhaps dubious reading of the commercialization of the book trade (as much a narrative of cultural decline as any other), Mailer's project becomes the search for a new way to produce belief in the novel—a new way to understand the novelist as outsider—after, in effect, declaring the old strategy obsolete. Shortly after making the deflating proclamation that there is no longer room for the writer as "figure in the landscape," Mailer asserts that the realization of the book trade's dark side makes him the very figure in the landscape he has just deemed impossible, even more of an outsider and lone wolf than he was before the fall. In much the same, paradoxical way as Paul Bowles does in his description of Port's refusal to write in *The Sheltering Sky*, Mailer uses the proclamation that literary writing is now impossible to enhance his own credentials as a literary writer. Realizing that "the publishing habits of the past were going to be of no help for my *Deer Park* . . . all I felt then was that I was an outlaw, a psychic outlaw, and I liked it" (234). In 1959, Mailer declares dead an old idea of the novel only in order to reinvent or reimagine it and, in so doing, he lays out the terms of his own literary rebirth. It is no longer sufficient to separate oneself from mass culture; one must also announce one's separation from the book trade.

But this is only the start of Mailer's advertisement, for it is after this realization, and in fact because of this realization, that Mailer decides, to Minton's consternation, to rewrite the draft of *The Deer Park* that Rinehart and many others had rejected and that Putnam has already agreed to publish; this is the "Last Draft" to which the title refers. (Minton opposed revision not because of belief in the novel's value but because "some interest in the book would be lost if the text were not identical to Rinehart's page proofs" [235]—more evidence of his interest in exploiting a literary controversy.) Mailer ties his desire to revise to his experience with the book trade and his original struggle to get *The Deer Park* published: "I wanted to take a look. After all," he writes, "I had been learning new lessons." Indeed, Mailer suggests, the experience had been transformative: "The book read as if it had been written by someone else. I was changed from the writer who had labored on that novel, enough to be able to see it without anger or vanity or the itch to justify myself" (235).

Song of Innocence

Those lessons, however, are not evident in *The Deer Park*, which perhaps surprisingly contains none of Mailer's newfound skepticism about the institutions that produce novels. On the contrary, the fact that Mailer's attack on the fallen book trade is meant to function as an advertisement for *The Deer Park* is wholly ironic because *The Deer Park*, for all of Mailer's attempts to shock, is itself an almost naïve advertisement for the cultural importance of the novel, an unlikely complement to *Fahrenheit 451*, a novel that echoes the promotional campaigns of contemporary literary institutions like the ABPC and adds to them a sizable dose of Mailer's cosmology. If the fourth advertisement is a song of experience, *The Deer Park*, despite Mailer's claim that he revised it in the light of his disillusion with the publishing industry, is a song of Mailer's peculiar brand of innocence, one that takes place in an odd prelapsarian age in which a rigid distinction between book culture and mass culture obtains, in which literature, specifically the novel, remains pure precisely because of its distance from commerce and its oppositional stance to the rest of American culture.

As *The Sheltering Sky* makes its case against mass culture by depicting the uncompromising flight from it, *The Deer Park*, narrated by Sergius O'Shaughnessy, an aspiring novelist amid Hollywood decadence, makes its case by depicting one writer's immersion in it. It begins as a conventional Hollywood novel, the story of Charles Eitel, a fallen director befriended by Sergius. Eitel is a hero to Sergius for his refusal to cooperate with the "Subversive Committee," a career-ruining choice: "He walked off a set one day in the middle of shooting a picture, and two days later he was called a hostile witness by an investigating committee of Congress" (18); little wonder that on meeting Eitel, Sergius says, "Seldom had I liked anybody so much" (29). Eitel's rebellion against the Subversive Committee, which happens before the action of the novel begins, has nothing to do with sympathy with the Communist cause; it is all about repositioning himself, the artist, as an outlaw, as Mailer himself aimed to do in *Advertisements*. In fact, the novel draws little distinction between the Communists, the Subversive Committee, and the Hollywood studios: all represent versions of totalitarianism. Becoming an outlaw will only pay off for Eitel if he can direct his next movie, his supposed masterpiece if he and the studio will stay true to his idea, which, he hopes, "'will justify so much bad work'" (44).

That the movie idea with which Eitel aims to redeem himself and his artistic career is the story of a television personality is telling; much like the Hollywood novel in which he is a character, Eitel's proposed movie aims to accrue artistic prestige to its creator by denouncing a medium with greater mass appeal. In it, a television star remarkably like today's talk-show hosts gives inauthentic, sentimental advice to real people, "converting their suffering to theatrical material" (126). The plot turns when the star's conscience compels him to start giving genuine advice to his guests, which "destroys the interest of his program" (126). The hero sinks "to the bottom of the world," aiming to help the downtrodden through honesty, but of course the people do not want honesty and so they turn on him. Eventually "he destroys himself with some pathetic violence" (127). This story-within-a-story is yet another version of *The Sheltering Sky* and *Fahrenheit 451*—and, for that matter, *The Deer Park* and *Advertisements for Myself*—a celebration and romanticization of the artistic hero as outlaw, the rebel against institutional constraints, the Mailer-esque novelist. Lest this last point not be obvious enough, Mailer suggests indirectly that Eitel's model for his movie's hero is Sergius himself: "'Elena thinks I have you in mind as the model for this improbable hero of mine,'" Eitel tells Sergius (127).

In *The Deer Park*, everyone is either an artist or a prostitute. The novel is built on a series of parallels and juxtapositions that suit both its author's typically Manichean worldview and the discourse of categorical distinctions between art and commerce, associating Hollywood and television with evil (and prostitution) and literary art with courageous, heroic, godly good.[20] Ultimately an artistic and a political sellout, who in the end partners with the Hollywood studio, turns his movie idea into sentimental pap, and cooperates with the Subversive Committee he had previously publicly snubbed, Eitel is paralleled with his girlfriend Elena, a prostitute. Eitel's ex-girlfriend, Lulu, is an actress who is also, in her way, a prostitute; she is put to work by the Hollywood studio that employs her to convince Sergius to sell his incredible life story to Hollywood and to convince Eitel to cooperate with congressional Communist-hunters. Before walking out on Eitel, Elena says, "'You always thought of me as a prostitute . . . but you don't know what I think of you'" (302). Moments later, Eitel confesses to Sergius about agreeing to testify before the committee as part of a deal struck with the studio to save his career: "'For the first time in my life I had the sensation of being a complete and total whore in the world'" (306).

The corruption of the Hollywood studios parallels that of the House Un-American Activities Committee, both led by opportunists—but more than that, the two nefarious institutions work together to revive Eitel's career as a hack director: " 'When I began to understand what sort of arrangement existed between the Committee and the studios we began to make progress' " (304). Earlier, in explaining his disdain for Communism, Eitel likens it to the Hollywood studios: "a political system which reminded him of nothing so much as the studio for which he worked" (36–37). Sergius reports that in the months leading to his deal with the Subversive Committee, Eitel, "if he had learned nothing else . . . had learned that he was not an artist, and what was a commercial man without his trade?" (298). After agreeing to cooperate with the committee to save his career, he takes out a paid advertisement in the newspaper, celebrating his choice. On reading it, Sergius comments, " 'It goes about par for the course' " (305). The moment provides a fitting measure of the distance Mailer traveled between 1955 and 1959: in *The Deer Park*, when the artist advertises himself, it symbolizes his ultimate debasement.

The novel begins with Eitel but gradually shifts focus to Sergius and his ambition to be a novelist. In fact, Sergius and Eitel face the same dramatic choice: whether to do business with corrupt Hollywood. Sergius's shining moment is his refusal, despite his own financial troubles, to sell his fascinating life story—an orphan, a war hero—to the studio. His choice here is oddly akin to that of Tom Rath in *The Man in the Gray Flannel Suit*, who was also asked to tell his life story—also as a war hero who has seen brutality—in exchange for a debased career and financial gain. Why Sergius, like Rath, refuses to do this has much to do with the attitude toward novels and commerce that *Advertisements* upends. (Both novels, in this sense, can be classified as stories of the veteran's struggle to adjust to the postwar world.) "The Last Draft" exposes the book trade; *The Deer Park*, however, contains its share of conventional, ABPC-styled encomiums to the novel and to the writer. The work of writing, Sergius reports, he "looked on with religious awe" (289). "I had the ambition," he explains at the start, echoing what Mailer would say many times in *Advertisements*, "that one day I would be a brave writer" (23).

But in what sense brave, and why is this kind of bravery admirable? The novel's inability or refusal to answer this question reflects the paradoxes of defining the novel in opposition to commercial culture. What is clear is that in the world of the novel, Sergius needs to turn down a Hollywood fortune, even if not especially when he's penniless, in order to maintain his integrity as a novelist. In explaining this decision, Sergius vacillates between concerns about his reputation and fears that Hollywood would rob him of his ability or power to express himself artistically. "'I don't want a slob movie made out of my name,'" he explains to his starlet girlfriend, Lulu (218), who dumps him soon after. Reputation is at stake, marking *The Deer Park* as a pre-*Advertisements* acknowledgment that notwithstanding his disdain for Eitel's paid advertisement, novelists, like Hollywood players, require good public relations. He elaborates a bit to Eitel, "'I can't help it. I guess I want to be a writer. I don't want somebody else to tell me how to express myself'" (228). But then: "I knew my decision didn't mean very much; if my movie was not made then others would be made, but at least my name would not be used" (228). Sergius then muses in a new vein, "I suppose what I really was thinking is that I would always be a gambler, and if I passed this chance by, it was because I had the deeper idea that I was meant to gamble on better things than money or a quick career" (228). The shift in rationales is followed by a studied uncertainty. Rather than report his feelings, Sergius qualifies ("I *suppose* what I was *really* thinking") and offers conditionals that suggest not artistic conviction but general confusion.

The novel suggests several explanations for Sergius's absence of clarity. One such explanation is that Sergius's artistry is instinctive or primitive, not something that he can intellectualize. Moments earlier, he has shown Eitel his poem, called "The Drunk's Bebop and Chowder," replete with Joycean language games. When Eitel comments on Joyce's influence, Sergius's response is "'Who's Joyce?.... I think I heard the name" (227). Perhaps the refusal is also instinctive, an indication of some deeply felt but inexpressible calling to be an artist. Another possible explanation, though, is that Mailer or Sergius or both struggle to articulate a sensible rationale for Sergius's decision because his decision is not sensible. Though it is clear that the decision is based on a principle, that principle is itself hard to discern. Allowing one's life story to be made into a movie, after all, is not comparable to testifying before the House Un-American Activities Committee. Nor does it preclude writing a novel. But *The Deer Park* seems to want us to think that it does; never is the possibility entertained that a person can write a novel while having attachments to commercial institutions.[21] The novelist in *The Deer Park* is a lone wolf, precisely what Mailer longs for him or her (though, in Mailer's case, usually "him") to be in his advertisement for it.

This is only possible because *The Deer Park* does not include the very people—publishers, agents, the entire machinery of literary production in the postwar era—who are featured in Mailer's advertisement for it; the novel does not even entertain the existence of this machinery, despite the fact that the novel was rewritten *after* Mailer's struggles with Rinehart and the rejections by Random House, Knopf, and six other publishers. In the novel, the choice is between novelist alone and Hollywood sell-out, between artist and prostitute. In the advertisement, however, that machinery of literary production assumes the starring role played in the novel by corrupt Hollywood executives. In this sense, Mailer's advertisement undermines a central idea of the novel it is designed to sell: in telling the story of its struggle to get published, of his dealings with publishers who are, in his view, philistines or cowards, Mailer debunks *The Deer Park*'s very claims for the novel's (*any* novel's) cultural importance. His ostensible advertisement for *The Deer Park* is, at the same time, implicitly, a brief against it, and as such a brief against the modernist ideology of the novel that had been used to market literary novels throughout the 1950s.

Mass Culture

What could replace this ideology? After completing revisions of the novel, Mailer had a new idea for *The Deer Park*, which he describes in his advertisement for it: "I could see that the new Sergius was capable of accepting the offer [from Hollywood], and if he went to Hollywood and became a movie star himself, the possibilities were good, for in Sergius I had a character who was ambitious yet, in his own way, moral, and with such a character one could travel deep into the paradoxes of the time" (243). *The Deer Park* is paradoxical and of its time, precisely because Mailer insists on an idea about art that his experience had told him no longer obtained. His newer idea—Sergius as movie star and literary hero simultaneously—suggests a novelist's escape from the "great divide" mentality, a way of thinking about literature that does not insist on its separation from mass culture but allows for the possibility of linking the two. In an odd way, Mailer had come around to Bennett Cerf's way of thinking. Cerf, whose efforts to prevent the publication of *The Deer Park* had, in fueling Mailer's animus against the book trade, unwittingly contributed to the making of *Advertisements*, had argued both to an audience at Columbia University and in *Variety* that television and literature were not necessarily natural enemies; Mailer belatedly came to agree. Sergius, he suggests, should have done what Mailer decided to do in the wake of his struggle to get *The Deer Park* published: participate in the world of commerce.

But Mailer does not try his new idea for the novel because, he writes, "I was not in shape to consider that book" (243), and his explanation constitutes the third section of Mailer's fourth advertisement: "By the last week or two, I had worn down so badly that . . . I was reduced to working hardly more than an hour a day. . . . I would come out of a seconal stupor with four or five times the normal dose in my veins, and drop into a chair to sit for hours" (244). More time to revise was unthinkable also because of commercial considerations ("The book could not be postponed beyond the middle of October or it would miss all chance for a large fall sale" [244]). In the throes of drug-fueled despair, Mailer becomes the mass-culture automaton about which so many critics and novelists of the 1950s warned readers: "I would sit in a chair and watch a baseball game on television. . . . Watching some afternoon horror on television, the boredom of the performers coming through the tense hilarities with a bleakness to match my own. . . . Then my mind would wear out, and new work was done for the day. I would sit around, watch more television and try to rest my dulled mind" (244). Mailer, who paints himself as the outlaw from all the rest of American culture, is in this story playing the role of the masses of *Fahrenheit 451*, watching television on all four walls, or he is the television-watching children of *Revolutionary Road* and *The Man in the Gray Flannel Suit*. In an interview shortly after the publication of *The Deer Park*, reprinted in *Advertisements*, Mailer is asked if television will "put an end to novel reading"; he answers, "It certainly seems to be cutting down on it" and that the novel has "a most doubtful future" (272). Mailer concludes his discussion of his bad condition with an acknowledgment of his limitations: "I had no magic so great as to hasten the time of the apocalypse" (247).

The advertisement for *The Deer Park* is thus doubly ironic; we are learning not only that the book trade is an unforgiving business like other unforgiving American businesses but also that outlaw writers will allow their avowedly sacred form of self-expression to be cheapened by drugs, television, and commercial considerations. Mailer has learned, however, that when one wants to be a "major" writer, the quality of the writing is not all that counts anyway. Far from the book-trade naïf that *Advertisements* presents him to be until the publication of *The Deer Park*, he exhibits a sense that the field of cultural production is competitive and complicated and that one's place in it is determined not by one's writing but by extraneous factors. His analysis, at the close of his advertisement, of what would determine the reputation of *The Deer Park* casts himself in the role of sociologist of culture. In the wake of a failure like that of *Barbary Shore*, Mailer writes, "A writer stayed alive in the circuits of such hatred only if he were unappreciated enough to be adored by a clique, or was so overbought by the public that he excited some defenseless nerve in the snob" (241). If *The Deer Park* were to sell 100,000 copies, Mailer continues, his reputation would be secure because "a serious writer is certain to be considered major if he is also a best-seller . . . [John] Steinbeck is better known than [John] Dos Passos, John O'Hara is taken seriously by people who dismiss [James T.] Farrell, and indeed it took three decades and a Nobel Prize before Faulkner was placed on a level with [Ernest] Hemingway" (241). Mailer is aiming to position himself as a "serious" writer (the seriousness with which Mailer uses terms like "serious" and "major" is another marker of his time) who speaks to the culture at large, or as a failure so large that it suggests he must be ahead of his time: "I discovered that I had been poised for an enormous sale or a failure—a middling success was cruel to take" (247). The fact that, for Mailer, middlebrow was death is one of the more conventional aspects of his literary worldview.

The fourth advertisement ends with a resurgence of optimism: "Now a few years have gone by . . . and I have begun to work up . . . a new book which will be the proper book of an outlaw, and so not publishable in any easy or legal way" (248). Mailer is again properly embattled, and he is again imagining the possibility of a writer standing alone, outside the machinery of literary production. It also ends with Mailer's own literal advertisement that he took out for *The Deer Park* in the *Village Voice*—a distant relation to Eitel's advertisement for himself in the novel and an anticipation of *Advertisements* as a whole—a collection of its harshest reviews ("Sordid and Crummy," says one publication, "Moronic Mindlessness," says another). The advertisement, Mailer writes, was a way of apologizing "for the bad flaws in the bravest effort I had yet pulled out of myself, and certainly for declaring to the world (in a small way, mean pity) that I no longer gave a sick dog's drop for the wisdom, the reliability, and the authority of the public's literary mind, those creeps and old ladies of vested reviewing" (248). It is a model of the kind of advertising, the kind of participation, that Mailer favors; it is a miniature version and a preview of *Advertisements* as a whole.

The Deer Park is not the first novel to advertise its negative reviews; what distinguishes Mailer's effort is his claim that the ad was produced by him alone. It is intended as an affirmation of his outlaw status, a point was made explicit in the advertisement itself, which said in small print at the bottom, "This advertisement has been paid for by Norman Mailer." Perhaps, Mailer suggests, the age of the old version of the solitary novelist is dead, killed by a corrupt book trade and the quasi-totalitarian America for which it now stands. But if the solitary novelist is dead, the solitary advertiser is born. One wonders, though, if even this advertisement belongs solely to the novelist. The idea for it might well have stemmed from Baxter's *The Image and the Search*, published by Putnam in 1955, shortly before *The Deer Park*. Baxter's British publisher had backed out on publishing the novel after a British newspaper condemned it for its sexual content. After publishing the novel, Minton, onetime advertising manager for Putnam's, wrote an advertisement for it in the New York *Herald Tribune* that quoted extensively from the British newspaper's attack. Mailer's purportedly solitary advertisement might well have been a collaborative effort (Tebbel 4: 216).

Talent in the Room

At the close of *Advertisements*, Mailer writes, "The novelists will grow when the publishers improve. Five brave publishing houses (a miracle) would wear away a drop of nausea in the cancerous American conscience, and give to the thousand of us or more with real talent, the lone-wolf hope that we can begin to explore a little more of that murderous and cowardly world which will burst into madness if it does not dare a new art of the brave" (473). The passage recapitulates not just much of what has already been said in *Advertisements* but much of the tension between the idealized novel and its reality throughout the 1950s, and it is as purposefully contradictory as anything else in the text. The "lone-wolf hope" can only be realized with the help of others, and writing is defined as the "art of the brave," though writers can only be lone wolves if publishers are also brave. As a prediction of what is needed for novelists to "grow," and presumably therefore for American culture to be saved, Mailer's pronouncement is not useful. Where, after all, will these publishers come from, when everything in American society militates against their existence? By calling five brave publishing houses a "miracle," Mailer suggests that, in fact, the novelists would not grow. Again, it is next to impossible to reconcile Mailer's ambitious proclamations with everything else he says about the state of the book trade. But again, reconciling contradictions is always beside the point in *Advertisements*. The point is always to reimagine the novelist as a rebel even in an age when novel production is big business. At least for Mailer, that project was successful. This is not to say that all of his post-1950s novels were successful, but rather that he maintained his status as an iconoclast to the end, aided by several outrageous television appearances. That he has had some influence on later self-promoting authors seems indubitable.[22]

In any event, few observers of postwar publishing would argue that the industry grew more courageous as the twentieth-century progressed, though whether the changes to publishing made the industry as a whole less courageous remains an open question. G.P. Putnam's Sons, the brave publisher that took on *The Deer Park* and *Lolita* when no other house would, was not immune to the changes to American publishing that began in earnest in 1959 with Random House's stock sale. In 1965, Putnam's purchased Berkley Books, a paperback house that had been founded in 1955. Ten years later, Putnam's and Berkley were acquired by MCA, one of the largest mass-culture conglomerates in the United States, producer of movies, television shows, and popular music. The purchase of Putnam's marked MCA's entry into book publishing. As publishers consolidated, novels continued to be published and read, but the ideology of the novel that animated *The Deer Park*, and along with it *Fahrenheit 451* and *The Sheltering Sky*, no longer obtained as it once had. New ideas, not necessarily Mailer's, would replace it.

Epilogue
Novels Today:
Oprah Winfrey, Jonathan Franzen,
and the Long Tail

I would have been happier if it could have been a sticker, but only because I am
uneasy with advertising on the front of a hardcover.
—*Jonathan Franzen, on the "Oprah's Book Club" label,*
October 21, 2001 (qtd. in Corcoran ST6)

The Disavowal That Failed

Norman Mailer aimed to look forward in 1959; Jonathan Franzen seemed
intent on reviving the literary world of the 1950s when he expressed
unease about advertising on the cover of his novel *The Corrections* and,
more generally, about participating in Oprah Winfrey's book club in
2001. Had it happened fifty years earlier, Franzen's public ambivalence
would have had a better chance of succeeding as a disavowal, the writer's
attempt to affirm his artistry by announcing his distance from the world
of commerce, which Bowles, Bradbury, and Mailer had used well in the
1950s. That Franzen's gesture fizzled in 2001 sets into relief some of the
ways in which the cultural and economic place of the novel has shifted
over the past half century.

Franzen was invited to participate in Oprah's Book Club in August
2001. His initial reaction, he told *People* magazine months after the fact,
was excitement: "I called my girlfriend in California and it was like, 'Oh
my god'" (Schindehette 83), a reaction that, Kathleen Rooney notes in
her account of the controversy, is "almost adolescent in its giddiness"
(36).[1] The excitement is understandable. The book club, participation
in which entailed an "Oprah's Book Club" label on the front of the hard-

cover edition of the book and an appearance on Winfrey's television show, had been a boon to the book trade since its inception in 1996, and it virtually guaranteed enormous sales for Franzen's novel: the initial, pre-book-club printing of 90,000 copies rose to 600,000 after the book-club selection (Farr 76).[2] But between the acceptance and the scheduled appearance came Franzen's public wavering—about the book-club label, the quality of the other books included in the club, and the effect that Franzen's participation would have on his audience's perception of his work. In response, Winfrey rescinded the invitation with a terse public statement: "Jonathan Franzen will not be on the *Oprah Winfrey Show* because he is seemingly conflicted about being chosen as a book club selection. It is never my intention to make anyone feel uncomfortable or cause anyone conflict. We have decided to skip the dinner and we're moving on to the next book" (qtd. in Rooney 33).

The purpose of the disavowal is to accrue symbolic capital; in the light of the near-unremitting criticism Franzen's stance provoked, however, there is little reason to believe that that occurred in this case. Why did this disavowal fail? One reason is surely that it was halfhearted and poorly articulated, an apparently defensive, uncalculated gesture, which, he suggested, again after the fact, was prompted by disapproval from his audience at readings: "I was bombarded with questions, mostly from the anti-Oprah camp" (qtd. in Kirkpatrick, "Oprah" E3). One of his more infamous comments illustrates the problem: "I feel like I'm solidly in the high-art literary tradition," Franzen said in an interview on National Public Radio (NPR), "but I like to read entertaining books and this maybe helps bridge that gap, but it also heightens these feelings of being misunderstood" (qtd. in Kirkpatrick, "Winfrey" C4). In the course of asserting a point of view, reversing himself, and then returning, Franzen betrays an unseemly concern for status. He repeats the gesture in the same interview: "She's picked some good books, but she's picked enough schmaltzy, one-dimensional ones that I cringe, myself, even though I think she's really smart" (qtd. in Kirkpatrick, "Winfrey" C4). Another problem is that Franzen seemed to be trying to have it all ways, pronouncing himself too good for the book club but not renouncing it or its commercial benefits.[3] Before Winfrey rescinded the invitation, Franzen told the *Portland Oregonian*, for example, that "the first weekend after I heard I considered turning it down," which contrasts curiously with his later, postcontroversy remarks to *People* about excitedly calling his girlfriend (qtd. in Kirkpatrick, "Winfrey" C4). Regardless, it was Winfrey who disinvited Franzen and not the other way around.

A second reason for the failure, evident in news coverage of the imbroglio, is that the contradictions inherent in Franzen's position were far more obvious to critics and to the reading public in 2001 than they might have been in 1951. (Another way to put it is that those who might agree with Franzen's position no longer occupied important positions in the cultural field.) About the book club's seal, Franzen said, "I see this as my book, my creation, and I didn't want that logo of corporate ownership on it. It's not a sticker, it's part of the cover. . . . The reason I got into this business is because I'm an independent writer, and I didn't want a corporate logo on my book" (qtd. in Rooney 44–45). As an invocation of the idea of the solitary writer, the attitude is not surprising; Franzen might have been Sergius O'Shaughnessy in Mailer's *The Deer Park*, not wanting his name associated with a Hollywood film, even though the film would have no bearing on whatever novel he might write. But within days of Franzen's comments, onlookers, including esteemed fellow writers, were pointing out the absurdity of his comments. Novelist Rick Moody asserted, "If you are being published by one of the big houses, you can't object that you are not commercial in some way: what book doesn't have the publisher's logo on the spine?" (qtd. in Kirkpatrick, "Oprah" E3). Franzen's publisher, Farrar, Straus & Giroux (FSG), is an excellent example of what has and has not changed with respect to the literary field over the past sixty years. Founded in 1946 as the book trade as a whole began to modernize, it is well known as a publisher of literary fiction and thoughtful nonfiction. But it is also a tiny piece of Verlagsgruppe, a German conglomerate that also owns other major American publishing houses such as Henry Holt and Macmillan, along with Germany's largest daily newspaper, *Die Zeit*; at the time *The Corrections* was published, Verlagsgruppe was one of five conglomerates that controlled 80 percent of American book sales (Schiffrin 2). Things have changed since 1946, but given FSG's continued existence as a respected literary brand if not an independent company, perhaps they have changed in ways more subtle than broad narratives of consolidation-fueled and commercialization-fueled decline suggest.

In any event, as Moody points out, Franzen's novel always had a logo of corporate ownership on it, and even Franzen's own editor at FSG, Jonathan Galassi, noted that "the jacket itself is advertising" (qtd. in Kirkpatrick, "Oprah" E3). Publishers, of course, had considerable incentive to stay on Winfrey's good side. Even granting that, the responses of Moody and Franzen's editor among others, and their immediacy, suggest that by 2001 the disavowal so central to literary-commercial success in the 1950s had lost much of its ability to generate symbolic capital, largely because the fact that books are always also a business, which Mailer "exposed" in *Advertisements* with help from *Fortune* and Wall Street in 1959, is no longer obscure. As early as the 1980s, James English argues, a "Flaubertian posture seems already a self-consciously dated and curmudgeonly one" (221).

Thus even if Franzen had more carefully stated his objections to Winfrey's book club, they would have been poorly received because the audience for literary fiction no longer believes that the cultural field conforms "in a broad way with what we habitually think of as the high-culture/mass culture opposition . . . that has prevailed since the nineteenth century" (English 220). And perhaps Franzen's expressions of ambivalence rather than renunciation—his initial decision to participate in the book club and his praise for its mission and for Winfrey that accompanied his denigrations—stem from his own partial recognition of this shift. His famous 1996 manifesto for the socially engaged literary novel, "Perchance to Dream: In the Age of Images, a Reason to Write Novels," is, among other things, an explicit exercise in belief production for a historical moment that is dominated not by mass culture but by cultural niches. In it, Franzen describes Paula Fox's novel *Desperate Characters*, from 1970, and the way the culture has changed since its publication:

A quarter-century has only broadened and confirmed the sense of cultural crisis that Fox was registering. But what now feels like the locus of that crisis—the banal ascendancy of television, the electronic fragmentation of public discourse—is nowhere to be seen in the novel. Communication for the Bentwoods meant books, a telephone, and letters. Portents didn't stream uninterruptedly through a cable converter or a modem; they were only dimly glimpsed, on the margins of existence. An ink bottle, which now seems impossibly quaint, was still thinkable in 1970. (58)

Franzen's nostalgia for an age in which the ink bottle remains thinkable is akin to Mailer's longing for the days of Perkins and Bradbury's for an age of fewer readers, but otherwise the passage is a bit jarring: 1970 is a historical moment that typically generates little nostalgia. Still, in the context of the novel's shifting place in the cultural field over the past four decades, it makes sense, and it suggests again that the emergence of mass culture in the 1950s was far less a problem for the cultural status of American novels than what came after. In 1970, moreover, Hollywood film was in the early stages of its most recent "golden age," led by a new generation of celebrity directors including Francis Ford Coppola and Martin Scorsese, and young writers at magazines like *Creem* (founded in 1969) and *Rolling Stone* (founded in 1967) were making the case for the cultural importance of popular music.[4] The point is not that starting in the 1970s mainstream rock music and Hollywood films surpassed novels as artistic achievements. Rather, the point is that other forms of popular culture besides novels, forms that decades earlier might have been casually disregarded as beneath the attention of highbrow critics, began to gain respect from intellectuals and from sizable audiences of educated consumers. The cultural field was growing more crowded, and so the novel's claim to cultural distinction was diminishing.

Simultaneous with this diminishing, a still bigger change was coming to television itself. Indeed, it is notable that Franzen looks back nostalgically to a moment—destined soon to end—in which network television dominated American culture to an extent far greater than it does in the twenty-first century. In 1970, cable television, television that was explicitly not aimed at the widest possible audience, was coming. Although the networks would remain strong throughout the decade, their decline was now imminent and perhaps inevitable. (Baughman names the 1980s the decade of the "shrinking mass" [*Republic* 211].) In short, as this book has argued throughout and as Franzen's nostalgia for 1970 implicitly suggests, network television was never the true enemy of the American novel. It was, rather, a foil. When its cultural power diminished, at the hands of cable television and later the Internet, the novel's cultural authority might have diminished as well. In the Introduction, I noted the conclusion of the study *Literacy in the United States* that book-buying by Americans was rising throughout the 1950s. That same study dates the reversal of this decades-long trend, the start of a decline in book buying, to 1974 (Kaestle, Damon-Moore, Stedman, Tinsley, and Trollinger 154). In this light, Franzen's nostalgia for 1970 becomes comprehensible.[5]

In 1996, Franzen drew two dispiriting conclusions. The first is the idea that the "serious" reader and the literary novel are endangered, a notion suggested in Franzen's description of the highbrow protagonist of *Desperate Characters*, with whom he at least partially identifies: "An unashamed elitist, an avatar of the printed word, and a genuinely solitary man, he belongs to a species so endangered as to be all but irrelevant in an age of electronic democracy" ("Perchance" 58). But this purported endangerment is a dubious notion. According to Chris Anderson, the editor of *Wired* magazine, we are now in the era of the "Long Tail," referring to the

ever-increasing length of the tail of a distribution curve. The implications
for Franzen's idea of the literary novel are significant. Booksellers in the
age of the Internet can now make profits even from low-selling books
because those books will not take up valuable shelf space in a store. Anderson explains: "New efficiencies in distribution, manufacturing, and
marketing were changing the definition of what was commercially viable across the board. The best way to describe these forces is that they
are turning unprofitable customers, products, and markets into profitable ones. . . . The story of the Long Tail is really about the economics
of abundance—what happens when the bottlenecks that stand between
supply and demand in our culture start to disappear and everything becomes available to everyone" (10–11). As Anderson notes, the average
Borders bookstore carries 100,000 titles; compared to other stores, it is
enormous, but still, shelf space is limited. However, 25 percent of Ama-
zon.com's book sales "come from *outside* its top 100,000 titles" (23). In
this age, the novel—the literary novel—is *never* endangered by market
forces because, as long as a tiny audience wants to read it, it is possible
and possibly even profitable to sell it. (This is especially so now that electronic reading devices are becoming increasingly popular.) In such a
world, anyone who chooses to be an "avatar of the printed word" will
never run out of reading material (though soon such a reader might
have to rely on electronic devices), and the fact that only a small group
of people would choose to live this way should hardly be a source of discomfort to an avowed highbrow.

But in a world of never-ending supply, the literary novel *is* more mar-
ginal than ever from the perspective of cultural authority because, although it survives, it survives only alongside an infinite number of other
cultural niche products—of the sort far less esteemed by Franzen—that
it is also profitable to sell, that also will not fade away. This was the second
dispiriting conclusion about the literary novel that Franzen drew in 1996
and the more credible one: that in the age of what he called "electronic
democracy," the literary novel is not at all central to the culture as a
whole, a perception registered in his disappointment about "no longer
mattering to a culture" ("Perchance" 61). In the 1950s, as the story of
Fahrenheit 451 shows, the idea that the novel was endangered, in a world
that was endangered, helped to constitute its cultural importance. It was
not true then that the novel's survival was threatened, either, but it was
easier to make the case then, and it was easier for that perceived endangerment to matter to an audience of readers with few alternatives
in the cultural field. In the age of the long tail, however, a strategy for

literary distinction that relies on the novel's perceived endangerment is not tenable.

After the Cold War

The emergence of niche culture is one reason that the 1950s strategy fails early in the twenty-first century; the end of the Cold War is surely another. As this book has described, during the Cold War, cultural supremacy was an imperative, and it was thus easy and natural to hitch concerns about the fate of literature to the larger geopolitical struggle. For novelists, critics, the ABPC, and all promoters of literary culture, mass culture was an obvious bogeyman, a stand-in for the Communist threat abroad and at home. That the post–Cold War world offers no analogous enemy was made clear in June 2004, when the National Endowment for the Arts (NEA) published "Reading at Risk: A Survey of Literary Reading in America." The report is an obvious analogue to the work done in the 1950s by ABPC-sponsored organizations like the Committee on Reading Development and the National Book Council: an expression of alarm about decline designed to double as a producer of belief in the importance of reading. In his preface, NEA Chairman Dana Gioia outlined what is at stake in the decline of literary reading: "The decline in reading parallels a larger retreat from participation in civic and cultural life. The long-term implications . . . not only affect literature but all of the arts—as well as social activities such as volunteerism, philanthropy, and even political engagement" (vii). (An update on this report from 2007, titled "To Read or Not to Read," draws the same conclusions about what it declares to be a further decline in reading.)

These are, of course, worthwhile reasons for concern about a decline in reading. But Gioia's list is notable for what it does not include, especially in the 2004 version: the regrettable, then-ubiquitous phrase "war on terror." That is, Gioia made no explicit attempt to hitch the cause of "literary reading" to the U.S.-avowed global war on terrorism, at a moment when the rhetoric of many other causes had been realigned to incorporate such concerns. Compared to Cold War–era jeremiads about literature and to contemporary rhetoric about other causes (immigration, for example), Gioia's list is tepid. Possibly Gioia declined to invoke the current war because it has been fought almost entirely as a military endeavor and barely at all as a war of ideas; to put it differently, it has not been embraced by liberal humanists in the way that the Cold War was. At

its most heated, the rhetoric of the "war on terror" was that of a battle between civilization and anticivilization, whereas the rhetoric of the Cold
War was that of a battle between two competing civilizations. Thus the
geopolitical situation of the first decade of the twenty-first century has
supplied no way analogous to the Cold War to promote the importance
of the book.

In the post–Cold War age of niches, Winfrey's astonishingly successful book club (successful for the book trade, that is—not for her television show, which typically generated lower ratings for its book-club shows
than for others [Farr 77]) does not seem like the instrument of cultural
decline—a fatal mixing of high and mass culture—that it might have
seemed in 1955. Rather, it registers as a return to something that has
been lost in the post–mass-culture age: common literary culture, the
novel as event, a brief moment when a novel can be restored to a central
place in American culture. As Farr summarizes, "In the first three years
of the Book Club, Oprah books sold an average of 1.4 million copies
each. Each book she invited her Book Club to read and talk about was an
instant bestseller, averaging seventeen weeks on the *New York Times* best-
seller list. Every book. In fact, from October 1996 through June 2002, the
length of the Book Club's first run, a week never went by without at least
one Oprah book on the national bestseller lists" (2).[6] Just as important,
Farr notes, the book club did more than just determine which novels
would be best sellers. It also increased the sales of novels relative to other
genres: "Self-help and computer instruction rules these bestseller lists
until the influence of Oprah's Book Club," at which point "literary fiction started appearing in surprising numbers" (3). Winfrey's endeavor,
because it prompted an unusually wide swath of the American public
to read novels, and Franzen's ambition, as expressed in "Perchance to
Dream," to make literary novels culturally relevant, should have been a
perfect match. The emergence of niche culture and the decline of mass
culture put television and the novel, neither of which had the cultural
authority or power that they once did, on the same side of a new version
of the culture wars.

How much this decline in cultural authority matters for American
novel producers is an open question, though it certainly has implications for the future of English departments and the future of literary
scholarship. Shifts in the cultural field, after all, did not stop Franzen's
ambitious novel from being published or from achieving a remarkably
large audience, and complaints that too many books are published seem
at least as common as complaints that too few good ones are published.[7]

But Franzen's failure to recognize how the cultural ground had shifted beneath the novel led to his public-relations mishap, and it points to a truth that Mailer recognized in 1959: strategies that helped make the case for the American novel's cultural importance in the 1950s would not work anymore.

Notes

Introduction

1. Sunstein addresses the implications of "niche culture" for American democracy. For more on the security implications of the Internet age, see Weimann. For a pre-2001 assessment of the cultural implications of the electronic age, see Birkerts.

2. See ch. 1, "Coming to Terms with Defining Terms," in Kammen.

3. See Menand 115–19 for a brief summary of television's emergence as a technology and a cultural force. On the FCC in the early days of television, see ch. 4, "The Regulators," in Baughman, *Same Time*.

4. Baughman's *Republic* is the best source on the impact of television's emergence on newspapers, magazines, and movies. For more on newspapers and magazines in the early decades of television, see Kaestle et al.

5. See Dickstein's *Leopards* and Schaub for versions of this argument. For an important dissent on the prevailing view, see the introduction to Hoberek.

6. See Wilinsky, Izod, and Stringer, in addition to Baughman's *Republic*.

7. For the classic attacks on mass culture, see Horkheimer and Adorno's *Dialectic of Enlightenment*, Macdonald's *Against the American Grain*, and, for a differently styled but related and influential critique, Eliot's *Notes Towards the Definition of Culture*. On the ideology of modernism as anticommerce, as opposed to the reality of modernism as a specific set of commercial strategies, see Rainey.

8. In addition to other sources, see ch. 3, "Art as Antidote: The Mass Culture Debates," in Jensen. See also Schaub; Cochran; Kammen.

9. "Excorporation is the process by which the subordinate make their own culture out of the resources and commodities provided by the dominant system, and this is central to popular culture, for in an industrial society the only resources from which the subordinate can make their own subcultures are those provided by the system that subordinates them" (Fiske 15).

10. See Schaub 25–39. See also McGurl.

11. On literature as the product of institutions, see especially the introduction to Rainey and Ziolkowski 6–10. On the sociology of literature generally, see the special issue of *Critical Inquiry* edited by Desan, Ferguson, and Griswold. On the need to study the book trade specifically, see Sutherland.

12. On novel production and the book trade after World War II, see especially Ohmann. See also Brouillette, *Postcolonial Writers*, and Young.

13. For more on this growth after World War II, see Frase 239.

14. On the production of nonfiction and fiction in the 1950s, see Murphy.

15. Although "nearly all scholars working on the 1950s in the United States," Nelson notes, "make a distinction between their own critical revisions of the

decade and mainstream nostalgia for the fifties as a time of prosperity, family togetherness, and national strength . . . scholars keep insisting that the idealization of the fifties remains so dominant that it crowds out the alternative" (11–12).

16. On the transformation of the university, see Bender and Lowen.

17. Price's *Reading for Life: Developing the College Student's Lifetime Reading Interest* exemplifies the collaboration of governmental, literary, and educational institutions to promote reading in a Cold War context. Sponsored by the National Book Committee, an offshoot of the ABPC, and published in 1959, the year Random House went public, the collection of essays addresses the "problem of developing reading interest in America" (vii) in the age "of the golf course and the television set" (vi), and notes that the average college student "lacks the 'know-how' to build sputniks" (v).

18. As Frase notes, "When the Council was established in 1946, the American book-publishing industry had not changed in its essential structure since the late-nineteenth century, when the functions of publishing had become separated from the functions of bookselling and book printing" (239). Earlier publisher associations include the American Publishers Association (formed in 1901), the American Association of Book Publishers (formed in 1921), the Book Publishers Bureau (1937), and the Council on Books in Wartime, "a cooperative endeavor responsible for the paperback books issued as Armed Forces Editions during World War II" (238).

19. Murphy aptly characterizes Melcher's editorials on the postwar book trade as "a rich source of expressions of angst, assessment, prediction, and . . . the mission of all involved in book publishing" (34).

20. The mission statement appears on the back cover of the pamphlet edited by Grambs.

21. On the story of Pocket Books, see Davis. On the emergence of the trade paperback, see Epstein and Barnhisel, *James Laughlin*.

22. English's *The Economy of Prestige* is an invaluable study of cultural prizes. See especially ch. 3, "The Logic of Proliferation."

23. See Bourdieu, "Production." As Sarah Brouillette has noted, Bourdieu recognized this blurring in his later work. See Bourdieu, *Rules of Art*, and see Brouillette, *Postcolonial Writers* 61–65.

24. See Dimaggio 152.

25. Hirsch's study is particularly significant because it was an attempt to address mounting concern that increasing concentration in the publishing industry would prevent adventurous works from finding publishers. For one iteration of this concern, see Whiteside. Hirsch's conclusion was that the trade's low barriers to entry would prevent concentration from having the negative effect that Whiteside and others feared. See also Powell, "Competition versus Concentration" and "The Blockbuster Decade."

26. Hirsch modifies Gans's terminology somewhat; the distinction Gans draws is between "creator-oriented" and "user-oriented" forms of culture. Gans explains, "High culture is creator-oriented," meaning that "the creator's intentions are crucial and the values of the audience almost irrelevant." The "popular arts," in contrast, are "user-oriented, and exist to satisfy audience values and wishes" (76).

27. This argument has been made most forcefully in the pages of two special issues of *Poetics* (12 and 14). See especially van Rees, "Advances" 285–86. The title of H. Verdaasdonk's article, "Empirical Sociology of Literature as a Non-

Textually Oriented Form of Research," effectively illustrates this move away from textual analysis in the pursuit of sociological insights.

Chapter 1

1. Bowles and Laughlin's relationship ended shortly after *The Sheltering Sky* was published in December 1949. Bowles and Strauss worked together until Strauss left the profession in 1967. See Strauss.

2. Bourdieu's term is "*denegation*," translated as "disavowal," "negation," or "denial" in "The Production of Belief." See the translator's note in "Production" 74.

3. Macdonald and Greenberg wrote the most famous of these critiques. On concerns specifically about fate of the literary novel, see also Schaub.

4. On the growth of the college-educated population, see Bender; see also Asheim 4–5. On the number of readers, see ch. 5, "Literacy as a Consumer Activity," in Kaestle, Damon-Moore, Stedman, Tinsley, and Trollinger.

5. These promotional strategies and specific examples of them are discussed in detail in Chapter 2 of this book.

6. Its immediate commercial success was matched by almost immediate critical attention. John W. Aldridge devoted a chapter to it in *After the Lost Generation* (1951; ch. 12) and Leslie A. Fiedler discussed it briefly in *Love and Death in the American Novel* (1960). Scholarly interest in Bowles waned in the 1960s and 1970s, but with the emergence of queer theory and postcolonial theory and with Bernardo Bertolucci's film adaptation (1990), it has spiked over the past two decades. See especially the special edition of *Twentieth Century Literature* (Butscher and Malin) and the *Review of Contemporary Fiction* 2 (1982). See also Morris Dickstein's *Leopards in the Temple*; Hout; Friend.

7. On art-house movies, see Wilinsky.

8. After reading a sampling of Bowles's poems, Stein remarked, "Well, the only trouble with this is that it's not poetry." When Bowles asked what it was, if not poetry, Stein replied, "How should I know what it is? You wrote it." (Sawyer-Lauçanno 99).

9. A discrepancy exists between Bowles's account of this in his autobiography and Sawyer-Lauçanno's later account. Bowles does not say—and Sawyer-Lauçanno does say—that Dial Press told him he would need to publish a novel before he could publish a collection of his short stories. Given that Bowles did in fact write a novel before publishing *A Delicate Prey*, his collection of stories, Sawyer-Lauçanno's version seems more plausible, especially because there is no evidence that Strauss ever tried to sell a short-story collection to publishers before the publication of *The Sheltering Sky*. See Sawyer-Lauçanno 275 and *Without Stopping* 164.

10. Bowles's passivity in this account is notable, particularly for someone known for following his will; in his letters to Laughlin, he attempted to distance himself from whatever it was his agent was doing, and here he distances himself from the very act of hiring her. Dial Press tells him he needs an agent; Dial Press even makes the phone call that introduces him to one.

11. My discussion of literary agents relies heavily on Coser, Kadushin, and Powell 285–307. See also Hepburn.

12. As Raymond Chandler described it, this is the "fall" for literary agents: the moment when the agent went "Hollywood" and left the independent New York literary scene.

13. See Rose. Rose's chronicle makes no mention of the literary department's formation; for that, see Strauss.

14. William Morris was apparently so sure that it wanted Strauss to head its department that it waited a full year for her to decide to take the job. Until she accepted, they did not even try to set up their literary department (Strauss 41).

15. Strauss, however, did not count herself a highbrow. Her favorite and most commercially successful client was James Michener.

16. See ch. 2, "The Politics of Realism," of Schaub for a discussion of the critical attention lavished on the novel as a work of art after World War II.

17. Sawyer-Lauçanno 274. Bowles retells the story in his preface.

18. Both Sawyer-Lauçanno and Carr, in the most recent biography of Bowles, devote less than a paragraph to Doubleday's rejection. See Carr 205.

19. The relevant comparison here is to Norman Mailer after Rinehart rejected his manuscript for *The Deer Park*. As an established novelist Mailer's advance was guaranteed ("a common arrangement for writers whose sales are more or less large," writes Mailer, though Rinehart did sue to try to recover the advance [*Advertisements* 228]).

20. Laughlin did not publish, and would not have published, *Tropic of Cancer* and, despite issuing earlier works by Vladimir Nabokov, he turned down *Lolita*. He also refused to allow New Directions to become a vehicle for Pound's anti-Semitism. See Barnhisel, *James Laughlin*; Laughlin, "New Directions" 41–42. See also de Grazia.

21. That indifference is conveyed in small print on the title page of every New Directions book: "New Directions Books are published for James Laughlin."

22. In 1952, Hellmut Lehmann-Haupt lauded New Directions for its "sole emphasis on literary and artistic quality" and "uncompromising idealism" (348, 351). See also *Conjunctions* 1 (Morrow), which is devoted entirely to tributes to Laughlin.

23. See Barnhisel, *James Laughlin* 96–99 for more on Laughlin's marketing strategies.

24. "I didn't limit myself," Laughlin said, "to publishing Ezra's friends and those he recommended. I also came strongly under the influence of various other people" (24).

25. Laughlin quotes Pound as telling him to "start printin things. None of my friends have any publishers." Later Laughlin adds, "Ezra immediately sent me to Bill [Carlos Williams]" (21, 23).

26. Laughlin said he initially thought *Siddhartha* was "Buddhism once over lightly. . . . wasn't too excited about it . . . but Henry kept after me. . . . So finally I heeded 'Uncle Henry'" ("New Directions" 44).

27. James Laughlin, "History," 224. Laughlin's explanation of Pound's commercial viability is questionable; the controversy surrounding the poet's Bollingen Prize had much to do with his later fame.

28. Levertov sets this phenomenon into relief as she pays tribute to Rexroth: "Most certainly it was he who persistently brought me to James Laughlin's attention and so . . . to the happiness and honor of becoming in 1959 a New Directions author" (ix).

29. Laughlin, "New Directions" 40–41. About Laughlin, Williams once said, "Among all the multitude of persons I've encountered in the world of letters and theatre . . . J. Laughlin remains the one I regard with the deepest respect and affection" ("Homage").

30. Bowles offered two quite different accounts of how the music for *The Glass Menagerie* came to be composed. In *Without Stopping*, he emphasizes that the work was done quickly but that he refused to work without a contract. Sawyer-Lauçanno relies on the account from Bowles that is quoted in Steen. There Bowles claims that he wrote the music without a contract. See Sawyer-Lauçanno 243–44.

31. Even after Bowles had mostly given up composing, he continued to compose for Williams's plays. He wrote music for both *Sweet Bird of Youth* and *The Milk Train Doesn't Stop Here Anymore* (1962).

32. Although Bowles never seems to have mentioned Williams's role in delivering the manuscript to Laughlin, Laughlin's account in the *Publishers Weekly* interview confirms Bowles's assertion that Strauss was bypassed in the effort to get *The Sheltering Sky* published by New Directions. The recently published *Selected Letters of Tennessee Williams, 1945–1957* includes a letter to Laughlin that touches on Bowles's manuscript: "Paul and Jane Bowles are in Tangier. Lehmann [Bowles's and Williams's publisher in England] . . . is very happy over advance reactions to Paul's novel and I suspect it will make a real impression there" (Williams 252). The letter, dated June 3, 1949, after Laughlin agreed to publish Bowles's novel but months before it was published, illustrates Williams's involvement with the novel before publication. Vidal, moreover, notes that Williams similarly sent one of *his* unpublished manuscripts to Laughlin with Williams's recommendation (*Point* 239).

33. In a recent memoir, Vidal says he played a similar role in getting *The Sheltering Sky* published in England, acting as an agent, bringing the manuscript to the publisher, John Lehman, Ltd. See Vidal, *Point* 114.

34. The classic example of the surprise best seller transformed into a "blockbuster" is Grace Metalious's *Peyton Place*. See Cameron and Chapter 4 of this book.

35. Laughlin did place advertisements for *The Sheltering Sky*; single ads appeared in three issues of the *Saturday Review of Literature* in December 1949 between the tenth and thirty-first. On December 17, when no advertisement appeared, the *Saturday Review* published Nelson Algren's largely unfavorable review of the novel.

36. Bowles was appreciative of Williams's work on his behalf: "Tennessee . . . went out of his way to write reviews of my first two or three books in the *New York Times*, the *Saturday Review*, and various other publications. He couldn't have been a better friend. No one I know has so consistently stood behind my writing as Tennessee during all these years" (Steen 36).

37. It might plausibly be argued that the fact that Port does not write does not mean that good writing is impossible. However, the novel's promotion insisted that Port is Bowles's alter ego and attributed the novel's artistry to Bowles's Port-like detachment.

38. This method links Bowles to the improvisatory aesthetic so prevalent in the postwar era. Bowles, however, does not celebrate the liberating potential of spontaneity. See Belgrad.

39. Bowles said frequently that *The Sheltering Sky* is a novel-length version of his noted short story, "A Distant Episode," in which an American linguistics professor, studying dialects in northern Africa, is kidnapped by a tribe, which cuts his tongue out, tortures him, and drives him to insanity. When asked if Port is a version of the professor, Bowles replied, "They're all [Port, Kit and Tunner] the professor . . . the desert is the protagonist" (*Conversations* 54).

40. The novel's major existential moment comes when Port's stolen passport is found. He literally runs from it, traveling deeper into the Sahara rather than

have this lone symbol of his identity brought back to him. Although Bowles's narrator makes clear that the fact of running away from his passport pleases Port, on a plot level, Port is *not* running from his passport. He is running from the man who is bringing him his passport: Tunner. Bowles describes Port's reaction to the news that his passport has been found and that Tunner will bring it to him this way: "The idea horrified him; faced with Tunner's imminent arrival, he was appalled to realize that he had never expected really to see him again" (171). Whatever horror Port felt was what impelled him to bribe his way onto the first bus out to El Ga'a and then to lie to Kit, to tell her that his passport was not and would not be found.

Kit, too, at the end of the novel, runs away only after finding out that Tunner is waiting for her.

41. At another point, the novel seems clearly to suggest that it was Port who invited him: "Tunner had been asked to come along, and perhaps that, too, had been subconsciously motivated, but out of fear; for much as [Port] desired the rapprochement [with Kit], he knew that he dreaded the emotional responsibilities it would entail" (105). This gibes with Bowles's own tendency to invite friends to visit to prevent being intimate with Jane.

42. Bowles retold this story several other times decades after the fact, suggesting that his anger never fully subsided. In a letter to Henry Miller in 1979, he writes, by way of introduction to a brief version of the story: "It's dangerous to have a publisher who has no interest in making money . . . but it's not interesting, that long saga (*In Touch* 489). Here we see again Bowles's desire to tell his story and his effort to distance himself from it. Bowles repeated this gesture in a letter to Phil Nurenberg five years later: after recounting the story of his relationship with Laughlin, Bowles writes, "Forgive this letter" (522).

43. Cerf also briefly discusses McDowell's hiring in *At Random* (242).

44. Epstein grew ambivalent about the popularity of his innovation: "My aim," he writes, "had been to restore and extend the *ancien régime* of literature, not to make a new world" (65–66). For more on the trade paperback, see Epstein 60–67.

Chapter 2

1. The occasion for the editorial was the announcement that Stephen King has been awarded the same Distinguished Medal in 2003 that Bradbury received in 2000.

2. The complete text can be found at Bradbury's official Web site: http://www.raybradbury.com/awards_NatBk.html.

3. In 1984, and only in 1984, separate National Book Awards for Science Fiction were awarded, one for hardcover books and one for paperbacks. The awards went to *Jem* by Frederick Pohl (hardcover) and *The Book of the Dun Cow* by Walter Wangerin (paperback).

4. This text is taken from the National Book Foundation's Web site: http://www.nationalbook.org/amerletters.html.

5. See, in addition to other pieces cited throughout, Bradbury's foreword to Rabinowitz and Kaplan.

6. Bradbury continues: "I have written poems about Melville, Melville and Emily Dickinson, Emily Dickinson and Charles Dickens, [Nathaniel] Hawthorne, Poe, Edgar Rice Burroughs, and along the way I compared Jules Verne and his Mad Captain to Melville and his equally obsessed mariner" (168).

7. The text of Martin's speech can be found at the National Book Foundation's official Web site: http://www.nationalbook.org/nbaacceptspeech_rbradbury_intro.html.

8. Cochran's *America Noir* is an exception in Bradbury scholarship and Patrick Brantlinger's *Bread and Circuses* is an exception among scholarship of the mass-culture debates: both note Bradbury's unlikely place in the debate.

9. From the science fiction and fantasy journal *Extrapolation* alone, see Connor; McGiveron; Hoskinson; Spencer. For edited collections on *Fahrenheit 451*, see Bloom; de Koster.

10. See English 58, 65–66. As English notes, the National Book Awards would in later decades lose credibility in the same way that the Pulitzers did at mid-century, and the result would be the launching of the (momentarily) more prestigious National Book Critics Circle Award.

11. Referring to the Book-of-the-Month Club in *A Feeling for Books*, for example, Radway writes, "Apparently the club was so successful in establishing itself as a key mediator in these years that it warranted renewed and even more vituperative criticism from writers such as [Dwight] Macdonald and Clement Greenberg and from the increasing numbers of literature professors whose cultural authority it challenged" (310).

12. See "Institutional Ads for Books Urged by Spier."

13. The other organizations, in addition to the ABPC, BMI, and ABA, were as follows: the Adult Education Association of the U.S.A.; Association of American University Presses; ALA; NCTE; Sears, Roebuck Foundation; and the United States Department of Agriculture Extension Service ("Widespread" 112).

14. For the complete story of New American Library, see Bonn.

15. For a detailed account of the story of the Modern Library, see Satterfield, which includes brief discussions of the Everyman's Library. See 25–27, 90–91. See also Cerf, *At Random*; Dardis.

16. See Satterfield 38–39. The antiadvertising argument is well expressed in "An Advertising Catechism," which appeared in *Publishers Weekly* in 1934. The anonymous author argues that advertising for individual books is so cost-ineffective that publishers should concentrate "the bulk of the advertising each season on the few books that might become best sellers" (128). As noted earlier, it was in part as a response to this problem that the book trade, led by the ABPC, began promoting "reading" rather than individual books. For a version of the argument for this kind of advertising, from 1949, see "Institutional Ads for Books Urged by Spier."

17. On the emergence of science fiction as a self-conscious genre, see Westfahl, *Mechanics* and " 'The Closely Reasoned Technological Story.' "

18. Bretnor's brief biography of Campbell in *Modern Science Fiction* says that he "has done more than any other man to develop modern science fiction as a mature literary form" (3). See also Rabkin, Mitchell, and Simon; and see Westfahl, " 'The Closely Reasoned Technological Story' " 193–94.

19. For the story of how Scribner's came to be involved with Bantam Books, see Cerf, *At Random*, 197–98. For Bantam's significance, see Davis, 103–9.

20. See Aronovitz.

21. Tebbel writes, "Ballantine's idea was not received with unanimous applause. Arguments for and against appeared in the press, the literary reviews, and in trade periodicals" (3: 396).

22. According to Weller, Doubleday's insistence on promoting Bradbury narrowly as a science fiction writer frustrated the author (203).

23. Stanley Kauffmann, Bradbury's editor at Ballantine, tells the story a bit dif-

ferently: "[Bradbury] got the galleys and wouldn't let go of them. He was fussing with them. So I had to fly out to California and work with him for a week out there" (qtd. in Davis, 167).

24. The dedication reads, "*This one*, with gratitude, is for Don Congdon" (emphasis added). The "this one" suggests that Bradbury is honoring Congdon's role in the creation of the novel, as opposed to the previous work, which Bradbury produced without collaboration from Congdon.

25. All quotes from *Fahrenheit 451* come from the Del Rey edition of the novel.

26. David Cochran explains Bradbury's relationship to his genre this way: "As many science fiction fans have argued, Bradbury is not really a science fiction writer at all. Unlike Isaac Asimov, for instance, Bradbury is not a scientist and knows little about physics, chemistry, or the other fields that form the basis for science fiction" (58).

27. Cochran observes that "the supreme irony" of *Fahrenheit 451* is that Bradbury's assault on mass culture is made "in the guise of a science fiction novel, one of the most debased forms of mass culture" (56). Cochran maybe overstates the critical disdain for science fiction, which for a variety of reasons attracted less criticism than other genres (the main reason probably being that it had less mass appeal than others, and thus was a less appealing target).

28. See ch. 2, "Mass Culture in the Twentieth Century," in Beaty for a discussion of Wertham's relation to the mass-culture critique of the 1950s. See also Medovoi and Hajdu.

29. See Tuttle for more on child-rearing during the Cold War.

30. These lines might seem to cast Bradbury as an early critic of the so-called political correctness that figured largely in the culture wars of the 1990s. But within the novel itself, Bradbury's concern is the preservation of the book and high culture from whatever might threaten them; these lines are thus rooted in the culture wars of the 1950s rather than those that took place four decades later.

31. Genette explains the idea of the "paratext" as follows: "A literary work consists, entirely or essentially, of a text, defined (very minimally) as a more or less long sequence of verbal statements that are more or less endowed with significance. But this text is rarely presented in an unadorned state, unreinforced and unaccompanied by a certain number of verbal and other productions, such as an author's name, a title, a preface, illustrations. . . . These accompanying productions, which vary in extent and appearance, constitute what I have called elsewhere the work's paratext" (1).

32. The January 23, 1954, issue of *Publishers Weekly* included as one of four major trends for the book trade in 1953 "a wave of censorship that had no previous parallel in the United States" ("Review of News and Trends of 1953" 286). In response, the ABPC and the ALA collaborated on a pamphlet titled "The Freedom to Read" (287).

Chapter 3

1. John Patrick Diggins asserts that the novel portrays a 1950s "conformist archetype" (216). In *Grand Expectations*, James T. Patterson, in the course of linking the novel with Whyte and Riesman, surmises that it "skewered the soulless, consumerist lives of suburbanites and the corporate world" (338). Robert Frank calls it a "quintessential text of Organization society" (38).

2. See ch. 2, "Quintessentially Middlebrow," in Wood. Jurca cites it as a repre-

sentative 1950s suburban novel. Long deems it a representative best seller of the "corporate-suburban" genre.

3. The "candle at midnight" reference alludes to a scene in the novel in Italy, when Tom is alone with Maria. It is this aspect of the novel that, as I'll argue in this chapter, is most obscured by the decision to call it *The Man in the Gray Flannel Suit*.

4. Today, the correct company name is Simon *&* Schuster (with the ampersand), but when it was founded, it was Simon *and* Schuster. Simon and Schuster themselves resisted the ampersand, but after they were gone the change was made. Viacom currently owns the company.

5. The most famous example of this is J. K. Lasser's lucrative annual books about income taxes. See Tebbel 3: 556 and Schwed 77–78.

6. On the distinction between producer- and consumer-oriented, see Gans; Hirsch.

7. See ch. 1, "A Cultural Perpetual Motion Machine: Management Theory and Consumer Revolution in the 1960s," of Frank's *Conquest of Cool* for more on the corporate culture of the 1950s.

8. Peter Schwed suggests that this decision was mutual; as much as Simon wanted autonomy, that is, the rest of Simon & Schuster wanted him away from the company's decision-making. "At about this time," Schwed writes, "it had been agreed that Dick Simon's books should be separated editorially from the regular publishing program of the firm" (193).

9. As Korda puts it, "The age of the entrepreneurial publisher, whose drive and personal taste was enough to make a publishing house grow and thrive, was over" (102).

10. James English observes that Bourdieu's "grand narrative of art's commercialization" depends on an "essentially modernist map of cultural fields" (8). Revising that map for a new age will be a crucial project for sociologists of culture going forward. See Bourdieu's *Rules of Art* for his acknowledgment of the changing cultural field.

11. When Simon became too ill to work, shortly before his death, Wilson's happy experience with publishers came to an end. See *What* 250–58, where he reports mistreatment by both Hollywood executives and agents.

12. Later Wilson adds still more detail, writing of "the exact moment when I had scrawled *The Man in the Gray Flannel Suit* with a pencil on a list of possible titles" and "the fact that my wife had backed this particular title when Dick Simon was arguing for another" (236).

13. See Jurca for the best critique of claims that Tom Rath is typical.

14. Orville Prescott's review in the *New York Times* identified one of its themes as "conformity-worship."

15. One example of how commonplace the critique of corporate culture had become can be found in Mills's review of *The Organization Man* in the *New York Times*. In a generally favorable review, Mills notes that Whyte's book mines "a very old theme" and that it "provides nothing new."

16. After mockingly summarizing the plot of the novel, Whyte notes that in a novel such as Wilson's, which he cites as symptomatic, "Society is so benevolent that there is no conflict left in it for anyone to be rebellious about" (251). See Frank and Jurca 135 and 137 for allusions to Wilson's Whyte-styled sociological aims. See also Brooks's essay about Donald Rumsfeld, which begins this way: "In 1955 Sloan Wilson published 'The Man in the Gray Flannel Suit,' and in 1956 William H. Whyte published 'The Organization Man.' Both books captured the spirit of the times."

17. As Jurca notes, Mills and Riesman both cited public relations as the paradigmatic example of dehumanizing corporate work. It "not only entails working with people and symbols rather than things but is one step further removed from material labor: it symbolizes the symbols" (151).

18. See Rainey 7, 108–12, 120 on patronage as a theme in classic high-modernist works.

19. Because these worries are intended to illustrate the perceived need to conform—the social ethic—required by the modern corporation, it is worth noting that Wilson seems to base it on his experience working not for a typical corporation but for a publishing company, Houghton Mifflin. Soon after World War II, Wilson worked there as a reader, and he describes the experience this way:

> Almost invariably I hated the books which the editors of the big publishing house planned to publish and loved the manuscripts which they were in the process of rejecting. Still, it would be quite possible for me to write reader's reports which would agree with Paul Brooks, I realized. All I would have to do would be to praise all the manuscripts I loathed and knock hell out of those I loved. This did not seem a good way to start a career in publishing. When I told Paul that I had concluded that publishing was not the best career for me, he looked immensely relieved. (*What* 153)

20. For more on Conant and meritocracy, see Hershberg and Lemann.

21. As Conant among others sought, the National Defense Education Act appropriated "federal aid for high school educational programs in fields relevant to national security" (Hershberg 711).

22. A more prosaic explanation for the omission of a Cold War context might be that Wilson himself was unaware of the Cold War implications of the work done by Better Schools. Nowhere in his memoir does he link the commission's work to a larger political context, and he notes, "At the age of twenty-seven, I was, as I am now, an almost completely unpolitical animal" (*What* 172).

23. See Jurca, especially the introduction and ch. 5, "Sanctimonious Suburbanites and the Postwar Novel."

24. See especially ch. 4, "The Unhappy Consciousness," in Schaub, and ch. 4, "On and Off the Road: The Outsider as Young Rebel," in Dickstein. See also Castronovo.

Chapter 4

1. See ch. 3, "Step Right Up: The World of Popular Amusement," in Bogdan.

2. Kammen deems the period from 1908 through 1938 the era of "proto-mass culture," a clumsy but useful term intended to correct for the indiscriminate use of the term "mass" to describe forms of culture that do not in fact reach the masses. See ch. 1, "Coming to Terms with Defining Terms."

3. On the Marxist logic of Greenberg's theory of culture, see Clark.

4. Kammen writes, "I draw a marked distinction between what British scholars refer to as 'traditional' popular culture (flourishing in the sixteenth to nineteenth centuries) and the considerably more commercialized and technologically transformed popular culture that emerged at the close of the nineteenth century and then blossomed exuberantly in the twentieth" (6). Carnivals fall into the latter category.

5. "The showmen working the Midway Plaisance, too, not only shared the same grounds and experiences but even met to discuss common problems. It was at this exposition . . . in the area around Buffalo Bill's Wild West Show, that the idea for a collective amusement company was first discussed and the carnival as we know it was born" (Bogdan 59).

6. For more on the story of the paperback, see Davis; Bonn.

7. See Bourdieu, "Field." *Publishers Weekly*'s attack on *Peyton Place* occurred in its annual "year in review" issue, which did always feature an assessment of the year in fiction.

8. Who, specifically, were "the pessimists" to which *Publishers Weekly* referred? Schaub asserts that "the most dramatic and consequential agreement among these critics was their uniform dismissal of most recent and contemporary American fiction" (41). This idea had filtered into mainstream magazines, where laments over the state of the novel became more common. See Schaub 57–58.

9. The passage is equally striking for its inaccuracy. There are no murders in the novel (Selena Cross is acquitted of the charge of murdering her stepfather) and there is only one suicide, and although most of the secondary characters are married, most of the important ones are not. Finally, the novel is concerned with the happiness of but a few, and the rest, consumed by their own hypocrisies, are presumably miserable.

10. In a similar vein, Fuller commented in his review: "'Kings Row' leaps immediately to mind in reading this book. Not since Henry Bellamann's sensational novel has anyone come along and applied quite the same kind of microscopic treatment to a small town with such relentless energy. Now a mere slip of a girl . . . has done it in a first novel" (B7).

11. In the *New York Times*, Manohla Dargis, a film critic, writes that soon after Britain's megaton bombs became known as "blockbusters," the term "entered the vernacular, appearing in advertisements before the end of the war, and as a clue in a 1950 crossword puzzle in this newspaper (46 across)." For more on the origins of the term *blockbuster*, see Neale 47–48.

12. See Stringer on blockbuster films. See also Powell's essay on media concentration in the 1970s, "The Blockbuster Decade."

13. For another, more personal discussion of the Random House consolidation, see Epstein 88–90. Random House is discussed in more detail in Chapter 5. See also Schiffrin and, for a review of Epstein and Schiffrin's accounts, see Heer.

14. More on the relationship between the process of making television shows from books and movies can be found in Christopher Anderson. As Anderson discusses, one of the early efforts to make a television show from a book or movie was *King's Row*, the novel by Henry Bellamann that was an influence on Metalious when she wrote *Peyton Place* (186–87, 192–93). On this influence, see Toth 76–77, 83–84, and 140–41.

15. For more rigorous, and inconclusive, sociological and economic studies of the effects of consolidation on literary production, see Hirsch; Powell, "Competition." I discuss the effects of consolidation in more detail in Chapter 5.

16. See especially ch. 4, "The Great RSV Controversy: Bible-Burning, Red-Hunting, and the Strange Specter of Unholy Scripture," in Thuesen.

17. On receiving it, Truman predicted "peace for all mankind" if only the Bible could make its way into the Soviet Union, but he also noted his love for the King James Version (Thuesen 90).

18. It seemed that everywhere in 1952, the book world and the religious world were mixing. *Time* reported on the sixth annual Christian Booksellers Convention in 1952, the largest yet, where Moody Press displayed religious and inspirational books that featured a pretty girl on one jacket and a rocket ship on another—all part of an effort to increase sales by 30 percent, to half a million copies. The magazine quotes the press's director: "Even faith can stand a little merchandising" ("Sales Appeal"). At the convention, *Publishers Weekly* reported, "Promotion, display and mailing were discussed, roadside promotion signs were offered, and it was reported that 163 dealers had taken the Christian Booksellers Association correspondence course in retailing." The publication of the RSV, moreover, was not the only Bible-related publishing event of its moment. On the same day it was published, Abingdon-Cokesbury published a third volume of "The Interpreter's Bible," Oxford University Press spent $60,000 to promote its Bibles, and Simon & Schuster issued a new printing of "The Bible, Designed to Be Read as Living Literature" ("Tips for the Bookseller" 700–701).

19. Macdonald's attack was a minor part of the end of the RSV's mass-culture honeymoon. Its commercial success, which no doubt benefited from the wave of Cold War religiosity, was in the end victimized by that wave. See ch. 4, "The Great RSV Controversy," in Thuesen for a discussion of what Thuesen calls "the greatest Bible translation controversy in American religious history" (94).

20. On the obscenity trials of the 1950s for literary novels, see de Grazia.

21. Cameron notes that Messner "staffed the firm almost entirely with women: women were the editors, sales directors, publicity agents, readers, and editorial assistants, as well as the company's typists and secretaries. What seems to have turned off other publishing houses fired the imagination of Messner and her staff" (xix).

22. See especially ch. 6, "Automated Book Distribution and the Negative Option," in Radway's *A Feeling for Books*.

23. On the strategies for marketing modernist culture, see especially Rainey; Turner.

24. Dardis puts it this way: Messner was "horrified and outraged at the prospect of the firm's losing, without a word of warning, its chief asset and glory as well as its bulwark against future bad times. Under no circumstances could Horace do something so monstrous!" (229). See also Satterfield 36.

25. Sussman was adaptable. While at the Modern Library, he argued for a low-key approach that employed "rational arguments"; he argued against advertising approaches that shamed readers or appealed to the consumer's sense of shame or snobbery. "As a result," Satterfield notes, "the Modern Library advertisements refused to shame the 'civilized minority'—a group Cerf and Sussman felt would be offended by such appeals—with promotions that belittled their intelligence" (49). Sussman receives a single mention in *At Random*, Cerf's memoir: "Aaron has been invaluable to us" (123).

26. See ch. 6, "How to Enjoy James Joyce's Great Novel *Ulysses*," in Turner. The famous ad "won praise from both the advertising and publishing industries for its 'dignity' and 'restraint'" (174).

27. As Wood notes, *Peyton Place* and Nabokov's *Lolita* share a plot element: a quasi-incestuous relationship between a stepfather and his underage stepdaughter. See ch. 1, "Lolita in Peyton Place."

28. See Toth 120–25.

29. See also Rainey 126–30.

30. Satterfield notes that Cerf's onetime boss, Horace Liveright, "appeared in

court on obscenity charges more often than any other publisher, and he risked financial instability and even jail to defend intellectual freedom." But his motives were also financial: "Liveright recognized that fighting censorship was good business: court battles sold books to a public intrigued by sexual scandal, while they also made friends in the avant-garde literary community" (32).

31. See Cameron vii–viii.

32. The primary cause of Allison's decision to leave is no doubt the revelation that her father had been married to a woman who was not Allison's mother at the time Allison was conceived. But Metalious suggests that the carnival incident and its aftermath were also factors in her decision to move to New York by having Tomas Makris, the novel's most brutally honest character, express the idea: " 'Her determination [to leave] took on form . . . after Kathy Ellsworth's accident, during the trial' " (273).

Chapter 5

1. For an overview of media concentration in this period, see Powell, "The Blockbuster Decade." See also Epstein; Schiffrin; Tebbel vol. 4.

2. See Frank 5 and ch. 3, "The Rise of a New Sensibility, or How the Fifties Broke Up," in Dickstein's *Gates of Eden*.

3. See ch. 10, "Mapping the Postmodern," in Huyssen; see also Jameson for theorizations of the postmodern.

4. Morris Dickstein characterizes Mailer's project this way: "*Advertisements* was the prototype for how [Mailer] turned his losses into strengths, his sense of failure, neglect, or misunderstanding into cultural meaning" (*Leopards* 152).

5. For more on the purchase of Pantheon, see Schiffrin 33–37.

6. RCA's motivation for buying a publishing house was to capitalize on the textbook market through the production of "teaching machines," an early version of personal computers that never did become profitable. See Schiffrin 74.

7. See Whiteside for an argument about the danger of concentration in publishing. I discuss Whiteside's argument in Chapter 4 of this book. For sociological approaches to concentration, see Altbach; Henderson; Hirsch. See also Neuman.

8. Whiteside's study was published first in the *New Yorker*, only four years before it too was purchased by Newhouse's Advance Publications.

9. Rigg did assert, however, that he would not have published *Peyton Place* despite its enormous success. His objections to it were neither literary nor moral. Lubar explains Rigg's rationale: "What would the teachers and school authorities who buy his textbooks think of a firm that published a book featuring incest and a school principal glorying in a lusty extramarital affair?" (107). (In fact, Makris is not involved in an extramarital affair in the novel.)

10. "For the last few years," Mailer acknowledges at the outset, "I have continued to run in that overcrowded mob of unconscionable egotists who are all determined to become the next great American writer" (18).

11. See also Castronovo, who calls *Advertisements* a book "about rebellion and the situation of the outsider" (14).

12. Advertising expenditures in the United States reached $11 billion in 1959, the year *Advertisements* was published, a $3 billion increase from 1955, and three times what was spent on advertising at the end of World War II (Cohen 301).

13. The emergence of these categories and of this research would ultimately contribute to the dissolution of mass culture's empire, as it would soon become

possible and profitable to narrowly target advertisements—on magazines and on television—to specific audiences.

14. "Packard had obtained most of his information from interested parties . . . who wanted to spread the gospel; taking their self-promoting claims literally, he therefore exaggerated the extent and importance of MR" (Fox 186).

15. Mailer's reaction is difficult to understand, in that earlier in *Advertisements* he denigrates "The Paper House" along with the other stories he wrote in 1951. After first saying that it is "not too bad," he adds that he has "no great pride in them. . . . This is the only time I took a retreat in my work" (108).

16. Tom Wolfe's introduction to the anthology of New Journalism pieces that he co-edited with E. W. Johnson is explicit about his effort to appropriate some of the cultural prestige that had previously gone only to novelists.

17. Haydn notes that despite what Mailer writes in *Advertisements*, he always wrongly blamed Cerf for Random House's rejection of *The Deer Park*, called him "Sally Cerf," and once challenged him to a fight at a party (263–64).

18. Haydn also assumes responsibility for Random House's later rejection of *Lolita*, and he asserts that Cerf wanted to publish it and embraced the possibility of controversy in the same way that he embraced the scandal of publishing *Ulysses* decades earlier (264).

19. According to Mailer, Simon & Schuster also rejected the novel, despite its editor's assertion that it "is the work of a serious artist," presumably out of a desire to avoid the controversies the novel would create (*Advertisements* 230–31).

20. Menand writes, "Mailer developed a Manichean version of [Jean-Paul] Sartre's left-wing existentialism and [Wilhelm] Reich's left-wing Freudianism. Every choice became a choice tween God and the devil with the margin separating the two always razor thin" (148).

21. The novel's celebration of the novelist-as-hero—the theme also mined in "The Man Who Studied Yoga"—reaches a pitch of perhaps self-conscious ridiculousness when Sergius, the storyteller, imagines Eitel telling him to reject Hollywood and pursue his solitary artistic ambition: "So do try, Sergius . . . try for that other world, the real world, where orphans burn orphans and nothing is more difficult to discover than a simple fact. And with the pride of the artist, you must blow against the walls of every power that exists, the small trumpet of your defiance" (374). That this is an instance of Sergius being a novelist within the novel, imagining what Eitel would say to him, rather than an actual plot element mitigates the sentiment a bit.

22. Though they are vastly different in many respects, the parodic advertisement for himself embodied in the title of Dave Eggers's confessional work from 2000, *A Heartbreaking Work of Staggering Genius*, bears Mailer's stamp, if only indirectly. Eggers, like Mailer, has been a critic of commercialized American publishing. See Brouillette, "Paratextuality," and Heer, "For Love."

Epilogue

1. I am indebted to Rooney and Farr's accounts of Oprah Winfrey's book club and of Winfrey's dust-up with Franzen.

2. As *Time* magazine noted in 1996, Winfrey's book club did more for Toni Morrison's book sales than did Morrison's Nobel Prize win in 1993 (Rooney 123).

3. "Even Harold Bloom," Farr notes, criticized Franzen. " 'It does seem a little

invidious of him to want to have it both ways,' Bloom said, 'to want the benefits of it and not jeopardize his high aesthetic standing'" (77).

4. On American film of the 1970s, see Biskind. On the history of *Rolling Stone*, see Draper.

5. For a discussion of the implications of these shifts for the 1980s, see Brier.

6. For more on sales, see Rooney 122–26.

7. For one example of this lament, see Zaid.

Works Cited

"An Advertising Catechism." *Publishers Weekly* 13 January 1934: 127–30.

Aldridge, John W. *After the Lost Generation: A Critical Study of the Writers of Two Wars.* New York: McGraw, 1951.

Altbach, Philip G. "Publishing and the Intellectual System." *Annals of the American Academy of Political and Social Science* 421 (1975): 1–13.

"American Book Publishing Is Organized for Expansion." *Publishers Weekly* 7 January 1951: 53.

Anderson, Chris. *The Long Tail: Why the Future of Business Is Selling Less of More.* New York: Hyperion, 2006.

Anderson, Christopher. *Hollywood TV: The Studio System in the Fifties.* Austin: University of Texas Press, 1994.

Aronovitz, David. *Ballantine Books: The First Decade: A Bibliographical History & Guide of the Publisher's Early Years.* Rochester: Bailiwick, 1987.

Asheim, Lester. "A Survey of Recent Research." Price 3–26.

"Aspects of Self: A Bowles Collage." *Twentieth Century Literature* 32 (Fall–Winter 1986): 259–99.

Baker, Carlos. "Small Town Peep Show." Rev. of *Peyton Place. New York Times Book Review.* 23 September 1956: 4.

Baldwin, James. "Mass Culture and the Creative Artist: Some Personal Notes." *Culture for the Millions: Mass Media in Modern Society.* Ed. Norman Jacobs. Boston: Beacon, 1971. 20–23.

Barnhisel, Greg. "Ezra Pound, James Laughlin and New Directions: The Publisher as Spin Doctor." *Paideuma* 29.3 (Winter 2000): 165–78.

———. *James Laughlin, New Directions, and the Remaking of Ezra Pound.* Amherst: University of Massachusetts Press, 2005.

"The Battle for the Book." *Saturday Review* 2 June 1956: 5.

Bauer, Raymond A., and Stephen A. Greyser. *Advertising: The Consumer View.* Boston: Harvard University Press, 1968.

Baughman, James L. *Henry Luce and the Rise of the American News Media.* Baltimore: Johns Hopkins University Press, 2001.

———. *The Republic of Mass Culture: Journalism, Filmmaking, and Broadcasting in America Since 1941.* Baltimore: Johns Hopkins University Press, 1997.

———. *Same Time, Same Station: Creating American Television, 1945–1961.* Baltimore: Johns Hopkins University Press, 2007.

Beaty, Bart. *Fredric Wertham and the Critique of Mass Culture.* Jackson: University Press of Mississippi, 2005.

Belgrad, Daniel. *The Culture of Spontaneity: Improvisation and the Arts in Postwar America.* Chicago: University of Chicago Press, 1998.

Bender, Thomas. "Politics, Intellect, and the American University, 1945–1995."

American Academic Culture in Transformation. Ed. Thomas Bender and Carl E. Schorske. Princeton: Princeton University Press, 1998. 17–54.

Berkley, Miriam. "The Way It Was: James Laughlin and New Directions." *Publishers Weekly* 22 November 1985: 24–29.

"Better Figures on Publishing." *Publishers Weekly* 15 January 1955: 219.

Birkerts, Sven. *The Gutenberg Elegies: The Fate of Reading in an Electronic Age*. New York: Fawcett Columbine, 1994.

Biskind, Peter. *Easy Riders, Raging Bulls: How the Sex-Drugs-and-Rock 'N' Roll Generation Saved Hollywood*. New York: Simon, 1999.

Bloom, Harold, ed. *Ray Bradbury's Fahrenheit 451*. New York: Chelsea House, 2001.

Bogdan, Robert. *Freak Show: Presenting Human Oddities for Amusement and Profit*. Chicago: University of Chicago Press, 1988.

Bonn, Thomas L. *Heavy Traffic and High Culture: New American Library as Literary Gatekeeper in the Paperback Revolution*. New York: Meridian, 1990.

"Booksellers Ordering Copies of Book Award Winners." *Publishers Weekly* 19 January 1952: 231.

Boucher, Anthony. "The Publishing of Science Fiction." Bretnor 24–42.

Bourdieu, Pierre. "The Field of Cultural Production, Or: The Economic World Reversed." *The Field of Culture Production*. Ed. Randal Johnson. New York: Columbia University Press, 1993. 29–73.

———. "The Production of Belief: Contribution to an Economy of Symbolic Goods." *The Field of Cultural Production*. Ed. Randal Johnson. New York: Columbia University Press, 1993. 71–111.

———. *The Rules of Art: Genesis and Structure of the Literary Field*. Trans. Susan Emanuel. Stanford: Stanford University Press, 1996.

Bowles, Jane. *Two Serious Ladies. My Sister's Hand in Mine: The Collected Works of Jane Bowles*. New York: Noonday, 1995. 1–203.

Bowles, Paul. *Conversations with Paul Bowles*. Ed. Gena Dagel Caponi. Jackson: University Press of Mississippi, 1993.

———. *In Touch: The Letters of Paul Bowles*. Ed. Jeffrey Miller. New York: Farrar, 1994.

———. Preface. Bowles, *Sheltering Sky* 5–6.

———. *The Sheltering Sky*. New York: Ecco Press, 1949.

———. *Without Stopping*. New York: Putnam's, 1972.

Bradbury, Ray. Afterword. Bradbury, *Fahrenheit 451* (1979) 167–73.

———. "Burning Bright: A Foreword by Ray Bradbury." Bradbury, *Fahrenheit 451*, 40th Anniversary Edition. 11–21.

———. "Coda." Bradbury, *Fahrenheit 451* (1979) 175–79.

———. "Day After Tomorrow: Why Science Fiction?" *The Nation* 176 (1953): 364–67.

———. *Fahrenheit 451*. New York: Del Rey, 1979.

———. *Fahrenheit 451*. 40th Anniversary Edition. New York: Simon, 1993.

———. "The Fireman." *Galaxy* 1 (1951): 4–61.

———. Foreword. *A Passion for Books: A Book Lover's Treasure of Stories, Essays, Humor, Love and Lists on Collecting, Reading, Borrowing, Lending, Caring for and Appreciating Books*. Ed. Harold Rabinowitz and Rob Kaplan. New York: Three Rivers, 1999.

———. *The Illustrated Man*. New York: Ballantine, 1963.

———. *The Martian Chronicles*. Garden City: Doubleday, 1950.

Brantlinger, Patrick. *Bread and Circuses: Theories of Mass Culture as Social Decay.* Ithaca: Cornell University Press, 1983.

Bretnor, Reginald, ed. *Modern Science Fiction: Its Meaning and Its Future.* New York: Coward-McCann, 1953.

Brier, Evan. "Reading in the 1980s: *In Country*, Minimalism, and the Age of Niches." *Lit: Literature Interpretation Theory* 19.3 (2008): 231–47.

Brockway, George P. "The Economics of Publishing—A Publisher's Point of View." *Publishers Weekly* 8 January 1955: 120–23.

Brooks, David. "The Good Fight, Done Badly." *New York Times* 16 April 2006: A23.

Brouillette, Sarah. "Paratextuality and Economic Disavowal in Dave Eggers' *You Shall Know Our Velocity.*" *Reconstruction: Studies in Contemporary Culture* 3.2 (Spring 2003). <http://reconstruction.eserver.org/032/brouillette.htm>

———. *Postcolonial Writers and the Global Literary Marketplace.* New York: Palgrave, 2007.

Burger, Peter. "Literary Institution and Modernization." *Poetics* 12 (1983): 419–33.

———. *Theory of the Avant-Garde.* Trans. Michael Shaw. Minneapolis: University of Minnesota Press, 1984.

Butcher, Fanny. "A Selection of Outstanding Books that Were Published in 1956." *Publishers Weekly* 21 January 1957: 34–37.

Butscher, Edward, and Irving Malin, eds. *Paul Bowles Issue.* Spec. issue of *Twentieth Century Literature* 32 (1986): 225–450.

"By and for the Public." *Time* 23 May 1949: 79–80.

Cameron, Ardis. "Open Secrets: Rereading *Peyton Place.*" Peyton Place *by Grace Metalious.* Boston: Northeastern University Press, 1999.

Campbell, John W. "The Place of Science Fiction." Bretnor 4–22.

Carr, Virginia Spencer. *Paul Bowles: A Life.* New York: Scribner's, 2004.

Carruth, Hayden. *Beside the Shadblow Tree: A Memoir of James Laughlin.* Port Townsend: Copper Canyon, 1999.

Casanova, Pascale. *The World Republic of Letters.* Trans. M. B. Devevoise. Cambridge: Harvard University Press, 2005.

Castronovo, David. *Beyond the Gray Flannel Suit: Books from the 1950s That Made American Culture.* New York: Continuum, 2004.

Cerf, Bennett. *At Random: The Reminiscences of Bennett Cerf.* New York: Random, 1977.

———. "Publishing Stocks Today: How They Stack Up." *Variety* 10 January 1962: 18.

Chambers, Whittaker. *Witness.* Washington: Regnery, 1978.

Chandler, Raymond. "Ten Percent of Your Life." *Atlantic* February 1952: 48–50.

Clark, T. J. "Clement Greenberg's Theory of Art." *Critical Inquiry* 9 (1982): 139–56.

Cochran, David. *America Noir: Underground Writers and Filmmakers of the Postwar Era.* Washington: Smithsonian, 2000.

Cohen, Lizabeth. *A Consumer's Republic: The Politics of Mass Consumption in Postwar America.* New York: Knopf, 2003.

Cominsky, J. R. "Let's Stop Salvaging." *Saturday Review* 2 June 1956: 9+.

Connor, George E. "Spelunking with Ray Bradbury: The Allegory of the Cave in *Fahrenheit 451.*" *Extrapolation: A Journal of Science Fiction and Fantasy* 45.4 (2004): 408–18.

Corbally, John E., and Ruth E. Seeger. "The National Citizens Commission for the Public Schools." *Educational Research Bulletin* 35 (1956): 141–46.

Corcoran, Monica. "On the Dust Jacket, to O or Not to O." *New York Times* 21 October 2001: ST6.

Coser, Lewis A. "Publishers as Gatekeepers of Ideas." *Annals of the American Academy of Political and Social Science* 421 (1975): 14–22.

Coser, Lewis A., Charles Kadushin, and Walter W. Powell. *Books: The Culture and Commerce of Publishing.* New York: Basic, 1982.

Dahlin, Robert. "Men (and Women) Who Made a Revolution." *Publishers Weekly* 2 July 1997: 51–60.

Daniell, David. *The Bible in English: Its History and Influence.* New Haven: Yale University Press, 2003.

Dardis, Tom. *Firebrand: The Life of Horace Liveright.* New York: Random, 1995.

Dargis, Manohla. "Defending Goliath: Hollywood and the Art of the Blockbuster." *New York Times* 6 May 2007: 2A1+.

Davis, Kenneth C. *Two-Bit Culture: The Paperbacking of America.* Boston: Houghton, 1984.

de Grazia, Edward. *Girls Lean Back Everywhere: The Law of Obscenity and the Assault on Genius.* New York: Vintage, 1993.

Desan, Phillipe, Priscilla Parkhurst Ferguson, and Wendy Griswold, eds. *The Sociology of Literature.* Spec. issue of *Critical Inquiry* 14 (1988): 421–660.

Dessauer, John P. "Pity Poor Pascal: Some Sobering Reflections on the American Book Scene." *Annals of the American Academy of Political and Social Science* 421 (1975): 81–92.

Dickstein, Morris. *Gates of Eden: American Culture in the Sixties.* Cambridge: Harvard University Press, 1997.

———. *Leopards in the Temple: The Transformation of American Fiction, 1945–1970.* Cambridge: Harvard University Press, 2002.

Diggins, John Patrick. *The Proud Decades: America in War and Peace, 1941–1960.* New York: Norton, 1989.

Dimaggio, Paul. "Market Structure, the Creative Process, and Popular Culture: Toward an Organizational Reinterpretation of Mass-Culture Theory." *Cultural Sociology.* Ed. Lyn Spillman. Oxford: Blackwell, 2002.

Draper, Robert. *"Rolling Stone" Magazine: The Uncensored History.* New York: Doubleday, 1990.

Dupee, Gordon. "Can Johnny's Parents Read?" *Saturday Review* 2 June 1956: 7–9.

Edes, Mary Elisabeth. "Fiction Forecast." *Publishers Weekly* 27 August 1956: 916–18.

Eggers, Dave. *A Heartbreaking Work of Staggering Genius.* New York: Vintage, 2001.

English, James. *The Economy of Prestige: Prizes, Awards, and the Circulation of Cultural Value.* Cambridge: Harvard University Press, 2005.

Eliot, T. S. *Notes Towards the Definition of Culture.* New York: Harcourt, 1949.

Epstein, Jason. *Book Business: Publishing Past Present and Future.* New York: Norton, 2001.

Farr, Cecilia Konchar. *Reading Oprah: How Oprah's Book Club Changed the Way America Reads.* Albany: State University of New York Press, 2005.

Ferlinghetti, Lawrence. *A Coney Island of the Mind.* New York: New Directions, 1958.

Fiedler, Leslie. *Love and Death in the American Novel.* New York: Stein and Day, 1975.

Fine, Benjamin. *1,000,000 Delinquents.* Cleveland: World, 1955.

"First National Book Award to Be Made March 16." *Publishers Weekly* 21 January 1950: 245–46.

Fiske, John. *Understanding Popular Culture.* Boston: Routledge, 2001.

Flesch, Rudolf. *Why Johnny Can't Read.* New York: Harper, 1955.

"For 1953, Sales Expansion Both Bottom and Top." *Publishers Weekly* 3 January 1953: 41.

"Four New Writers: Unknown Names Fill the Publishers' Lists." *Life* 30 January 1950: 35–36.

Fox, Paula. *Desperate Characters.* New York: Harcourt Brace, 1970.

Fox, Stephen. *The Mirror Makers: A History of American Advertising and Its Creators.* Urbana: University of Illinois Press, 1997.

Frank, Thomas. *The Conquest of Cool: Business Culture, Counterculture, and the Rise of Hip Consumerism.* Chicago: University of Chicago Press, 1998.

Franzen, Jonathan. *The Corrections.* New York: Farrar, 2001.

———. Introduction. *The Man in the Gray Flannel Suit* by Sloan Wilson. New York: Four Walls Eight Windows, 2002.

———. "Perchance to Dream: In the Age of Images, a Reason to Write Novels." *Harper's* April 1996: 35–54.

Frase, Robert W. "American Book Publishers Council." *Encyclopedia of Library Information and Science.* Ed. Allen Kent and Harold Lancour. New York: Marcel, 1968. 238–43.

Friend, Tad. "Years in the Desert: *The Sheltering Sky* at Fifty." *New Yorker* 15 January 2001: 90.

Fuller, Edmund. "New Hampshire: Activities for Strong Stomachs." Rev. of *Peyton Place. Chicago Sunday Tribune* 23 September 1956: B7.

Gans, Herbert J. *Popular Culture and High Culture: An Analysis and Evaluation of Taste.* New York: Basic, 1999.

Genette, Gerard. *Paratexts: Thresholds of Interpretation.* Trans. Jane E. Lewin. Cambridge: Cambridge University Press, 1997.

Ginsberg, Allen. "America." *Howl and Other Poems.* San Francisco: City Lights Publishers, 1956.

Gioia, Dana. Preface. "Reading at Risk: A Survey of Literary Reading in America." Washington: National Endowment for the Arts, 2004.

———. Preface. "To Read or Not to Read: A Question of National Consequence." Washington: National Endowment for the Arts, 2007.

Grambs, Jean D. *The Development of Lifelong Reading Habits: A Report of a Conference called by the Committee on Reading Development, June 25–26, 1954.* New York: Bowker, 1954.

Greenberg, Clement. "Avant-Garde and Kitsch." *Art and Culture: Critical Essays.* Boston: Beacon, 1989. 3–21.

Gussow, Mel. "James Laughlin, Publisher with Bold Taste, Dies at 83." *New York Times* 14 November 1997: D19.

"Gutenberg Joint Committee Formed to Plan New Awards." *Publishers Weekly* 5 November 1949: 1980.

Habermas, Jürgen. *The Structural Transformation of the Public Sphere: An Inquiry into a Category of Bourgeois Society.* Cambridge: MIT Press, 1991.

Hajdu, David. *The Ten-Cent Plague: The Great Comic-Book Scare and How It Changed America.* New York: Farrar, 2008.

Hall, Donald. "The Difference of James Laughlin." Morrow 273–83.

Haydn, Hiram. *Words and Faces.* New York: Harcourt Brace Jovanovich, 1974.

Heer, Jeet. "For Love—and Money—A Heartbreaking Tale of Mega-Success." *National Post* 12 October 2002: SP5.

———. Rev. of *The Book Business: Publishing Past Present and Future* and *The Business of Books: How International Conglomerates Took Over Publishing and Changed the Way We Read. National Post* 3 February 2001: B7.

Hemley, Cecil. "The Problem of the Paper-backs." Rosenberg and White 141–46.

Henderson, Bill. "Independent Publishing: Today and Yesterday." *Annals of the American Academy of Political and Social Science* 421 (1975): 93–105.

Hepburn, James G. *The Author's Empty Purse and the Rise of the Literary Agent.* Oxford: Oxford University Press, 1968.

Hershberg, James. *James B. Conant: Harvard to Hiroshima and the Making of the Nuclear Age.* New York: Knopf, 1993.

"Highlights of 1956 News and Trends in the U.S. Book Industry." *Publishers Weekly* 21 January 1957: 47–60.

Hirsch, Paul M. "U.S. Cultural Productions: The Impact of Ownership." *Journal of Communication* 35 (1985): 110–21.

Hoberek, Andrew. *The Twilight of the Middle Class: Post–World War II American Fiction and White Collar Work.* Princeton: Princeton University Press, 2005.

Horkheimer, Max, and Theodor W. Adorno. *Dialectic of Enlightenment.* Trans. John Cumming. New York: Continuum, 2001.

Hoskinson, Kevin. "*The Martian Chronicles* and *Fahrenheit 451*: Ray Bradbury's Cold War Novels." *Extrapolation: A Journal of Science Fiction and Fantasy* 36.4 (1995): 345–59.

Hout, Syrine C. "Grains of Utopia: The Desert as Literary Oasis in Paul Bowles's *The Sheltering Sky* and Wilfred Thesiger's *Arabian Sands*." *Utopian Studies* 11 (2000): 112–36.

Huyssen, Andreas. *After the Great Divide: Modernism, Mass Culture, Postmodernism.* Bloomington: Indiana University Press, 1986.

"Institutional Ads for Books Urged by Spier." *Publishers Weekly* 26 November 1949: 2007–8.

Isherwood, Christopher. "A Review of *The Martian Chronicles*." *Tomorrow* October 1950: 56–58.

Izod, John. *Hollywood and the Box Office: 1895–1986.* New York: Columbia University Press, 1988.

Jacobs, Norman, ed. *Culture for the Millions? Mass Media in Modern Society.* Boston: Beacon, 1959.

Jameson, Fredric. *Postmodernism: Or, The Cultural Logic of Late Capitalism.* Durham: Duke University Press, 1991.

Jensen, Joli. *Is Art Good for Us? Beliefs About High Culture in American Life.* Lanham: Rowman, 2002.

Jurca, Catherine. *White Diaspora: The Suburb and the 20th Century Novel.* Princeton: Princeton University Press, 2001.

Kaestle, Carl F., Helen Damon-Moore, Lawrence C. Stedman, Katherine Tinsley, and William Vance Trollinger Jr. *Literacy in the United States: Readers and Reading Since 1880.* New Haven: Yale University Press, 1991.

Kammen, Michael. *American Culture, American Tastes: Social Change and the 20th Century.* New York: Basic, 1999.

Kenner, Hugh. *The Poetry of Ezra Pound.* New York: New Directions, 1951.

Kirkpatrick, David D. "Oprah Gaffe by Franzen Draws Ire and Sales." *New York Times* 29 October 2001: E1+.

———. "Winfrey Rescinds Offer to Author for Guest Appearance." *New York Times* 24 October 2001: C4.

Korda, Michael. *Another Life: A Memoir of Other People.* New York: Random, 1999.

de Koster, Katie, ed. *Readings on Fahrenheit 451.* San Diego: Greenhaven, 2000.

Krim, Seymour. "The Real World of Science Fiction." *Commonweal* 5 (1953): 252–54.

Laughlin, James. "New Directions: An Interview with James Laughlin." Interview with Susan Howe. *The Art of Literary Publishing: Editors on Their Craft.* Ed. Bill Henderson. Yonkers: Pushcart, 1980. 13–48.

———. "Some Irreverent Literary History." *Random Essays: Recollections of a Publisher.* Mt. Kisco: Mayer Bell, 1989.

Lehmann-Haupt, Hellmut. *The Book in America.* 2nd. rev. Amer. ed. New York: Bowker, 1951.

Lemann, Nicholas. *The Big Test: The Secret History of American Meritocracy.* New York: Farrar, 1999.

Levertov, Denise. *Collected Earlier Poems 1940–1960.* New York: New Directions, 1979.

Levine, Lawrence W. *Highbrow/Lowbrow: The Emergence of Cultural Hierarchy in America.* Cambridge: Harvard University Press, 1988.

Long, Elizabeth. *The American Dream and the Popular Novel.* Boston: Routledge, 1985.

Lowen, Rebecca S. *Creating the Cold War University: The Transformation of Stanford.* Berkeley: University of California Press, 1997.

Lubar, Robert. "Henry Holt and the Man from Koon Kreek." *Fortune* December 1959: 104+.

Macdonald, Dwight. *Against the American Grain: Essays on the Effects of Mass Culture.* New York: Random, 1962.

———. "A Theory of Mass Culture." Rosenberg and White 59–73.

Mailer, Norman. *Advertisements for Myself.* Cambridge: Harvard University Press, 1992.

———. *The Deer Park.* New York: Vintage, 1997.

———. "The Mind of an Outlaw." *Esquire* November 1959: 87–94.

Mann, Peter H. "The Novel in British Society." *Poetics* 12 (1983): 435–48.

May, Elaine Tyler. *Homeward Bound: American Families in the Cold War Era.* Rev. ed. New York: Basic, 1999.

May, Lary. *Recasting America: Culture and Politics in the Age of the Cold War.* Chicago: University of Chicago Press, 1989.

McGiveron, Rafeeq O. "What 'Carried the Trick'? Mass Exploitation and the Decline of Thought in Ray Bradbury's *Fahrenheit 451.*" *Extrapolation: A Journal of Science Fiction and Fantasy* 37.3 (1996): 245–56.

McGurl, Mark. *The Novel Art: Elevations of American Fiction After Henry James.* Princeton: Princeton University Press, 2001.

Medovoi, Leerom. *Rebels: Youth and Cold War Origins of Identity.* Durham: Duke University Press, 2005.

Melcher, Frederic G. "An 'Industrial Family that Serves the Nation.'" *Publishers Weekly* 17 January 1953: 204.

———. "Bibles Seeking New Readers and Readers Seeking New Bibles." *Publishers Weekly* 16 August 1952: 698.

———. "1000 Meet to Honor Books." *Publishers Weekly* 25 March 1950: 1508.

Menand, Louis. *American Studies.* New York: Farrar, 2002.

Metalious, Grace. *Peyton Place.* Boston: Northeastern University Press, 1999.

Mills, C. Wright. "Crawling to the Top." Rev. of *The Organization Man. New York Times Book Review* 9 December 1956: 6.

———. *The Power Elite.* Oxford: Oxford University Press, 2000.

———. *White Collar: The American Middle Classes.* Oxford: Oxford University Press, 2002.

Mills, Hilary. *Mailer: A Biography.* New York: Empire, 1982.

Morrow, Bradford, ed. *Inaugural Double-Issue.* Spec. issue of *Conjunctions* 1 (1981–82): 1–295.

Murphy, Priscilla Coit. " 'Down with Fiction and Up with Fact': *Publishers Weekly* and the Postwar Shift to Nonfiction." *Publishing Research Quarterly* Fall 1998: 29–52.

Nadel, Alan. *Containment Culture: American Narratives, Postmodernism, and the Atomic Age.* Durham: Duke University Press, 1995.

"National Book Award Plans Are Now in Full Swing." *Publishers Weekly* 12 January 1952: 141–42.

"National Book Awards Given by Book Industry." *Publishers Weekly* 18 March 1950: 1420.

"National Book Committee." *Publishers Weekly* 22 January 1955: 328.

"Nation's Business at High Level: 1951 to Bring Retail Boom." *Publishers Weekly* 13 January 1951: 127–29.

Neale, Steve. "Hollywood Blockbusters: Historical Dimensions." Stringer 47–60.

Nelson, Deborah L. "Introduction." *Women's Studies Quarterly* 33 (Fall–Winter 2005): 10–23.

Neuman, Susan B. "The Business Behind the Book." *English Journal* 74 (November 1985): 68–71.

Ohmann, Richard. "The Shaping of a Canon: U.S. Fiction, 1960–1975." *Critical Inquiry* 10 (1983): 199–223.

"Our Country and Our Culture: A Symposium." Ed. William Phillips and Philip Rahv. *Partisan Review* 19.3 (1952): 282–326.

"Our Country and Our Culture: II." Ed. William Phillips and Philip Rahv. *Partisan Review* 19.4 (1952): 420–50.

"Outsiders Don't Know." Rev. of *Peyton Place. Time* 24 September 1956: 100.

Packard, Vance. *The Hidden Persuaders.* Brooklyn: Ig, 2007.

"Paperback Movie Tie-Ins." *Publishers Weekly* 14 January 1956: 151–52.

Patterson, James. *Grand Expectations: The United States, 1945–1974.* New York: Oxford University Press, 1996.

Pease, Donald E. "Moby Dick and the Cold War." *The American Renaissance Reconsidered.* Ed. Walter Benn Michaels and Donald E. Pease. Baltimore: Johns Hopkins University Press, 1985. 113–55.

"People Who Shaped the Book Business." *Publishers Weekly* 20 July 1997: 18–31.

Peterson, Richard A. "Six Constraints on the Production of Literary Works." *Poetics* 14 (1985): 45–67.

"Poet of the Pulps." Rev. of *Golden Apples of the Sun. Time* 23 March 1953: 114.

Poirier, Richard. *Norman Mailer.* New York: Viking, 1972.

Pounds, Wayne. *Paul Bowles: The Inner Geography.* New York: Peter Lang, 1985.

Powell, Walter. "The Blockbuster Decade: The Media as Big Business." *Working Papers for a New Society* July–Aug. 1979: 26–36.

———. "Competition versus Concentration in the Book Trade." *Journal of Communication* 30 (Spring 1980): 89–97.

———. "Control and Conflict in Publishing." *Society* 17 (1979): 48–53.

Prescott, Orville. Rev. of *Is Anybody Listening?* by William H. Whyte. *New York Times* 7 April 1952: 23.

Price, Jacob, ed. *Reading for Life: Developing the College Student's Lifetime Reading Interest.* Ann Arbor: University of Michigan Press, 1959.

"The Promotion of Reading Will Be Vigorous in 1953." *Publishers Weekly* 10 January 1953:133.

"Publishers' Trade Book Sales." *Publishers Weekly* 3 January 1953: 25.

Publishers Weekly 1872–1997: Our Industry and Its Magazine Through the Years. Spec. issue of *Publishers Weekly* 2 July 1997.

Rabkin, Eric S., James B. Mitchell, and Carl P. Simon. "Who Really Shaped Science Fiction?" *Prospects* 30 (2005): 45–72.

Radway, Janice A. *A Feeling for Books: The Book-of-the-Month Club, Literary Taste, and Middle-Class Desire.* Chapel Hill: University of North Carolina Press, 1997.

———. *Reading the Romance: Women, Patriarchy and Popular Literature.* Chapel Hill: University of North Carolina Press, 1984.

Rainey, Lawrence. *Institutions of Modernism: Literary Elites and Public Culture.* New Haven: Yale University Press, 1998.

"Reading Promotion Activities by Many Groups." *Publishers Weekly* 21 January 1956: 215–16.

"Review of News and Trends of 1953." *Publishers Weekly* 23 January 1954: 286–89.

"Review of News and Trends of 1954 in the Book Industry." *Publishers Weekly* 22 January 1955: 322–29.

Rexroth, Kenneth. "An Interview with Kenneth Rexroth." Morrow 48–67.

Reynolds, Wade E. "*Fahrenheit 451*: Three Reasons Why It's Worth Teaching." *Virginia English Bulletin* 36.2 (1986): 117–21.

Riesman, David, with Nathan Glazer and Reuel Denney. *The Lonely Crowd: A Study of the Changing American Character.* New Haven: Yale University Press, 1950.

Robinson, Michael J., and Ray Olszewski. "Books in the Marketplace of Ideas." *Journal of Communication* 30 (1980): 81–88.

Rooney, Kathleen. *Reading with Oprah: The Book Club That Changed America.* Fayetteville: University of Arkansas Press, 2005.

" 'Roosevelt and Hopkins' Wins BMI's Gutenberg Award." *Publishers Weekly* 16 April 1949: 8–9.

Rose, Frank. *The Agency: William Morris and the Hidden History of Show Business.* New York: Harper, 1995.

Rosenberg, Bernard, and David Manning White, eds. *Mass Culture: The Popular Arts in America.* New York: Free, 1957.

Rosenberg, Harold. "Pop Culture: Kitsch Criticism." *The Tradition of the New.* New York: Da Capo, 1960.

Ross, Andrew. *No Respect: Intellectuals and Popular Culture.* New York: Routledge, 1989.

"Sales Appeal." *Publishers Weekly* 13 September 1952: 992.

Satterfield, Jay. *The World's Best Books: Taste, Culture, and the Modern Library.* Amherst: University of Massachusetts Press, 2002.

Saunders, Frances Stonor. *The Cultural Cold War: The CIA and the World of Arts and Letters.* New York: New Press, 1999.

Sawyer-Lauçanno, Christopher. *An Invisible Spectator: A Biography of Paul Bowles.* New York: Ecco, 1989.

Schaub, Thomas Hill. *American Fiction in the Cold War.* Madison: University of Wisconsin Press, 1991.

Schatz, Thomas. *The Genius of the System: Hollywood Filmmaking in the Studio Era.* New York: Pantheon, 1988.

Schiffrin, André. *The Business of Books: How International Conglomerates Took Over Publishing and Changed the Way We Read.* London: Verso, 2000.

Schindehette, Susan. "Novel Approach: Author Jonathan Franzen Insults Oprah—and Gets Dumped from Her Show." *People* 12 November 2001: 83–84.

Schwed, Peter. *Turning the Pages: An Insider's Story of Simon & Schuster, 1924–1984.* New York: Macmillan, 1984.

"The Shining Moment." *New York Times.* 16 September 2003: A24.

Showalter, Elaine. "Emeralds on the Home Front." *The Guardian* Feature and Reviews 10 August 2002: 27.

Sklar, Robert. *Movie-Made America: A Social History of American Movies.* New York: Random, 1975.

"Specialists to Confer on Book Use and Reading." *Publishers Weekly* 13 January 1951: 6–7.

Spencer, Susan. "The Post-Apocalyptic Library: Oral and Literate Culture in *Fahrenheit 451* and *A Canticle for Leibowitz.*" *Extrapolation: A Journal of Science Fiction and Fantasy* 32.4 (1991): 331–42.

Spigel, Lynn. *Make Room for TV: Television and the Family Ideal in Postwar America.* Chicago: University of Chicago Press, 1992.

Spock, Benjamin. *Baby and Child Care.* New York: Pocket, 1946.

Steen, Mike. *A Look at Tennessee Williams.* New York: Hawthorn, 1969.

Stefferud, Alfred, ed. *The Wonderful World of Books.* Boston: Houghton, 1953.

Steinberg, Heinz. "Socio-Empirical Reading Research: A Critical Report About Some Revealing Surveys." *Poetics* 12 (1983): 467–79.

Stewart, Lawrence D. *Paul Bowles: The Illumination of Northern Africa.* Carbondale: Southern Illinois University Press, 1974.

Strauss, Helen. *A Talent for Luck.* New York: Random, 1979.

Stringer, Julian, ed. *Movie Blockbusters.* New York: Routledge, 2003.

"Summary of Events and Trends of 1950 in the American Book Trade." *Publishers Weekly* 20 January 1951: 221–26.

"Summary of Events and Trends, 1952, in the American Book Trade." *Publishers Weekly* 24 January 1953: 269–72.

Sunstein, Cass. *Republic.com.* Princeton: Princeton University Press, 2002.

Sutherland, John. "Publishing History: A Hole at the Center of Literary Sociology." Desan, Ferguson, and Griswold 574–89.

Talese, Gay. "Random House Will Buy Knopf in Merger." *New York Times* 17 April 1960: 1+.

Tebbel, John. *A History of Book Publishing in the United States.* 4 vols. New York: Bowker, 1972–81.

"Three Literary Prizes." *New York Times* 18 March 1950: 12.

"Tips for the Bookseller." *Publishers Weekly* 16 August 1952: 700–701.

Thuesen, Peter J. *In Discordance with the Scriptures: American Protestant Battles over Translating the Bible.* New York: Oxford University Press, 2002.

Tolchin, Martin. "Publisher Defends TV as Intellectual 'Tonic.'" *New York Times* 30 April 1960: 13.

Toth, Emily. *Inside Peyton Place: The Life of Grace Metalious.* Jackson: University Press of Mississippi, 1981.

Trilling, Lionel. *The Liberal Imagination: Essays on Literature and Society.* New York: Scribner's, 1950.

Turner, Catherine. *Marketing Modernism Between the Two World Wars.* Amherst: University of Massachusetts Press, 2003.

Tuttle, William F. "America's Children in an Era of War, Hot and Cold: The Holocaust, the Bomb, and Child Rearing in the 1940s." *Rethinking Cold War Culture.* Ed. Peter J. Kuznick and James Gilbert. Washington: Smithsonian, 2001.

"TV Effect on Book Buying Is 'Nil,' ABA Reports." *Publishers Weekly* 6 January 1951: 38.

"U.S. Economy Now at Record High: How Will it Affect the Book Trade?" *Publishers Weekly* 5 January 1952: 21.

van Rees, C. J. "Advances in the Empirical Sociology of Literature and the Arts: The Institutional Approach." *Poetics* 12 (1983): 285–310.

———. "Empirical Sociology of Cultural Productions." *Poetics* 14 (1985): 5–11.

Verdaasdonk, H. "Empirical Sociology of Literature as a Non-Textually Oriented Form of Research." *Poetics* 14 (1985): 173–85.

Vidal, Gore. Introduction. *Collected Stories.* Paul Bowles. Santa Rosa: Black Sparrow Press, 2001.

———. *Point to Point Navigation: A Memoir, 1964–2006.* New York: Vintage, 2006.

Watson, John B. *Psychological Care of Infant and Child.* New York: Norton, 1928.

Weimann, Gabriel. *Terror on the Internet: The New Arena, the New Challenges.* Washington: US Institute of Peace, 2006.

Weller, Sam. *The Bradbury Chronicles: The Life of Ray Bradbury.* New York: Morrow, 2005.

Wertham, Fredric. *Seduction of the Innocent.* New York: Rinehart, 1954.

Westfahl, Gary. "'The Closely Reasoned Technological Story': The Critical History of Hard Science Fiction." *Science Fiction Studies* 20.2 (1993): 157–75.

———. *Mechanics of Wonder: The Creation of the Idea of Science Fiction.* Liverpool: Liverpool University Press, 1999.

Whiteside, Thomas. *The Blockbuster Complex: Conglomerates, Show Business, and Book Publishing.* Middletown: Wesleyan University Press, 1981.

Whyte, William H., Jr. *Is Anybody Listening?* New York: Simon, 1952.

———. *The Organization Man.* Philadelphia: University of Pennsylvania Press, 2002.

"The Widespread Promotion for 'The Wonderful World of Books.'" *Publishers Weekly* 10 January 1953: 112–13.

Wilinsky, Barbara. *Sure Seaters: The Emergence of Art House Cinema.* Minneapolis: University of Minnesota Press, 2001.

Williams, Tennessee. "An Allegory of Man and His Sahara." *New York Times* 6 December 1949: 7.

———. "Homage to J." Morrow 45.

———. *The Selected Letters of Tennessee Williams.* Ed. Albert J. Devlin and Nancy M. Tischler. New York: New Directions, 2004.

"Will the 'Award Books' Be Featured in Your Store?" *Publishers Weekly* 5 January 1952: 40.

Wilson, Edmund. "Who Cares Who Killed Roger Ackroyd?" Rosenberg and White 149–53.

Wilson, Sloan. Afterword. Wilson, *The Man in the Gray Flannel Suit.*

———. "Bygones." *New Yorker* 19 June 1949: 55–59.

———. *The Man in the Gray Flannel Suit.* New York: Four Walls Eight Windows, 2002.

————. *What Shall We Wear to This Party? The Man in the Gray Flannel Suit Twenty Years Before and After.* New York: Arbor, 1976.

Wolfe, Tom. Introduction. *The New Journalism.* Ed. Tom Wolfe and E. W. Johnson. New York: Harper, 1973.

Wolin, Richard. *Heidegger's Children: Hannah Arendt, Karl Lowith, Hans Jonas, and Herbert Marcuse.* Princeton: Princeton University Press, 2003.

Wood, Ruth Pirsig. *Lolita in Peyton Place: Highbrow, Middlebrow, and Lowbrow Novels of the 1950s.* New York: Garland, 1995.

Yates, Richard. *Revolutionary Road.* New York: Vintage, 2000.

"A Year of Reading Promotion." *Publishers Weekly* 20 January 1959: 79.

Young, John K. *Black Authors, White Publishers: Marketplace Politics in Twentieth-Century African American Literature.* Jackson: University Press of Mississippi, 2006.

Zaid, Gabriel. *So Many Books: Reading and Publishing in an Age of Abundance.* Trans. Natasha Wimmer. Philadelphia: Paul Dry Books, 2003.

Ziolkowski, Theodore, *German Romanticism and Its Institutions.* Princeton: Princeton University Press, 1990.

Index

Acknowledgments

In a book that aims to shine a light on the kinds of collaborations that produce all books, I am especially pleased to acknowledge the many people without whom this project could not have happened. Foremost among them are Morris Dickstein, Louis Menand, and Nancy K. Miller, all of whom have provided generous amounts of encouragement, critique, and advice. I am grateful also to everyone in the English departments at Louisiana State University in Shreveport and the University of Minnesota Duluth (UMD). In particular, Paul Cannan, Helen Taylor, Larry Anderson, Deshae Lott, Kristie Weeks, Diane Boyd, and Jeffrey Hole have been good friends and colleagues and valuable sources of advice and support. Thanks also to Linda Krug, David Reynolds, Michele Larson, Deloris Wright, Sam Cohen, and Scott Kaufman. I greatly appreciate various grants that I received from UMD in support of my research. Not least, I thank the students in my classes in Shreveport and Duluth.

At the University of Pennsylvania Press, Jerry Singerman's patience and counsel as editor have been much needed and greatly appreciated, as have the insightful comments of the anonymous readers to whom he sent the manuscript.

Finally, I am blessed with a wonderful family, for whom words continue to fail. Thanks most of all, then, to my parents, Carol and Al Brier, and to Lisa and Peter Cole, David and Jen Brier, and Sally, Ethan, Sarah, and Benjamin. I am looking forward, as always, to my next visit to the Northeast.

Earlier versions of Chapters 1 and 4 were published previously. Chapter 1 was published as "Constructing the Postwar Art Novel: Paul Bowles, James Laughlin, and the Making of *The Sheltering Sky*" in the January 2006 issue of *PMLA*. Chapter 4 was published as "The Accidental Blockbuster: *Peyton Place* in Literary and Institutional Context" in the fall/winter 2005 issue of *WSQ: Women's Studies Quarterly*, edited by Deborah Nelson, published by the Feminist Press at the City University of New York. Many thanks go to the editors of both publications for their thoughtful critiques.